Conflict in Sri Lanka

Internal and External Consequences

Conflict in Sri Lanka
Internal and External Consequences

Editor

V.R. Raghavan

Published for
Centre for Security Analysis
Chennai, India

Vij Books India Pvt Ltd
New Delhi, India

Published   by

Vij Books India Pvt Ltd

2/19, Ansari Road, Darya Ganj
New Delhi - 110002
Phones: 91-11-65449971, 91-11- 43596460
Fax: 91-11-47340674
e-mail : vijbooks@rediffmail.com
web : www.vijbooks.com

Centre for Security Analysis
"9-B" Ninth Floor,
Chesney Nilgiri, 71, Ethiraj Salai,
Egmore, Chennai-600008
Tamil Nadu, India
+91-44-65291889
office@csa-chennai.org
www.csa-chennai.org

First Published : 2011

ISBN 13 : 978-93-80177-96-0

Acknowledgement

The Centre for Security Analysis (CSA) has undertaken a three year research project **Internal Conflicts and Transnational Consequences** supported by the John. D and Catherine. T MacArthur Foundation. This volume is part of the ongoing project and its publication has been possible by the project grant.

The Editor acknowledges the assistance and support provided by Prof Amal Jayawardane, Executive Director, Regional Centre for Security Studies (RCSS), Colombo in organizing the seminar on which this book is based.

TABLE OF CONTENTS

Foreword

This book forms a part of a four nation project supported by John. D and Catherine. T MacArthur Foundation called *Internal Conflicts and Trans Border Consequences* and includes the conflicts in India, Nepal, Myanmar and Sri Lanka. Since the causes of these endemic conflicts have been examined over several years; therefore with this project Centre for Security Analysis (CSA) felt that a focus on the consequences will be instructive. Whole generations have lived with the consequences of conflict for decades and overtime these consequences have in turn become the drivers of conflict. The project looks at how such consequences have evolved and taken deep root to find directions for policy formulations to manage the consequences and even try to resolve the conflicts. Four countries that form a part of this project also represent four unique governance systems. India with a stable and deep rooted democracy has responded to conflicts in its own way. Nepal was a monarchy that responded differently to the conflict involving Maoists and pro-democracy elements. The consequence of this was the removal of the monarchy itself and the subsequent impasse on the formation of the government. Myanmar under its military Junta is a remarkable example of how long standing internal conflicts affect multiple countries such as Bangladesh, China, Thailand and India. The stakeholders in this conflict extend all the way from Belgium to Singapore. Sri Lanka, with a presidential form of government has had a very long and traumatic conflict experience. The consequences are felt not only in Tamil Nadu in the South of India but also in Delhi and Malaysia, Singapore, Canada, New Zealand and several European countries because of the phenomenon called Diaspora. The project, therefore, seeks to understand the consequences of conflicts, how these have become drivers of the conflict and what policy options/ choices that the governments can evolve.

This book brings together a remarkable analysis on the economic, political and social consequences of the conflict in Sri Lanka with distinctive chapters from experienced authors. Adding special meaning to the book is the piece by the Honorable External Affairs Minister of Sri Lanka Prof. G.L. Peiris who conceptualized, initiated and led the famous Peace Process in Sri Lanka. He was face to face with the insurgent leaders and brought to bear his enormous constitutional expertise in finding newer ways of making the peace process inclusive of the adversaries. The fact that his efforts did not succeed showed up of the behavioral pattern of LTTE as it sought to utilize and sometimes exploit the peace process to its advantage.

The book breaks new ground in understanding the emerging scenario in Sri Lanka and analysis of the future course of actions required by the Government of Sri Lanka, the civil society as well as the international community and will be a useful tool in the hands of policy makers, scholars and students alike.

Lt Gen (Retd) V R Raghavan
President
Centre for Security Analysis

INTRODUCTION

Brig K Srinivasan (Retd) and Ms Ancy Joseph

The Centre for Security Analysis (CSA) has been studying the conflict in Sri Lanka progressively since 2004. A number (over 60) of experts, academicians, journalists, strategic analysts and Sri Lankan political personalities have addressed several aspects of the conflict at various stages and their analyses, observations and recommendations as well as differing views were presented at various seminars organized by CSA in collaboration with think tanks in Colombo. The same have been brought out in the form of edited volumes.

The issue of *Conflict over the Fisheries in the Palk Bay Region* was addressed as a research project and the study was published in 2005. The book *Conflict Resolution and Peace Building in Sri Lanka* was the result of a seminar organized in Chennai during December 2004. Based on the suggestions from papers presenters and participants of this seminar, ten experts addressed the concept of federalism as might be relevant to Sri Lanka and the same were presented at the seminar organized in May 2005 in collaboration with Sri Lanka Foundation Institute (SLFI), Colombo. This resulted in an edited volume titled *Federalism and Conflict Resolution in Sri Lanka*. While the ceasefire between LTTE and the Government was in place, analyses by some experts were presented through a timely seminar jointly organized by CSA and SLFI in February 2006 at Colombo. The proceedings have been published as a book *Peace Process in Sri Lanka: Challenges and Opportunities.* As the conflict progressed, when the Government of Sri Lanka (GOSL) had cleared eastern part of the island and was poised to militarily address LTTE in the North, CSA organized a conference in March 2008 in collaboration with Bandaranaike

Centre for International Studies (BCIS), Colombo. This conference looked at various dimensions of the conflict and analyzed as to how Sri Lanka would be looking forward. Three ministers from GOSL, Secretary General of the Secretariat for Coordinating the Peace Process, economists, political analysts and retired diplomats from India and Sri Lanka presented their views and analyses. The book *Conflict in Sri Lanka: The Road Ahead* was the product reflecting their ideas and views on the future course at that phase of the conflict.

While the armed conflict ended in May 2009, it was generally recognized that a lot more needed to be done on many fronts. Merely winning the war did not solve the problem, many political and administrative steps were needed to win peace. Against this backdrop, CSA organized a seminar in collaboration with Regional Centre for Strategic Studies (RCSS) Colombo in August 2009 wherein experts from varied background addressed many issues relevant to Post- war rebuilding of the Sri Lankan society. The themes addressed were economic reconstruction, socio-ethnic cohesion and political management. Papers presented in this seminar are contained in the book *From Winning the War to Winning Peace: Post-war rebuilding of the society in Sri Lanka.*

Subsequently, CSA has undertaken a research project to understand the conflict by studying and analyzing the consequences and to draw useful conclusions on managing the consequences and even to resolve the conflicts. The study covers internal conflicts in India, Myanmar, Nepal and Sri Lanka. The *Conflict in Sri Lanka: Internal and External Consequences* is an excellent case study. Experienced journalists, capable administrators, knowledgeable academicians have addressed different facets of internal and external consequences of conflict in Sri Lanka and the same were presented at a seminar organized in collaboration with RCSS in October 2010. This volume contains these presentations.

Prof G L Peiris, honourable External Affairs Minister of Sri Lanka, has been deeply involved in resolution of the conflict for years. He had headed the GOSL negotiating team for talks with LTTE mediated by Norway and subsequently too, has been addressing the conflict in many ways in various capacities. He has been regularly taking part in the programmes organized by CSA on the conflict in Sri Lanka. Prof Peiris while delivering the key note address explained the major consequences of the conflict which deserved immediate and foremost attention and how the GOSL was addressing the same. He highlighted the accomplishment of Government of Sri Lanka, a small nation state with limited resources in wiping out insurgency without any spillover of the conflict outside the country. He highlighted the state of internally displaced people (IDPs) and what was being done to rehabilitate them at the earliest. In his talk he also appreciated the support and assistance provided by the Government of India for settling the IDPs, particularly, building new houses for them; rebuilding and repairing old houses. While discussing the political management, he elucidated the plans of GOSL to repair the war torn areas so as to hold elections at local body level and subsequently provincial council elections. Another significant point brought forth by Prof Peiris was the need to revisit and refine many of the International Laws, particularly laws relating to the refugees, as many terrorist organisations and insurgent groups were able to derive considerable advantage in its present form. He emphasized the need for a re-modulation of the conceptual foundations of public international law in order to make the fight against insurgency/ terrorism much more effective taking into account the asymmetrical warfare between the actors i.e. legitimate state and insurgent/terrorist groups. Prof Peiris highlighted that the internationalization of the efforts/actions by government to address internal conflict as another major fall out of the conflict. Internationalization of the conflict, he asserted, questions the national sovereignty and is a deterrent to effective action by the state and a source of tremendous strength to the terrorist groups.

Keethaponcalan in *Ethno-political Conflicts and the Civil War: Domestic and International Impact* explores the impact of the conflict on polity, society, security and demography. On political front, the conflict led to erosion of democracy and democratic values, over-centralization of political power, and strengthening of ethnic politics, especially among the minority communities and the adoption of racially motivated policies and strategies by the Government. He lists out introduction of stringent anti-terrorism laws, the politicization of military and militarization of politics and civil administration as security related consequences. While discussing the international dimension of the consequences, he explores the involvement of India, as a mediator, negotiator and deployment of the Indian armed forces in Sri Lanka under the banner of the Indian Peace Keeping Force. He examines the role of Tamil Diaspora, initially chose to settle abroad due to lack of security and eventually transformed into a major financial contributor for the conflict which in turn sustained the war machinery of the LTTE. He recommends accommodative policies and minority friendly approach of the Sri Lankan state and the Sinhala people to weaken the anti-Sri Lankan activities of the Tamil Diaspora. In order to minimize the impact of ethnic politics, the larger parties should become truly national and accommodative of the minority concerns. This could be achieved through constitutional reforms that entail measures for devolution of power.

Military victory of the Sri Lankan Armed Forces over the LTTE brought an end to one of the most violent ethno-political conflict in the world. Though the war is over, conflict still persists and transition from conflict to post conflict is not a simple process but a long drawn out process which needs clear vision, objectives and goals. In *Pursuit of Sustainable Peace after the Military defeat of LTTE: Some insights into the post war scenarios*, **Gamini Keerawella** elucidates various factors that need to be addressed in order to bring peace and stability in post war Sri Lanka. Transitional security constitutes an important aspect of post-conflict peace and reconciliation. Militarization is inevitable when a war is going on. Therefore, reframing of security concerns and security arrangements which takes into account the individual and collective identities to suit the post conflict scenario should receive priority attention. He articulates the need for the resettlement of internally displaced people in the post war situation. Rehabilitation and reconstruction along with integrated programmes to promote sustainable livelihood of the IDPs can prove to be effective tools of reconciliation. The government's approach towards former LTTE combatants is also vital in this context. Prof Keerawella emphasizes on capacity building and construction of civil society in the post war setting. Keerawella is of the view that Government needs to recognize the diversity of the Tamil nationalism and engage in a constructive dialogue with them. A political space must be created to integrate it as vital part of civic nationalism. He also recounts the role of Tamil Diaspora which constitutes a very important aspect of the political equation to the post conflict peace building process. He emphasizes the need to get the Tamil Diaspora to be partners in the post-war peace building process. To enable this, the government needs a clear perspective, direction and work plan with a thorough understanding of the internal dynamics and a realistic assessment of the strength as well as the limitations of the Tamil Diaspora.

With the emergence of a multi-dimensional international order, a number of other actors have acquired prominence in international politics that include inter-governmental organizations, UN instruments with new roles, International NGOs, interest groups and academic bodies. He points out the importance of international trust and confidence building not only for averting unacceptable external probes, but also for promoting the stability and progress of the post-war peace building process. The central element of the post-war peace building process that determines the long-term stability and peace of the country is political and constitutional reforms widening the democratic political space in the country. He is of the opinion that these political and constitutional reforms are needed to strengthen good governance and devolution of power.

Estimating the cost of a conflict is an onerous task. **Deshal de Mel** in *Economic Dimensions of the Conflict* explores economic impact of the conflict at national and regional level. The direct costs of the conflict include destruction of physical and human capital, military expenditure, exclusion of natural resources and resources required for refugee care. In 2008 defense expenditure was 3.8% of GDP or 17.1% of total government expenditure. It was estimated that a 1% increase in defense expenditure causes a 2.4% decline public investment. However, defense expenditure has acted as an important stimulus to the economy, particularly in terms of rural employment and livelihoods with a multiplier effect. He notes that though the national economy has not suffered large scale damage, the local economy of the North and East has suffered severe damage as these regions were home to many major industries, all of which either halted production or substantially cut down on production.

The indirect costs of conflict are numerous but hard to estimate quantitatively. High military expenditure has led to reduced Foreign Direct Investment (FDI), domestic investment and tourism losses. Its adverse impact is felt on business competitiveness, the delays to economic reform processes and high fiscal deficits. Social infrastructure (schools, health centers) has also been adversely affected due to the conflict, with potentially damaging impacts on long term economic performance, particularly in the conflict zones. The Sri Lankan conflict also had an important international dimension. The conflict in Sri Lanka at various stages had influenced other governments policy on overseas developmental assistance (ODA) to Sri Lanka and trade policies.

According to Deshal de Mel, post conflict economic priorities should include- in short term labour intensive economic activity with substantial backward and forward linkages. However, in the medium term, economic activity be directed towards creation of higher end employment; employment opportunities for youth and ex-LTTE combatants through reconstruction activities; revival of traditional sectors like agriculture and fisheries and small scale industries in the North and Eastern Provinces. He is of the view that economic growth needs to be inclusive and sustainable. In this context macroeconomic policy needs to support an environment that will encourage economic growth. Therefore, he says, the government must prioritize expenditure to create the necessary fiscal space to effectively respond to the needs of reconstruction in the post conflict areas.

Vivekanandan in *The Plight of Fishermen of Sri Lanka and India: The legacy of civil war* discusses impact of the conflict on fisheries sector-traditional sector of Northern and Eastern provinces of Sri Lanka and Tamil Nadu. The Northern Province was the leading fish producing region of Sri Lanka and played a significant role in catering to the nutritional security of the island nation. Maritime boundary in the Palk Bay and Palk Straits was fixed as per Katchathivu agreement of 1974. This was a politically contentious issue in Tamil Nadu, but it did not make any difference to the fishing activities and the fishermen on both sides. However, civil war adversely affected the fishermen and fisheries industry in Sri Lanka particularly in Northern Province where more than one generation of fishing community lost out on their livelihood. The conflict triggered changes in the fishing, in and around Palk Bay. Decline in the fishing activity on the Sri Lankan side led to the exploitation of fish resources on Sri Lankan side by Indian fishermen.

Post war, the fishermen from Northern Province is reclaiming the space lost during the war but find Indian trawlers as a big hurdle. Any attempt at controlling the Indian trawlers leads to political repercussions in India with potential to harm Indo-Sri Lankan ties. This is preventing the Sri Lankan Government from taking a hard stance on the issue. In the south and west of Sri Lanka, the emergence of multi-day fishing boats has resulted in a new dynamic fishery that involves trans-border fishing in India's Exclusive Economic Zone. Moreover the shooting of Indian fishermen by Sri Lankan Navy has complicated the issue. He views the problem of trans-border fishing as not just a question of experts or administrators or politicians working out a solution. He says it requires a deeper process involving fishermen on both sides and negotiating a settlement that is acceptable to both the fishing communities.

In the chapter *Impact of the Conflict on Tamil Nadu,* **Alexander** highlights the exodus of people from Srilanka, either as repatriates or refugees as a major consequence of the conflict in Sri Lanka, causing considerable strain on the state administration and the law and order machinery. On arrival, the repatriates were given cash doles, provided with ration, free accommodation, free water and electricity, educational facilities and they were permitted to take up local jobs to support their livelihood. The bulk of them were settled in Tamilnadu; a few were sent to Andhra Pradesh, and a few others to Kerala and Karnataka. Many youngsters among the refugees with professed allegiance to different militant groups established recruiting centers in the landing points and established contacts with different political parties and different Indian intelligence agencies and subtly played one against the other. They recruited cadres from the refugee camps and these resulted in rival pamphleteering, skirmishes, kidnappings, abductions, tortures, murders, assaults and shootouts and assassinations. They also indulged in gunrunning, drug peddling, smuggling of medicines, petrol, explosives, ammunition etc. These activities had put considerable strain on the law and order, crime machinery and judiciary. It was difficult to proceed against these criminals and law breakers as they enjoyed the political patronage and common man's sympathy. However, Tamil Nadu police disarmed all the groups including former LTTE leader Prabhakaran. Following the assassination of Rajiv Gandhi, LTTE was banned. On the issue of firing and attacks on Indian fishermen by Sri Lankan Navy, he mentions that whenever there had been attacks and shootouts on the fishermen it had its political and law and order echo in the state. Political parties and common man felt that the remedy was in getting back Katchathivu Island.

Laksiri Fernando in *Long Distance Reactions to the conflict and their Ramifications* delves on reactions of the Diaspora, Non Government Organizations and International Non Governmental Organizations and select Western Governments and UN to the conflict. While commenting on the reactions of the Tamil Diaspora, it was generally believed that the Diaspora in the west was the main lifeline for the LTTE for a long time. Political activism of the Tamil Diaspora was controlled by the LTTE until recently and no other Tamil party was allowed to function in many countries. The LTTE created easy avenues for the Tamils to migrate and professional human traffickers were employed for the task. Long distance Nationalism is very strong even after the defeat of LTTE and might pose a challenge to 'reconciliation and development' in the country.

While exploring reactions of NGOs and International NGOs he traces the stand taken by them right from the beginning of the conflict. In the earlier days human rights violations advocated against the government were largely valid. But in late 1980s, when LTTE had transformed itself to a militant movement, these NGOs chose to turn a blind eye. Fernando points out that NGOs critically view the actions of the state and state actors virtually ignoring actions of the non state actors or even the terrorist organizations. This encouraged anti-state forces to gather political momentum against Sri Lanka. He also mentions the accusation of war crimes and human right violations by the GOSL during the final stage of the war prevented a genuine dialogue between GOSL and rest of the world. India, China, Russia and Pakistan were empathetic but the West and Japan repeatedly called for ceasefire and to restart the stalled peace talks. Post conflict, Western government's exerted pressure on Sri Lanka on certain contentious issues – IDPs and War Crimes. While the Sri Lankan government chose to ignore or resist what appear to be 'interferences,' Fernando emphasizes on the need to constructively engage with these governments for the betterment of Sri Lankan society and of the world community.

Sathiya Moorthy in *Sri Lanka: Trans-Border Consequences of an Internal Conflict* explicates the political fall out of the Sri Lankan Conflict on India and particularly the southern state of Tamil Nadu. He explains that Tamil Nadu was an accident entrant and did not have any role to play until the mass exodus of the Tamil refugees. Thereafter he explains the Tamil Nadu factor in Indo-Sri Lankan relations, exploitation of the ethnic issue of the Sri Lankan conflict for electoral advantages in Tamil Nadu and competitive politics of the mainstream Dravidian Parties which may have influenced the approach of government of India towards the conflict in Sri Lanka. Dealing with strategic and security related consequences he points out the increase of 'gun culture' in the state which perpetrated violent acts by militants backed by LTTE. This became a major law and order problem in the state. Adding to this was the establishment of the international linkages with drug-trafficking and gun-running with Tamil Nadu as transit point. Expansion of the LTTE's air and navy wings was of security concern to India as the southern coasts of India were accessible to LTTE and needed to be guarded. Though not direct fallout of the internal conflict in Sri Lanka, the presence of external actors in the Indian Ocean waters shared between India and Sri Lanka is also a cause of concern for India.

Exploring the future of the LTTE, he believes that rebuilding or reviving LTTE is difficult, though a lot would depend on what the Sri Lankan state has to offer Tamil community and polity in terms of political solution. It also depends on what the Tamils in Sri Lanka and afar think that they are capable of and would want to do in the future in terms of politics. If the Tamil militancy were to rear its head again on the Sri Lankan soil, Tamil Nadu could become a logistics base and a natural sanctuary for them, a base to stockpile weapons and supplies needed for a long drawn out engagement with Sri Lankan state. On the fisheries issue he is of the opinion that it needs to be addressed at the political and community levels by the governments and people concerned.

The analysts have enumerated many of the consequences of the internal conflict which need more detailed attention by political actors, government and society. There are some issues which are common to many of the internal conflicts and they are very much prevalent in this case too. The variable of the ethnic/religious/linguistic identity as a cause of the conflict stands out needing greater analysis. The way internal conflicts are addressed is an area of specialized study of the political management given the political set up and environment. There is another factor which is ever present in all conflicts i.e. the economy. All these aspects in the case of Sri Lanka are worth studying in greater detail.

The impact on international environment is another major issue that warrants greater attention by the governments. In this case, the conflict has certainly impacted Sri Lanka in many ways like trade policies, Overseas Development Assistance (ODA) and Report of the UN Panel on Human Rights Violations. The conflicts also bring about certain other consequences which nations generally tend to ignore, for example, civil-military relations. These consequences are major challenges to any and every government and need to be addressed taking into account all the stakeholders involved.

INTERNAL CONFLICT IN SRI LANKA: MANAGING THE CONSEQUENCES[1]

G.L. Peiris

There has indeed been a copious amount of discussion on the causes of the conflict in Sri Lanka and at this juncture a shift in focus on the consequences is most warranted as it would complete the analysis on the conflict.

I believe that the international community has not given adequate recognition to Sri Lanka's efforts in controlling the negative consequences of the conflict. The conflict was sustained by a terrorist organization recognized by the United States FBI as the most feared and ruthless terrorist organization in the world. The conflict spanned the greater part of three decades in various forms but it came to an end. A small country with very limited resources was able to handle an exceedingly complex situation in a way that sought to contain and control the fall out of the conflict within the island as well as on the world at large.

I proceed to some concrete illustrations of the fact that Sri Lanka managed to contain some of the negative consequences. It has been the empirical experience of nations that when a conflict of this kind comes to an end there is considerable instability in the region arising from a variety of causes, not least of which is the proliferation of small arms. For

---

[1] This chapter is based on the transcribed version of the Keynote Address delivered by the author at the Seminar on " Conflict in Sri Lanka: Internal and External Consequences" held on 26-27 October 2010 in Colombo organised by the Centre for Security Analysis and the Regional Centre for Strategic Studies.

example, this was particularly the case in the aftermath of the conflict in Cambodia. This was a very serious problem along with a turbulence of considerable magnitude within an extensive geographical region with the proliferation of weapons and lawlessness. This did not happen at the end of the conflict in Sri Lanka, neither within the country nor in the neighboring countries. This did not happen as a co-incidence but because of perceptive and properly structured policies that had been formulated and implemented. The manner in which Sri Lanka dealt with the rehabilitation of the people in the North and the East who were directly affected by the conflict is also a point of discussion here. The ability of the Government of Sri Lanka to reduce the number of IDPs within a span of 15 months from 297,000 to the current figure is 18,000 of which about 11,000 are moving in and out, is not recognized. The Government also rehabilitated 5,700 of a total of 11,700 ex-combatants. They are being prepared actively and rigorously for re-integration into the community and it is only the hard core ex-combatants who are being held with a view to institute criminal proceedings against those among them who have been involved in serious criminal activities.

There is also a whole cluster of initiatives connected with the resuscitation of the economy of those parts of the country that have been ravaged by the conflict. The Government of Sri Lanka acknowledges its appreciation of the support that it has received from foreign Governments, particularly the Government of India. On a recent visit to New Delhi, we had detailed discussions on the logistics, especially in a meeting with Shri P Chidambaram, Minister of Home Affairs, Government of India. There are 50,000 houses for IDPs being constructed at a cost of approximately 250 million USD and the cost is being borne by India. There are about 1000 houses being constructed on state land and 32,000 houses which are being constructed by the owners but the wherewithal is being provided for by the Government of India. There are also 17,000 houses which are capable of being repaired and the Government is undertaking these activities with great vigor and enthusiasm.

Sri Lanka also focused on elections in the Eastern and the Northern Province. Holding elections in war-torn areas is a difficult task but we began the process in the East with local Government elections and graduated to holding provincial council elections in the province. In the Northern Province we have already held elections to local Government institutions in Jaffna and Vavuniya followed elections to the other local Government bodies in the north. Sooner than later, we will hold Provincial Council elections in the Northern Province. It is, therefore, a multi-faceted strategy which is sequenced beginning with priority on the humanitarian conditions of the people who have been displaced, then ensuring that those efforts are reinforced by economic and political initiatives that would help complete the strategy that is being embarked upon by Government of Sri Lanka.

Another familiar aspect with regard to consequences of the conflict is the high degree of collaboration among insurgent groups in the region. It is a matter of practical experience that they do not operate in isolation and have links and synergies. They work together by exchange of information, money laundering, movement of weapons, movement of people, training etc. Sri Lanka has ensured that this did not happen in the case of its conflict. If one takes Waziristan in the Swat valley in Pakistan, the North Eastern region in India and the current situation in Nepal, there is clear evidence that there is collaboration and interaction among insurgent groups. This is not the case in Sri Lanka. When I was asked by New Delhi, soon after the Pune Bakery Blast whether the terrorists were trained in Sri Lanka, I was able to state categorically that there is no evidence whatsoever of such training. This allegation was taken seriously and was investigated by GOSL and we came to the conclusion that there is no reason to believe that this had happened. We have seen to it that there is no spill over and collaboration among the different insurgent groups within the South Asian region.

Taking the issue of refugees, in conflicts of this nature one of the most prominent consequence would be problems connected with refugees. Sri Lanka has been actually commended for the steps taken to prevent the problem from escalating and assuming serious proportions. I had a very fruitful meeting with the Senator John Faulkner, the then Defence Minister of Australia on the sidelines of the Shangri La Dialogue.

He thanked the Government of Sri Lanka profusely for actions that had led to the mitigation of the refugee problem in Australia and said that his Government appreciated the action taken by the Government of Sri Lanka to extenuate the problems that Australia would have to deal with on Christmas Island or elsewhere with regard to refugees. The Government of Australia in recognition of the very useful action being taken by Sri Lanka made the policy decision to suspend the processing of applications for refugee status from Sri Lanka for a period of one year. They declared that they are satisfied that there is nothing happening in the country from which people need to run away. This was supported by the United Nations High Commissioner for Refugees who said that there is absolutely no evidence of systemic discrimination of a group of people in Sri Lanka and there was no reason for people to flee the country claiming fear for their lives or safety. This is why I stated to a leading Canadian newspaper, the Toronto Sun that these people seeking refuge at this stage are really economic refugees hoping to improve their life. The Government of Sri Lanka objects to the fictitious basis on which refugee status is sought. The international community clearly recognized, as was explicitly articulated by the Government of Australia, that there was no refugee problem in Sri Lanka.

Another consequence of conflicts of such nature is the security of sea lanes. We are familiar with the rather serious problems in this regard in various parts of the world. As far as the Indian Ocean is concerned, we have done everything we possibly can and these attempts have been considerably successful given the security and safety of the sea lanes in the Indian Ocean. We had a useful discussion in Galle, called the Galle Dialogue where 23 Navy's from around the world participated. Nirmal Verma, the Commander of Indian Navy visited us just before this dialogue and spent almost a week in Sri Lanka, visiting Trincomalee and other parts. There is very active collaboration in this field between India and Sri Lanka and therefore matters connected with the safety of sea lanes, piracy, gun running and trafficking have been dealt with in a systematic way. The results are there for the world to see.

For all these efforts there has been inadequate acknowledgement of the quality and the magnitude of the Sri Lankan achievement. It was not just a question of achieving a military victory over a dangerous insurgent group, which was a difficult task but also the task of bringing in peace which is an equally daunting task. The post conflict phase has to be handled with finesse and sensitivity in order to prevent the exacerbation of some of the problems outlined above. However in the overall setting of consequences emanating from a conflict of this nature we need to be perennially conscious of potential dangers. Let us not forget that the military action is over and there is no likelihood of the LTTE having the strength to re-arm and re-group. Nevertheless they continue to have some assets particularly large pecuniary resources which they have accumulated over almost a quarter of a century and highly sophisticated communications network which they have consolidated. If one looks at the events unfolding in North America and Western Europe it would be very unreal to regard all issues connected with this conflict as being completely ceased. Certainly the military aspect has come to an end, and it will not raise its ugly head again. There are however other ramifications that calls for active attention and appropriate action. For instance, the matters connected with the so called Transnational Government of Tamil Eelam (TGTE). Purported elections were held in different parts of the world, the Canadian constituency, as it is called, supposed to have elected 25 persons. There is also a person actively associated with the LTTE who claims to have been elected as Prime Minister in this Transnational Government of Tamil Eelam. The matter reached this far in spite of no government recognizing it. When I discussed this matter with the Canadian Foreign Minister[2], he assured us that they are not recognizing it and are doing everything possible consistent with the laws of Canada to suppress it. In the United Kingdom there is a Tamil Global Forum which is equally active. These are the organizations that are putting constant pressure on politicians in their host countries and getting involved in electoral politics

---

[2] When I accompanied His Excel lency President Rajapakse to New York for the UN General Assembly elections, I met the F oreign Minister of Canada, Mr. Lawrence Cannon, on the sidelines.

to make themselves useful to the powers that be. Even more active than the wings of this movement in Northern America and the United Kingdom is the activity that is undertaken in Norway. That is even more vigorous. We have a reason to believe that the Norwegian wing have a great deal to do with the arrival of the ship, Ocean Lady in Canada. This was the situation where about 87 people on board this vessel went to Canada and among them were persons against whom there are serious charges including murder and who are wanted in Sri Lanka. The granting of refugee status to such people leads to letting them into the society with an impact on the social order of the society. All of them would find themselves on the dole of the host Government, so they would be supported by the tax payers of those countries and they generally have no fixed employment. The natural and inevitable consequence of this situation would be the proliferation of crime, social unrest and disorder in the community. This is accompanied by the equally distressing developments - gun running, narcotics, human trafficking and frauds connected with passports and visas. The international community would have to be conscious of such consequences. The moral obligation on them is to respond appropriately in order to contain consequences of this nature which emanate from a conflict at the post-war stage.

I would like emphasis in the light of this situation that the orthodox assumptions and conceptions of international law, principles and international governing of the reception of refugees need a fresh look. However, the problem is broader and deeper. It is my view that the traditional corpus of international law does not adequately serve the international community at this time. I read a speech by Dr. Manmohan Singh, the Prime Minister of India where he made some relevant remarks on the subject of the role of force in defence strategy. He made the point that in the present time insurgents and terrorists are able to derive very considerable advantage from the manner in which international law is structured. There is a need to make it very clear that we have the resolve to grapple with terror and we have the means at our disposal to accomplish that objective. There must be no ambiguity on this point. This is a message that must go out loud and clear to insurgents wherever they may be active in any part of the world. In the backdrop of these views, we need to reflect upon the fact that the principles of international law were developed in a particular context. The orthodox setup in which these principles received expression and were subsequently refined and developed was in the context of conflicts between and among sovereign states. Today the problem is totally of a different dimension. Some of the most dangerous conflicts in South Asia are not conflicts between states but situations where the legitimate authority of the established state is being challenged and jeopardized by an insurgent group. The most striking characteristic of this situation is the asymmetry between the sovereign state and the insurgent group. This puts the insurgent group at a decisive advantage. Former United Kingdom Prime Minister Margaret Thatcher made a very perceptive remark soon after an assassination attempt on her. Thatcher was able to save her life only by a whisker. The next morning she addressed the media and said that we must remember what a decisive advantage a terrorist has against the lawful Government. "The terrorist chooses the time, the place and the opportunity. How do you protect every temple, church, bus halt, and railway station in the whole country? It is they and they alone who know where the next bomb is going to explode". The response of the Irish Republican Army which attempted the assassination was even more interesting. They said "Madam, we have to be lucky only once, you have to be lucky every time". This is also true. Hence the point being that in a conflict of such nature the insurgent has a decisive advantage. The principles of international law which are evolved to deal with such situation must obviously take this reality into account. There cannot be reciprocity and uniformity. There is a need to look at established corpus of law, for example, the right to preemptive action. We do not believe in preemptive action outside of our territorial borders and certainly self defence under national law does not arise only after you have been attacked. The substantive criminal laws of India, Sri Lanka, Pakistan, all these countries recognize right of self defence when there is reasonable apprehension of danger. This is certainly a principle that needs to be developed and applied in situations involving conflict between the states and insurgent groups. There has to be a re-modulation of the conceptual foundations of public international law in order to make the fight against terrorism much more effective than it is at the present time.

This brings us to the question of national sovereignty and local action v/s internationalization. Today one of challenges that Sri Lanka faces is the belief that whatever is done in the aftermath of a conflict should be under international auspices. Only then will it be credible and effective. This belief is being pursued very powerfully and emotionally by several INGOs in Sri Lanka, sometimes with a vengeance. Internationalization brings in its wake very formidable problems. The clearest example today is Nepal. The situation on the ground is that the elected Government of Nepal does not have full authority to deal with problems connected with arms and ammunition because the final authority to deal with these matters is the United Nations. In many critical situations the Government becomes a kind of atrophy and its hands are tied. This immeasurably strengthens and emboldens the terrorists. Therefore this degree of internationalization is a disincentive to effective action by the state and a source of tremendous strength to the terrorist groups. We believe that the international order today must be constructed on the premise that countries must be encouraged to deal with their own problems. This is very essential. This is not an era where one can still preach the colonial mentality that emerging nations lack the resources, wherewithal and the intellectual acumen, in terms of empirical experience to deal with matters of this nature. This is a wholly condescending, patronizing attitude which is out of sync with the morals of the contemporary world. We believe in keeping with the spirit of the United Nations Charter and the values which lie at the core of the UN as an instrument that the central endeavour must be to give every encouragement to countries to work out their own solutions in keeping with their own historical antecedents, their social traditions, and their cultural values. Solutions that states adopt change significantly from culture to culture, from country to country and there is no 'one size fits all' solution. When we were contemplating the legislatures, the structures and the lessons learnt in the reconciliation commission we were certainly happy to benefit from useful experience elsewhere. In particular we looked at the experience of South African Truth and Reconciliation Commission, the Chilcot Committee in the

United Kingdom. However, we took care to ensure that it was suitably adapted to suit the combination of circumstances in Sri Lanka. This is absolutely essential. If it has to work on ground it must be in harmony with local circumstances and priorities. Any attempt to impose in a country such as Sri Lanka situated in these circumstances is bound to be futile and counter-productive.

In the aftermath of the conflict, Sri Lanka has been deeply conscious of the need to address the potential consequences by itself and put in place viable strategies and mechanisms to extenuate the gravity of those consequences. There is a multi pronged strategy developed for this purpose. Political development and political innovation in the face of economic contentment may not yield the desired results. Most of all we believe that economic revival is absolutely crucial and that there is an intimate correlation between economic resuscitation and political innovation. This has required the collaboration of the private sector. The Government of Sri Lanka has been able to persuade the private sector to go to Jaffna and Kilinochichi and open up factories. Tamil speaking girls have become the bread winners in their families in these regions. We are also reviving fisheries and agriculture and these activities are bringing about an economic revival in these parts. The first element of the multi-pronged strategy has been the economy. The second element is addressing the emotional side of aftermath, the scars in the minds of people. There is the need to remove the pain and anguish and encourage people to put their negative experiences behind them to face the future with courage and fortitude. The Reconciliation Commission has been put in place to enable this task.

The Diaspora is another crucial element. Whether we like it or not the Diaspora have an indispensable role to play. When I was in Washington to meet the US Secretary of State, Hillary Clinton, she told me that she would not advise me but talk about some the US experiences in this matter. She said that the Clinton Administration invested very considerable effort, time and money in reaching out to the Diaspora referring to the Americans in Northern Ireland. Although it took a great deal of time, it was well worth it. The results were commensurate with the expenditure that was expended on the task. The idea is to soften attitudes. It is not the intention of the Government of Sri Lanka to isolate the Diaspora, much less to demonize them. We want to reach out to them. Mr. Gothabaya Rajapakse, Secretary to the Ministry of Defence in Sri Lanka and I have been talking to the Diaspora. The central message that we are sending out to the Diaspora is that we want them to be involved in the political and economic advancement of the people in the conflict torn regions. We are asking them "Would you not really derive a deep sense of satisfaction by seeing the substantially improved economic conditions of the people of North and the East". There is an honest effort that is being made with regard to the development of infrastructure; highways, irrigation systems, schools, hospitals etc. We are asking them to be associated with these projects. I am happy to note that the responses have been for the most part very encouraging and promising. We are working closely with them and many of them have chosen to come back. They may not be coming to settle down but they are at least coming with their families to the country to see for themselves the conditions that prevail. There is no substitute for first hand observation and the Diaspora is doing this. This makes the situation in Sri Lanka very sanguine and full of hope for the future.

We are at a very critical juncture in the history of our country and to formulate progressive policies there must be a deep analysis. The Government of Sri Lanka is working to address the ramifications of the conflict and in doing so it intends to work with academics, intellectuals and professionals. In the new environment there is scope for all academics and professionals of the universities to participate fully. The President openly asks Tamil academics, intellectuals and professionals to participate in politics actively and has also offered them nominations from the SLFP, the ruling political party. This was not possible until the war came to an end as the LTTE claimed exclusivity that any Tamil speaking person who contested elections was not going to live for long. Today this situation has changed, with the absence of fear, duress and intimidation.

INTERNAL CONSEQUENCES

ETHNO-POLITICAL CONFLICT AND THE CIVIL WAR: DOMESTIC AND INTERNATIONAL IMPACT

S. I. Keethaponcalan

As one of the major violent ethno-political conflict in the world the confrontations between the Tamils and the Sinhalese in Sri Lanka attracted much attention academically and otherwise. Consequently, a great deal has been written on the conflict and the civil war paying particular attention to causes, consequences, and possible ways to resolve the conflict. However, no source exclusively deals with the consequences of the conflict in a systematic way. This chapter has been written with the intension of providing an in-depth analysis of the impact of the conflict, internally as well as internationally. As an introduction, the chapter delves briefly into the origin and development of the conflict. However, the focus is on the consequences rather than the origin and development of the conflict. The ethnic conflict and the civil war have had a tremendous impact on the polity and led to severe consequences. In fact one may argue that the basic premises of the Sri Lankan society have been altered irreversibly due to the conflict and its consequences. This chapter explores these consequences under two broad categories: (1) domestic consequences and (2) consequences with an international dimension. Under domestic effects three major aspects are being examined: (1) political, (2) security and (3) demographic. In terms of consequences with international dimension, the Indian intervention and the impact on India, the politics of the Tamil Diaspora, and the changes that took place in the recent past within Sri Lanka's foreign policy have been analyzed.

Ethnic Conflict and the Civil War

Much has been written on the ethnic conflict and the civil war in Sri Lanka. Therefore, this chapter does not intend to delve too much into this question. However, as an introduction, a brief section has been allocated to the origin and the development of the conflict before we move into the central theme of the chapter, the consequences of the conflict. As far as the origin of the conflict is concerned, there is obviously no agreement among scholars and even general public as to when exactly the problems began in Sri Lanka. At the societal level most people prefer to see the 1983 ethnic riots as the beginning of the conflict, as it marked the instigation of a new phase in the relations between the two largest ethnic communities in the country, the Sinhalese and the Tamil. Others however, consider 1956 as the watermark year because it was in this year the Sinhala Only Act, which made Sinhala the only official language of the state much to the chagrin of the Tamil community, was enacted. The Act almost permanently damaged the relations between the two communities and to large extent radicalized the Tamil nationalist groups. It was however clear that ethnically oriented disagreements and grievances existed even before the Sinhala Only Act. Others trace the origin of the conflict to the ancient history where, according to the Mahavamsa, the great Sinhala chronicle, Tamil and Sinhala kings were fighting each other centuries ago. For instance Mahavamsa claims that Dutugemunu, a Sinhala prince unified the island by defeating and killing the Tamil king of Ellalan in the battle field.

During the colonial period, especially the British occupation, the Sinhala – Tamil relations seemed cordial and the elite certainly coexisted without much difficulty. For instance, when the Sinhala leaders such as D.S and F.R. Senanayake were imprisoned by the British Government following the 1915 ethnic riots between the Sinhala and the Muslim communities, Ponnampalam Ramanathan, a leading Tamil political figure of the day carried forward a sustained campaign to seek justice for the Sinhala community.[1] The early days of the Ceylon National Congress (CNC) also witnessed greater collaboration between Sinhala and Tamil

---

[1] K.M. de Silva, *History of Ceylon* (Peradeniya, Sri Lanka: The University of Ceylon, 1973).

leaders. However, a split occurred in the CNC along ethnic lines on the question of a Tamil seat in the Western province leading to Ponnampalam Arunachalam's exit from the CNC. Arunachalam, the founder leader of the CNC, in 1921, formed his own organization called the Tamil Mahajana Sabha. The establishment of an ethnic based political institution marked the beginning of ethnic politics and contestation between the two communities. The trend that started in 1921 never was reversed and in the later stages escalated into a high intensity violent confrontation.

The Tamils, although small in numbers in relations to the majority Sinhalese played a vital role in the politics of the British Ceylon. For instance, Ponnampalam Ramanathan, was elected to the legislative council as the first representative of educated Ceylonese in 1911. The Tamils also were in the forefront of the movement for constitutional reform. In addition, largely due to the advantage they had in terms of English language education, the Tamils were slightly over-represented in the public sector employment. This created the impression especially within the Sinhala community that the Tamils were offered undue advantage and favored by the British. When the concept of self rule was introduced gradually, the Sinhalese started to assert their position as the predominant ethnic community. For instance, in 1936, a pan-Sinhala cabinet of ministers was formed excluding the Tamil and Muslim representatives. Alarmed by the obvious trend, the Tamils proposed a formula called the fifty-fifty to the Soulbury Commission, which was sent to Sri Lanka before independence. The fifty-fifty formula proposed by the All Ceylon Tamil Congress (ACTC) leader G.G.Ponnampalam envisaged fifty percent seats in the national legislature for the minority communities and the rest for the Sinhalese. The proposal amply demonstrated the gulf and the mistrust, which had developed between the two communities on the eve of the independence. Since the proposal did not fit into the liberal democratic ideals that the British Government was systematically inculcating within the Sri Lankan society and since the Sinhala leaders of the day were vehemently opposed to the Ponnampalam proposal, it was shot down by the Soulbury Commission.[2]

---

[2] A.Jeyaratnam Wilson, *Sri Lankan Tamil Nationalism, Its Origins and Development in the 19* *and 20th Centuries* (New Delhi: Penguin Books, 2000).

Although the British were accused of favoring the minority Tamil community, on the eve of the independence they had evolved into favoring the majority Sinhala community as political power was transferred, justified by liberal democratic principles, to the Sinhalese dominated political institutions, be it the newly formed United National Party (UNP), Parliament, or the Cabinet of Ministers. The only protection the Soulbury Commission or the independent constitution called the Soulbury Constitution provided to the minority communities was the Article 29 (2) which prevented parliament from enacting laws that favor one community over another.

Founded on the notion that the majority Sinhala community was discriminated against by the British, the new Governments formed in the immediate aftermath of independence began to introduce a series of measures that literally excluded the minority communities in general and the Tamil community in particular, from the process and the machinery of the state formation. The Citizenship Acts of 1948/49, the Sinhala Only Act, the nationalization projects, and the standardization schemes were some of the examples of these measures. One of the salient features of the Tamil politics in the first half of the 20th century was that it was extremely Colombo centric. Since the focus of the Tamil leadership was Colombo and Colombo centric politics, regionalism did not figure prominently in their schemes. Even the fifty-fifty proposal was a Colombo centric scheme; not a regional formula. The flip side of the argument is that the (north-east) regions were neglected not only by the Governments, but also the Tamil leadership. In the second half of the 20th century however, they were convinced that they cannot share power with the Sinhala leadership in Colombo and in anticipation of more anti-minority designs, they turned to regionalism.

The Federal Party, a splinter group of the ACTC, headed by S.J.V. Chelvanayagam, demanded greater regional autonomy for the North-East provinces, which was considered by the Tamils as their "homeland." The party carried on a non-violent campaign and signed two agreements with Governments in Colombo, but failed to achieve a solution to their problems. Frustrated by the inability of the moderate Tamil parties to win over their political demands, the Tamil youth, in the 1970s turned to violence in favor of a separate state for the Tamils. In the late 1970s and the early 1980s, several Tamil militant groups were in operation fighting effectively the Sri Lankan armed forces. In 1971, when the Janatha Vimukthi Peramuna attempted to violently overthrow the Government, the country possessed only a small and nominal armed force, which lacked modernity, training and sophisticated weaponry. It was with the generous assistance from friendly states that the insurgency was brought under control. However, in response to the challenge posed by the Tamil armed groups, the state armed forces also grew into a modern force and were able to resist the pressures emanating from the North East. With the LTTE evolving in to the sole armed group fighting the state in the name of the Tamil cause, a civil war resulted between the state armed forces and the LTTE, which continued for over two decades. During these two decades several attempts were made to resolve the conflict through peaceful means and several battle field successes were achieved by parties. Eventually however, the armed forces, in May 2009, managed to crush the LTTE violently. Consequently, the LTTE leadership, organizational structure, at least domestically and the membership were terminated and the state stands victorious.

Domestic Impact

Internally, the conflict had tremendous impact on the political and social life of all segments of the people. They could range from psychological impact to the change in the demographic composition of some of the regions. In order however, to preserve the focus of the chapter, only the political, security related and demographic changes have been analyzed in this section. Politically, the conflict has led to erosion of democracy and democratic values, over-centralization of political power, and strengthening of ethnic politics. In terms of security related consequences, introduction of stringent anti-terrorism laws and the politicization of military and militarization of politics and civil administration have been noted. The other major domestic impact of the conflict is the changes that took place in the demographic composition of some of the regions close to the conflict.

Political Consequences

Erosion of Democracy

One of the areas where the major impact of the conflict was felt was on democracy and democratic governance. Sri Lanka boasts of a long tradition of democracy as institutions of representation were established by the colonial powers and in fact universal franchise was granted to Ceylon as early as in 1931, well before many of the European states adopted it. The Ceylonese people and the political leaders readily accepted the democratic political culture and parliamentary democracy introduced by the British rulers. In a way, the values introduced by the colonial masters shaped and determined the nature of the Ceylon national movement. In contrast to Indian nationalist movement, which pursued the objective of total independence and carried on a radical movement, the Sri Lankans adopted a conciliatory approach and were more interested in constitutional reform than independence. Sri Lankans were trying to win political power through democratic means. In India even the non-violent campaign headed by Mohandas Gandhi bordered on political radicalism. The Sri Lankans on the other hand confined their entire campaign to parliamentary methods. Largely due to this trend Ceylon was considered by many as a model democracy in the third world region. Even in the early days of independence Sri Lankans adhered to the democratic principles rather strongly. Electoral principles and parliamentary methods remained strong despite the effort of some of the leaders to extend the life of their Governments, illegitimately. For instance, Prime Minister Sirimavo Bandaranaike's regime that was elected in 1970 for a five year period wanted to extend the life of the Government well beyond five years. It however could not do so for long and was forced to dissolve parliament and opt for an election in 1977. The party lost the election very badly partly due to its authoritarian tendencies and abuse of power. This was because democracy was valued as a way of life and people wanted to protect the value.

Democracy as a value lost its power and appeal however in the recent past largely due to the ethnic conflict. As the ethnic conflict escalated radicals in the North as well as in the South began to argue that democratic values may be compromised in order to win the war. On this argument human rights were violated and democratic ideals of social and political institutions were sacrificed leading to almost total collapse of democratic values in the country. Democratic governance was also compromised as authoritarianism and abuse of power have become the norm. In the post-war period, development discourse replaced the "winning the war" slogan and is being used as an excuse for furthering authoritarian tendencies. The Government on this front has been ably assisted by radical nationalist parties. If not resisted, the gradual erosion of democratic values may lead to the transformation of Sri Lanka into a one party state like Singapore.

Centralization of Political Power

When the foreign powers arrived in the Island in the early 16th century, there were three distinct kingdoms in the territory, two Sinhalese and one Tamil. Since then however a process of unification and centralization was set in motion and eventually it was the British who succeeded in unifying the whole island under one political and administrative structure. Therefore, centralization was not a new phenomenon to Sri Lanka. Yet, the Soulbury Constitution that facilitated transfer of power devised a loose structure with space for sharing of power among at least a few institutions. Although the Prime Minister was the chief executive officer, he or she was dependent to a large extent on the cabinet of ministers and even on Parliament. Political groupings other than the two main parties were also able to exercise some influence on the ruling regime and have a say in public policy making. Also the constitution did not specifically label Sri Lanka or rather Ceylon as a unitary state. The British in fact left an ambiguous state structure as elements of federalism were also present. For instance, the national legislature left by the British was a bi-cameral institution with the Senate as an integral part of the legislative process. The 1972 charter, the First Republican Constitution, effectively paved the way for further centralization by declaring the country a unitary state. It is imperative to note that when the First Republican Constitution was devised the Tamils were fighting hard demanding a federal state. In fact the Federal Party made a proposal before the Constituent Assembly to transform the state into a federal structure. Therefore, the decision to make the state a formal unitary structure could be depicted as nipping the Tamil demand in the bud.

However, further centralization took place when the executive Presidential system was introduced by altering the First Republican Constitution in 1978. This constitution concentrated the entire system and political power on one person, the President. According to this constitution the President is the head of state and the Government, he or she is the Commander in Chief of the Armed Forces, and takes all important public policy decisions. Therefore, this constitution created an all powerful President. The interesting aspect however is that the powerful Presidential system in Sri Lanka was justified by the need to have stable Governments and strong leaders, first to ensure economic development and second, to face the challenges created by the ethnic conflict and Tamil militancy.[3]

Excessive centralization on the other hand led to abuse of power and authoritarianism. Almost all Sri Lankan Governments in the recent past stand accused of abuse of power. J.R.Jayewardene for instance deprived Sirimavo Bandaranaike, the leader of the opposition Sri Lanka Freedom Party and the main challenge to the Jayewardene presidency, of her civic rights in order to prevent her from contesting the Presidential election. An oppressive policy was adopted by President Premadasa especially in terms of his political opponents and during his time in office, civil liberties were severely curtailed. In response a sort of a democracy movement evolved contributing to the election of Chandrika Kumaratunga as the President in 1994. The abuse of power and authoritarianism prevailed after the introduction of the Second Republican Constitution led to the popular demand for the abolition of the present charter and reverting back to the Westminster style of governance.[4] Chandrika Kumaratunga

---

[3] K.M.de Silva & Howard Wriggins, *J.R.Jayewardene of Sri Lanka, A Political Biography* (London: Leo Cooper, 1994).

[4] This does not mean that authoritarianism was the result of 1978 constitution. Political authoritarianism prevailed even before the introduction of Presidential system and caused by multitude of factors. To be precise one can argue that it was in the early 1970s, under the United Front Government headed by Prime Minister Sirima Bandaranaike, the slip towards authoritarianism originated in Sri Lanka.

came to power on the promise to abolish the Presidential system. As the President she never was serious about getting rid of the present constitution as promised and in fact, in the later years, she was also accused of political authoritarianism.

The South[5] that vehemently opposed the existing constitution, in 2010, supported further consolidation of Presidential powers under the same constitution. Mahinda Rajapaksa, like his predecessor from the SLFP, promised to do away with the Presidential system and won the presidency in 2005. Rajapaksa pursued the war against the LTTE with determination and with the assistance from friendly states like India, China and the United States of America defeated the LTTE comprehensively. The military victory boosted the image of the President and his popularity in the South shot up. Without wasting too much time, the President went for re-election and won handsomely. The parliamentary election was also wrapped up with much ease as the ruling coalition came close to winning a two thirds majority.[6] Constitutional change in Sri Lanka requires a two thirds majority in the national legislature. By eliciting the support of some of the opposition members of parliament, the Government mustered the necessary strength to amend the Constitution. In September 2010, the Government, through constitutional change, lifted the two term limit of a President. Originally the Article 31 (2) specified that a person shall hold the office of the President only for two terms. This clause was removed. Also the 17th amendment to the constitution, which in 2001 transferred some Presidential powers to the Constitutional Council, was altered transferring the powers back into the President. Therefore, the Sri Lanka presidency currently is much stronger and far too centralized. The present Government was able to do this only due to its achievements in terms of ending the war.

Ethnic Politics

As indicated elsewhere in this chapter the Tamils and Sinhalese co-

---

[5] Meaning the Sinhala people.

[6] Presidential and the parliamentary elections were conducted in January and April 2010 respectively.

existed rather peacefully during the early stages of the British rule and they were working together towards the common aim of greater constitutional reform. Some commentators argue that it was the system of ethnic representation adopted by the British that ignited the ethnic politics and later the conflict. However, the introduction of the universal franchise in 1931 had the potential to exasperate ethnic differences.[7] Ethnic slogans or in other words racism became an important tool to win elections in the post 1931 period. Taking advantage of the fears of their own communities in relation to other ethnic or social groups ethnically oriented political parties were formed and ethnic slogans against other communities were used to win election. Racism was and is a sure fire vote catcher in Sri Lanka.[8] The 1956 general election was an excellent example of this trend. There was sort of a competition between the two mainly Southern parties, the United National Party and the Sri Lanka Freedom Party, to offer the best Sinhala nationalist stance to the Sinhala voters. For instance, the SLFP adopted the Sinhala only policy while the UNP was still in favor of two languages, Sinhala and Tamil. In response to the growing SLFP popularity within the Sinhala community the UNP also declared that it was also adopting the Sinhala only policy. Immediately, the SLFP announced that it will make Sinhala the only official language of Sri Lanka within 24 hours if it won the election. The SLFP in fact rooted the UNP out by winning a landslide in this election.

The conventional wisdom is that these two parties, the SLFP and the UNP are national parties and other parties especially the minority parties are ethnic parties. It is however, imperative to note that although these two groups are called national parties, they are essentially Sinhala parties as their primary vote base is among the Sinhala people. These parties have no option but focus primarily on the Sinhala people due the on-going competing ethnic nationalisms. For instance, SLFP hardly attract minority votes unless extremely prominent minority leaders represent the party. The SLPF especially in Colombo was able to attract considerable

---

[7] Jane Russell, *Communal Politics Under the Donoughmore Constitution,* 1931-1947 (Dehiwala, Sri Lanka: Tisara Prakasakayo Ltd., 1982).

[8] S. Vanniasingham, *Sri Lanka: The Conflict Within* (London: Sangam Books, 1989).

Muslim votes due to the influence of prominent Muslim leaders like A.H.M. Fowzie. Increasingly the Tamils refrain from voting the Tamil candidates running for office on the SLFP ticket. The UNP on the other hand has the tendency of fielding minority candidate and tend to win minority votes, which has created the impression that the UNP is comparatively less Sinhala nationalist or pro-minority. It is however, pointed out that the UNP has also introduced some of the most dangerous anti-Tamil measures. For instance, the 1983 (July) ethnic riots were unleashed under the watch of the UNP Government, which wanted to teach the Tamils a lesson. The Prevention of Terrorism Act (PTA), which was described as draconian by most of the independent observers and the Tamil commentators, was originally introduced by the UNP Government.

In sum, one can argue that the nationalistic attitude of the two largest parties was a cause and consequence of the ethnic conflict and it also served as a cause for further escalation. However, as the conflict escalated and with the radicalization of Tamil nationalism, these two parties began to soften their stance vis-à-vis ethnic relation and the Tamil role in the affairs of the state as they increasingly became accommodative. For instance, in the middle of the 1990s, under the leadership of Chandrika Kumaratunga, the SLFP, which hitherto, demonstrated hard-line Sinhala nationalist attitude turned substantially accommodative of minority concerns and became pro-peace. Due to this transformation the party was able to absorb the sympathy of the Tamil people, which was evident from the unprecedented support she received from the Tamil people in the early days of her tenure as the President. In the late 1990s, under the leadership of Ranil Wickremesinghe the UNP also turned pro-peace and contested the 2001 general election on a peace platform and won.

Interestingly, the accommodative policies and attitude of the two largest political parties created a vacuum in Sinhala nationalist politics as no major political grouping represented this segment of the political opinion. First it was the Janatha Vimukthi Peramuna (JVP) and then the Jathika Hela Urumaya (JHU), which stepped into fill the vacuum left by the two major parties. The JVP started its political journey as a Marxist entity with the aim of capturing state power through violent revolution. Despite its Marxist conviction the JVP could not shed the ethnic prejudices as it believed that the Tamils were the "fifth column" or Indian agents.[9] The party believed that there was no ethnic conflict in Sri Lanka, justifying the notion that devolution of power to address the Tamil concerns was unnecessary. This stance enabled the party to oppose the peace talks between the Government of Sri Lanka headed by Ranil Wickremesinghe and the LTTE in 2002. Mass agitation was used as the primary weapon against the peace process, through which the party was also able to magnify its parliamentary strength from mere 16 seats in 2001 to 39 in 2004. The JVP despite its Marxist label was effectively doing ethnic politics. In this process the party transformed itself into the "protector" of the Sinhala Buddhist constituency and the state, a role traditionally played by the Buddhist Sangha. The peace process and the new role the JVP was playing ignited a new phenomenon within the Southern polity as some of the politically motivated Buddhist monks organized themselves into a political party called the Jathika Hela Urumaya,[10] among other objectives, but primarily, to oppose the peace attempts and prevent possible devolution of political power. In the 2004 parliamentary election, which the new party faced for the first time, the JHU won nine seats, an impressive performance by any standard. The ideological foundation of both the JVP and the JHU in relation to the ethnic conflict brought the two parties into direct contestation as both were competing to win the same voter base, i.e the Sinhala Buddhist constituency. Through this competition however, they were able to determine the state policy towards the minority communities and especially the peace process in the early 2000s. This was possible only because the two main Southern partiers or at least their leadership were advocating an accommodative approach towards the minorities.

In 2005, with the nomination of Mahinda Rajapaksa as the Presidential candidate, the SLFP went back to its traditional ideological

---

[9] David Rampton & Asanga Welikala,*The Politics of the South, Part of the Sri Lanka Strategic Conflict Assessment 2005* (Colombo: The Asia Foundation, 2005).

[10] National Heritage Party.

foundation where accommodative policies were abandoned in favor of a relatively hard-line approach. Rajapaksa announced that he intends to achieve an honorable peace and any solution to the ethnic conflict should be achieved within the existing unitary structure of the state. By "an honorable peace" Rajapaksa meant that the peace talk will not be conducted according to the dictates of the LTTE, but according to the rules set by the state. The "solution within the unitary structure" slogan shut down any hope of an amicable solution. Interestingly, due to the ideological similarities, the JVP and the JHU endorsed Rajapaksa candidacy and worked tirelessly for his electoral victory. Following the electoral victory, Rajapaksa focused on the war and managed to wipe out the LTTE completely. The way the war was pursued and the victory, helped co-opt almost all nationalist Southern parties except the JVP.

A parallel process of ethnic politics took place within the Tamil community, which since 1921, was pursuing an ethnically oriented but Colombo centric politics. Almost all major political groupings formed by Tamil leaders in the first half of the 20th century were ethnic in nature. *Tamil* Mahajana Sabha, the All Ceylon *Tamil* Congress and the Federal Party, which was called the *Tamil* Arasu Katchi in Tamil language, were some of the examples of this trend. Almost all of these parties extensively used Tamil racist or nationalist slogans to win votes, in a mirror image of the Southern politics. Tamil nationalist groups were brought together to form the Tamil United Liberation Front in 1976, which demanded a separate state for the Tamil people in the North-East.

Leadership of the Tamil nationalist movement was transferred effectively to the Tamil militant groups in the mid 1980s. Although a small group of Muslim youth was involved in the struggle, almost all the armed groups were ethnic Tamil in nature in the early days of separatist insurgency. Also they were fragmented as several armed groups were fighting the state at the same time. Through a process of elimination and integration, the LTTE, in the early 1990s, emerged as the sole fighting force. Armed groups like the Eelam People's Revolutionary Liberation Front (EPRLF) and the Tamil Eelam Liberation Organization (TELO) were violently eliminated and the groups like Eelam Revolutionary

Organization (EROS) were integrated with the LTTE. The LTTE policies and strategies further fragmented the Tamil polity as many of the groups that were targeted by the LTTE joined the Government and the state armed forces and fought against the LTTE. The centralization of armed struggle in the LTTE and to a large extent one person, Velupillai Prabaharan, the founder leader of the LTTE, made the subjugation of the struggle by the state armed forces possible.

The conflict also forced other ethnic and social communities in the island to pursue ethnic politics. For instance, the Sri Lanka Muslims, the third largest ethnic group in the country also in the later stages of the conflict got in to the ethnic politics by forming a separate Muslim identity. Based on the newly formed separate identity the Muslims also created their own ethnically based political party, the SLMC. Currently there are several Muslim parties or splinter groups in operation. Although the Muslim parties are fragmented, the community had achieved remarkable success in political bargaining with the successive Governments. The Indian Tamils in the plantation sector also have their own ethnically oriented parties, slogans, campaigns and strategies. Therefore, it is clear that the Sri Lankan polity is fragmented very seriously by ethnic factors. Ethnic conflict and ethnic fragmentation could be explained as cause and consequence of the conflict.

Security

Stringent Anti-terrorism Laws

One of the direct impacts of the conflict is the introduction of stringent anti-terrorism laws, which in turn generated very serious questions of human rights violation in the later years. There are two important pieces of legislations in this regard: (1) the Emergency Regulations and (2) the Prevention of Terrorism Act (PTA). It is however, imperative to note that the Emergency Regulations were reintroduced in response to the first JVP insurrection of 1971. The PTA however was a direct result of the increasing violence that emanated from the ethnic conflict.

Since the mid-1970s, a series of robberies were reported from the North, some of the Tamil political leaders affiliated to Southern political parties and civilians collaborating with Sinhala polity were either attacked or killed, and especially Tamil members of the police were targeted and killed. For instance, Puthur branch of the Peoples Bank was robbed on March 5, 1975. On July 2, a Tamil civilian who was suspected of collaborating with the Sri Lankan Government was shot and killed in Urumpirai. Alfred Thuraiappa, Jaffna Mayor and a leading member of the ruling Sri Lanka Freedom Party, was shot dead on July 27. On May 18, 1977 two Tamil police constables were shot dead in Inuvil in Jaffna. On August 16, *Yarldevi*, the Colombo–Jaffna express train was attacked in Pungankulam. Police Inspector Bastiampillai and four other policemen belonging to the police intelligence branch were shot and killed in Murunkan-Madhu road on April 07, 1978.[11]

Hence, it was clear that the security situation in the Northern Province in general and Jaffna district in particular was fast deteriorating and the security forces and the police stationed in Jaffna were losing control. Violence perpetrated against suspected Tamil militants and civilians did not yield any results in favor of the armed forces. Instead counter insurgency methods employed by the armed forces and police alienated the people to a great extent and the Army was perceived as an alien occupying force. The political leadership in the South and the security apparatus were frustrated as they received little or no assistance from the Tamil people to arrest the growing trend of violence. Furthermore, the fact that the Tamil militants could easily cross the Palk Strait to seek refuge in Tamil Nadu after attacks added to the sense of helplessness.[12] It was against this backdrop, in April 1978 the LTTE officially communicated to the world of its existence and claimed responsibility for eleven assassinations. The communiqué sent shockwaves in the South and the Government responded with a piece of legislation to ban the LTTE called the

---

[11] For further details on violent incidents in Sri Lanka see, Ahmar Moonis,   *Violence and Terrorism in South Asia, 1971-2004* (Karachi: University of K arachi, 2005).

[12] K.M.de Silva & Howard Wriggins, 1994. p.352.

Proscription of the Liberation Tigers of Tamil Eelam and Similar Organizations Act No 16 of 1978, which also failed to end the violence and increasing popularity of the militant movements in the North.

In 1979, the United National Party Government headed by President J.R.Jayewardene decided to replace the Proscription Act of 1978 with what is called the *Prevention of Terrorism (Temporary Provisions) Act No 48 of 1979*. Some of the observers who had examined the PTA had imparted the impression that the Government's primary response to the troubles in the North was legal.[13] It is however necessary to note that the J.R. Jayewardene Government never was dependent exclusively on legal instruments to counter the challenges posed by the Tamil militants. The Government adopted a combined strategy of counter-insurgency violence, threat, for instance of ethnic riots, and of course special legislations. Before the PTA was introduced in Parliament Brig. Tissa Weeratunga was appointed as the overall commander for Jaffna with instructions to eliminate terrorism before December 31, 1979. The armed forces were granted greater freedom to achieve the objective of curbing terrorism. However, the existing Emergency Regulations, in the view of the ruling party, were not adequate for the task in hand, leading to the enactment of the PTA, which granted excessive powers to the armed forces and the executive branch in dealing with the violence in the North. Hence, one could argue that the primary response of the Government to the Tamil militancy was not legal; it depended heavily on counter insurgency violence and the PTA and other legal instruments were enacted only to bolster the military approach.

Significantly, a closer look at the political developments in this period also indicates that the PTA had a definite political dimension. Therefore, it is safe to assume that the PTA was not only a response to Tamil militancy, but also ethnic politics of the Tamil parties, particularly the Tamil United Liberation Front (TULF). The emerging trends in the Tamil politics was not only worrying but also irritating the President. Leaders of the TULF, which was formed incorporating a number of

---

[13] Ibid.

Tamil political parties to bolster the Tamil cause, won the parliamentary election in 1977 on a campaign for separate state. If this was not bad enough for the Sinhala polity, Appapillai Amirthalingam, leader of the TULF and a Tamil became the leader of the opposition in Parliament for the first (and only) time in the post colonial history of Sri Lanka. Not many Sinhalese were happy about this development. K.M.de Silva points out "There was no precedent in the history of the parliamentary democracies of the commonwealth for the position of the Leader of the Opposition being held by the head of a party committed to a separatist programme, and thus to the dismemberment of the polity."[14]

The TULF leadership while serving as the main opposition party was still maintaining relationship with the Tamil militant organizations and in times guiding and manipulating the violent youth to facilitate its own agendas. Hence, the close relationship between the so called non-violent democratic political party and violence in the North was evident.[15] This trend annoyed J.R.Jayewardene and many other Sinhala leaders in the South. In response to an interview granted by Appapillai Amirthalingam to *Newsweek* of 8 August 1977 in support of a separate state, President J.R.Jayewardene contended "...when statements of that type are made the news chapters carry them throughout the island, and when you say that you are not violent but that violence may be used in time to come, what do you think the other people in Sri Lanka will do? How will they react? If you want to fight, let there be a fight; if it is peace, let there be peace. That is what they will say. It is not what I am saying. The people of Sri Lanka say that."[16] Moreover the Sansoni Commission that investigated the 1977 ethnic riots against the Tamils contended that some of the action of the TULF and speeches made by leaders of the party contributed to the ethnic violence.[17] The parliamentary

---

[14] Ibid.

[15] Loganathan, Ketheshwaran, *Sri Lanka: Lost Opportunities – Past Attempts at Resolving the Ethnic Conflict* (Colombo: Center for Policy Research and Analysis, 1996).

[16] de Silva, & Wriggins, 1994. p.352.

[17] Sansoni Commission Report, *Report of the Presidential Commission of Inquiry into the Incidents Which Took Place between 13 th August and 15 th September 1977* (Colombo: Government Press, 1980).

debate on the proposed Prevention of Terrorism Act was marked by verbal attacks on TULF for complicity with Tamil militants and for unsettling ethnic harmony, by especially Justice Minister K.W. Devanayakam and Lalith Athulathmudali. Therefore, the Government wanted to curb the activities of the TULF as well. It is against this backdrop that the Section 2 (h) of the PTA, which stipulates that "Any person who… by words either spoken or intended to be read or by signs or by visible representations or otherwise causes or intends to cause commission of acts of violence or religious, racial or communal disharmony or feelings of ill-will or hostility between different communities or racial or religious groups…shall be guilty of an offence under this Act," gains significance. This provision was clearly aimed at the TULF leadership and it was also politically motivated.

Although the immediate aim of the PTA was prevention of violence in the North, it had much broader provisions, which had the potential to be used in other situations as well. This created a sense of anxiety among Southern political parties, some of which charged that the Act could be used to suppress political activities in the South. That was why the Sri Lanka Freedom Party proposed an amendment to confine the Act to the Jaffna peninsula, only to be rejected by the Government. In 1982, pointing to the Section 2 (e), which provided that "any person who…commits the offence of mischief to the property of the Government, any department statutory board, public co-operation bank, co-operative union or co-operative society or to any other public property… shall be guilty of an offence under this Act," Sarath Muttetuwegama of the Communist Party argued that the law could be used to suppress trade union actions and political resistance in the South.[18] Indeed, it is imperative to note that the PTA was used in the South against political rivals including journalists and trade unionists. The PTA was extensively used in the late 1980s to suppress the second JVP rebellion. Hence, it is obvious that although the immediate objective of the PTA was defeating the Tamil militancy in the North, it was motivated heavily

---

[18] "That Terrorism Act Amendment Bill," *Saturday Review*, 27 March 1982. p. 9.

by broader political schemes. The PTA has been criticized heavily by international human rights organization and commentators from the Tamil community for assisting severe human rights violations.

Politics and the Military

Currently, Sri Lanka has a sophisticated and in a way over sized armed force. The evolution of the armed forces commenced with the creation of the Ceylon Army in 1949 through a parliamentary legislation.[19] A ceremonial force grew from mere thousands to approximately 200,000 men and women in the early 2000. Today Sri Lankan armed forces comprise of a fully developed Army, a sophisticated Navy and a reasonably well equipped Air Force in addition to a police force. The armed forces also include several affiliated bodies such as intelligence agencies and possibly secret operation units like the Long Reconnaissance Units. This growth and the sophistication were a direct result of the ethnic conflict and the civil war.

Although the Sri Lankan armed forces are a powerful institution and very influential, except on a couple of occasions they have stayed out of politics and political issues. In 1962, a group of military and police officers planned a coup to overthrow the Government of Prime Minister Sirimavo Bandaranaike. Since one of the conspirators, a police officer, on the eve of the coup, informed the Government of the impending military scheme, the Government moved in swiftly and arrested almost all the officers involved in the planned military coup. Many of them were sentenced to lengthy jail terms. It was clear that this failed attempt to overthrow a democratically elected Government was undertaken by a very small number of displeased officers without large scale support within the military or the population. It was also not very well planned. In Pakistan and Bangladesh, two key members of the South Asian polity, the armed forces are tempted more often than not by political power and have staged several successful military coups. The fact that despite a

---

[19] Army Act No. 17 of 1949.

problematic polity and social milieu, the Sri Lankan armed forces did not nor could not take-over political power by extra legal means was depicted as an indication of the strength of the country's democratic tradition.

The other major incident where the military intervened in political issues occurred during the recent peace process.[20] As the ethnically oriented conflict progressed and transformed into an internal civil war, the military began to occupy large portion of the territory in Jaffna peninsula and other parts of the Northern Province declaring them as High Security Zones (HSZ). The gradual expansion of the HSZs created a humanitarian situation within the Tamil community as many families were forced to move to other areas as internally displaced people (IDPs). The LTTE, demanding shrinking of the HSZs, raised the issue as a precondition for further progress of the peace process. The military high command in the North, particularly Major General Sarath Fonseka, who would later become a major issue and an important factor in Sri Lankan politics, openly opposed any move to alter the HSZs by writing directly to the media. Except for these two major incidents, the Sri Lankan armed forces stayed under the control of the civilian-political leadership and took pride in playing the second fiddle to the political leadership.[21]

However, a closer look at the military and the political culture in Sri Lanka indicates elements of militarization of politics and civil administration and the politicization of the military. As the size, capacity and value of the armed forces magnified, its political role and ambitions also increased. Although no major or known attempts were made to stage a military coup after 1962, the role of the military personnel in politics has multiplied. Unlike in the early days of independence, several military leaders have entered active politics in the recent past. For instance, Major General Janaka Perera, a revered military hero of the South contested

---

[20] The recent and final peace process was undertaken between the Government of Sri Lanka and the LTTE from 2002 – 04.

[21] S.I.Keethaponcalan, *Sri Lanka: Politics of Power, Crisis and Peace, 2000-2005* (Colombo & Chennai: Kumaran Book House, 2009), pp. 103-05.

the provincial council election in 2008 representing the main opposition UNP.[22] General Sarath Fonseka who led the Army as its commander and provided leadership to the entire campaign during the final war with the LTTE entered politics even before he was completely discharged from active duties. He contested the 2010 Presidential election as the common candidate of the major opposition parties and posed an enormous challenge to the incumbent President, who otherwise was extremely popular for winning the war. Immediately after the election, the Government detained him on claim that he was conspiring to overthrow the Government with the help of deserted military officers. General Fonseka was sentenced to 30 months of rigorous imprisonment. General Fonseka could be depicted as a symbol of the growing influence of military in politics.

The growing political clout of the military has also led to greater accommodation of the military personnel by successive Governments. A large number of former leaders of the armed forces have been appointed to civil service, diplomatic corps, and brought into the state mechanism as chairmen, governors, commissioners and so on. Rear Admiral (retd) Mohan Wijewickrama serves as the Governor of the Eastern Province. Major General G.A. Chandrasiri was appointed as the Governor of the Northern Province in 2009. The prison system is headed by Major General V.R. de Silva. Some of the military leaders have been sent abroad as ambassadors. For instance former Air Force Commander and Chief of Staff Donald Perera is currently serving as the Sri Lankan Ambassador to Israel. The present Defence Secretary, who commands substantial authority, also served in the military. A significant turn of events is that some of the civilian structures for instance the non-Governmental organizations, and urban development authority has been placed under the Minister of Defence, currently. It is also possible that Sri Lankan Governments in the recent past have been accommodating substantial number of military and police leaders in order to mitigate the temptation to overthrow elected Governments.

---

[22] He was killed by a suicide bomber during the election campaign.

Demography

Like many other factors that are linked to the conflict, demographical changes or alterations also influenced the conflict as a cause and consequence. First the issue of demography came up in the discourse when the Tamil people began to complain about what they called systematic state sponsored colonization schemes in the historical habitat of Tamil people in the North-East provinces. Post-independent Governments of Sri Lanka under the pretext of development schemes began to settle Sinhala people mainly from the South in the North-East provinces, in a way altering the demographic composition of the areas thereby reducing the dominance of the Tamils in these areas. Consequently, the Tamils lost dominance in regions like the Eastern province and Vavuniya in the Northern Province. Weakening of the population strength in these regions also had the potential to reduce Tamil representation in institutions of representation including the national legislature. Sensing the danger of state sponsored colonization schemes, the Tamils made "land" and "land settlements" a major issue in any negotiation with the Governments of Sri Lanka in the past and managed to gain concessions. For instance, the Bandaranaike-Chelvanayakam Pact of 1957 and the Dudley Senanayake - Chelvanayakam Pact of 1965 had provisions on land issues. These provisions were included to ensure the Tamil community that their population strength will not be altered artificially.

The evolution of the conflict into a civil war however, had unavoidable impact on the ethnic composition of areas that are linked to the war. For instance, as violence intensified many Tamils, in order to avoid the security threat emanated from the battle, moved to other areas domestically and internationally. They moved to India and Western countries. Many of them at the same time moved to Colombo. The Tamil displacement had dual impact. For instance, the number of Tamils in Jaffna and other major Tamil cities dwindled while their strength in some of the Southern cities especially Colombo increased dramatically. During the war, it seemed that by fighting for Jaffna, meaning the land in the North, the Government lost Colombo to the Tamils. The flip side of the story is that as the conflict intensified the number of armed forces increased drastically in the Tamil areas necessitating the possession of land to set up military camps. According to the statistics provided by Tamil activists about one thirds of the land in Jaffna peninsula alone has been acquired by the state as High Security Zones, where the civilian habitat has been completely prevented. The military however, maintained that only 18% of the land has been taken over by the military to be used as HSZs.

An important dimension of the displacement and demography is the predicament of the Muslims of the Northern Province. The LTTE, influenced by its own security analysis, expelled all the Muslims in the North without any warning in 1990. The expelled Muslims in large numbers settled in the district of Puttalam, which in turn gave way to new conflicts and tension in the district. The expulsion of the Muslims from the North transformed monolithically the population of the LTTE controlled areas.

International Dimension

Some of the consequences of the conflict had an international dimension but they essentially occurred within the Sri Lankan soil. For instance, key activities related to the Indian intervention and the deployment of the Indian military essentially took place in Sri Lanka. However, assassination of former Indian Prime Minister Rajiv Gandhi could be called an international consequence. This section also examines the politics of Tamil Diaspora in the West. Of late, Sri Lankan foreign policy as well changed drastically due to the necessities created by the decision to terminate the LTTE militarily. Important consequences in this regard have also been explored in this section.

Indian Intervention

The violent conflict unavoidably led to the greater foreign involvement and interference in Sri Lanka. Primary among them was the Indian intervention which began in the late 1970s covertly and a more direct and official involvement began following the anti-Tamil ethnic riots in 1983. Sri Lanka due to its geographical location is critical for India's security and national interest. In the immediate aftermath of independence it was suggested by some analysts that Ceylon should be annexed with the Indian union.[23] Also due to its regional ambitions and its role as a potential regional super power, India assumed the task of "security manager" of the South Asian region.[24] Although these concerns and projects did not lead to concrete political measures from New Delhi, it was important to ensure that the island nation did not transform into a base for powers that are hostile to India and its international projects. When President J.R.Jayewardene's Government since the late 1970s leaned radically towards the West in general and the US in particular, Sri Lanka began to go against the interest of the neighboring regional super power. Since Sri Lanka was making foreign policy decisions based on the notion of state sovereignty, India could do very little to stop the slide.

In order, therefore to influence the Government of Sri Lanka, India began to take advantage of the ethnic conflict and started to arm and train Tamil militant groups, leading to the setting up of several training camps in India itself. The decision to espouse the Tamil militant groups was also influenced by the relations between the Sri Lankan Tamils and the Tamils in India and the impact of the conflict on the politics of the Southern state of Tamil Nadu. The Tamil militants were also using Tamil Nadu as a base to stage attacks in Sri Lanka. Tamil Nadu also served as a safe haven for militants wanted by the Sri Lankan authorities. At this stage, the Indian assistance to Tamil militancy however, was unofficial and remained as a covert operation by the Indian secret services.

The covert involvement however, turned to direct and more official intervention following the 1983 anti-Tamil ethnic riots. Prime Minister Indira Gandhi sent her foreign minister for a fact finding mission to Sri Lanka and based on his report, appointed a special envoy in G.Parthasarathy for peace making. The Indian intervention as a peace

---

[23] Shelton Kodikara, *Foreign Policy of Sri Lanka* (Delhi: Chanakya Publications, 1992).

[24] P. Venkateshwar Rao, Ethnic Conflict in Sri Lankan: India' s Role and Perceptions, *Asian Survey*, 28 (4), April 1988, p. 419.

maker in Sri Lanka in the early 1980s had two primary targets: (1) managing the conflict, and (2) keeping the Sri Lanka Government within its own policy orientations. The second objective was to be achieved through the peace maker role. Under Indian auspices, several peacemaking attempts were made. Prominent among them were the All Party Conference convened in Sri Lanka to discuss, among other proposals, the "Annexure C" framework formulated by Parthasarathy himself, and the Thimpu Talks, conducted primarily between representatives of the Government of Sri Lanka and the Tamil militant groups in the capital city of Bhutan. These two peace attempts failed largely due to the confidence both parties had on military solution. Both at this point in time believed that they could achieve their goals militarily.

The conflict led to the deployment of foreign military forces, for the first time in the post-colonial history of the country, when the Indians frustrated by the inability of the parties in conflict to reach an agreement, transformed their role from mediators to negotiators. Especially after the collapse of the Thimpu Talks, India began to negotiate directly with the Government of Sri Lanka. Using threat of punishment and reward as a strategy it successfully negotiated an agreement with the Sri Lankan Government, which while devising a mechanism to devolve powers, ensured the Indian control over the affairs of its Southern neighbor. The Indo-Lanka Accord of July 1987 paved way for the establishment of the provincial councils through the 13th Amendment to the constitution of Sri Lanka. Indian influence over the island nation was preserved, rather formally through provisions that prevented Sri Lanka for example from allowing unfriendly states to use Sri Lankan ports, especially the Trincomalee harbor, and Sri Lankan soil for gathering intelligence on India.[25] Critics pointed out that these provisions of the Indo-Sri Lanka deal violated Sri Lankan sovereignty. The Agreement also allowed Indian armed forces in Sri Lanka as a peace keeping force. Clause six of the Annexure to the Agreement stated that "The President of Sri Lanka and

---

[25] Alan J. Bullion, *India, Sri Lanka and the Tamil Crisis 1976 – 1994* (London: Cassel Publishers, 1995).

the Prime Minister of India also agree that in the terms of paragraph 2.14 and paragraph 2.16 (c) of the agreement, an Indian peace keeping contingent may be invited by the President of Sri Lanka to guarantee and enforce the cessation of hostilities, if so required." It was however clear from the inception that the Sri Lankan President did not have much liberty in this matter as it was part of the deal. The Indian Peace Keeping Force (IPKF) arrived in the island immediately after the signing of the agreement.

The arrival of the IPKF in Sri Lanka amidst much controversy ignited two new dimensions of the already existing high intensity violence. First, an armed conflict ensured between the so called peacekeeper, the Indian armed forces and the LTTE. While signing the agreement, on behalf of the Tamils in Sri Lanka, the Indian Government attempted to gain the consent of the Tamil groups, including moderate political parties as well as the militants. Almost all the groups, including the TULF, openly declared their approval. But the LTTE had to be forced through armed fist tactics to accept the deal.[26] Under pressure, the LTTE consented to the agreement and to surrender arms, but in the first available opportunity attacked the IPKF leading to a sustained violent campaign. The confrontations between the LTTE and the IPKF led to killing and maiming of large number of men on both sides and violation of the rights of the civilian population in the North-East including the right to life.

Second, the JVP, which had already attempted to capture state power through violent rebellion, went underground following the proscription of the organization after the 1983 riots and started a fresh violent campaign. Slogans against Indian intervention in Sri Lanka formed the basis of this campaign. The brutal violence and counter violence unleashed by the JVP and the armed forces led to the extra judicial killing of large number of suspected JVP cadres, members of the armed forces and public servants, and civilians. Civil liberties were curtailed severely during this period and second insurgency turned the down-South into a killing field.

---

[26] JN Dixit, *Assignment Colombo* (Delhi: Konark, 1998).

President Premadasa, who from the inception opposed the Accord, and the Indian military presence in the country, used full military strength at his command to deal with the JVP problem. Paradoxically, the fact that the presence of the IPKF was taking care of the "northern insurgency," enabled President Premadasa to deal firmly with the JVP. Consequently, the JVP, including its leadership was crushed in 1989, bringing the revolution to an end.

The conflict in Sri Lanka not only invited direct Indian intervention but also had an impact on the Indian polity as well. One could safely argue that the major consequence on India was the assassination of former Prime Minister Rajiv Gandhi by the LTTE. It was under Rajiv Gandhi's premiership that India's position on the Sri Lankan conflict changed radically. Under Prime Minister Indira Gandhi, who was killed in October 1984, India was pro-Tamil and it extended all possible assistance to the Tamil militant groups. Coming to power of Rajiv Gandhi following the assassination of his mother Indira Gandhi, altered India's Sri Lanka policy drastically as it became relatively pro-Sri Lankan Government. The Sri Lankan Government was treated with respect and the "boys" were placed in their due place. Also it was under Rajiv Gandhi's leadership that the Indo-Lanka Accord of 1987 was signed, which forced the Tamil militant groups to surrender their struggle. In the LTTE scheme of thinking, the Rajiv Gandhi Government, through the Accord, unfairly exploited the Tamil struggle to ensure the hegemonic postures of India in Sri Lanka. This, for the LTTE was a betrayal of the trust the Tamils had placed on India. The violent confrontation between the LTTE and the IPKF led also to the killing of large number of LTTE cadres including some of the prominent leaders. It was also believed that at the societal level, some of the worst atrocities were committed by the IPKF on the civilian population in the North-East. Therefore, the antagonism between Rajiv Gandhi and the LTTE leadership was evident. In 1989, Rajiv Gandhi was unseated and the new Government headed by V.P.Singh decided to withdraw the Indian troops from Sri Lanka. Commentators however believe that it was the possibility of Rajiv Gandhi's return to power in 1991 that motivated the LTTE to assassinate the former Prime Minister.

Rajiv Gandhi was killed by a suicide bomber, believed to be a member of the LTTE, in an election rally in Sriperumbudur in the state of Tamil Nadu.

Due to the ethnic affiliation between the Sri Lankan Tamils and the Tamils in India, the people of Tamil Nadu in general and the political parties in particular began to support the Tamil separatist movement and militancy in Sri Lanka. Tamil militants received shelter and financial and moral support from Tamil Nadu. On the one hand activities of the Tamil militants in India raised the nationalism of the Tamils of the Southern Indian state and they also led to tension and law and order problems in the state. The first element was significant because it was Tamil Nadu that demanded cessation from the Indian union first in the early 1960s. The movement however died a natural death due to the accommodative policies adopted by the central Government in relation to the demands and aspirations of the states of the Indian Union. Yet, there are still residues of radical Tamil nationalism and the people involved in these movements were able to express their own nationalism through the issues of Tamils in Sri Lanka, because it is practically impossible to go against the India Union. The *Nam Thamilar* movement that was regenerated by film director Seeman is a good example of this trend. It is also imperative to note that many political parties including the two major parties, the DMK and the AIADMK have at one or another point in time supported the Tamil militancy for political purposes. The assassination of Rajiv Gandhi however to a large extent evaporated the support for militancy. In the recent past especially with the escalation of the violence during the last phase of the civil war, support for the Sri Lankan Tamil cause increased largely in response to the emerging humanitarian catastrophe. Despite the defeat of the LTTE in May 2009, pro-Tamil activities in the state of Tamil Nadu are still continuing. It is however too early to predict whether the ethno-nationalist sentiments ignited by the conflict in Sri Lanka will lead to a more vibrant movement in Tamil Nadu in the future or will face a slow but natural death.

Politics of Tamil Diaspora

Tamils of Sri Lanka historically had the habit of traveling abroad in search of wealth and a small number of them had already settled in the Western states for political as well as economic reasons. The process of migrating to the West as refugees however was intensified following the escalation of ethnic violence especially with the 1983 riots. Immediately after the nation-wide attack on the Tamil targets in July 1983, the Tamils in large number began to move towards India, a natural refuge and Western states. It was the underprivileged segment of the Tamil community that chose to move to Tamil Nadu while the more affluent segment of the community preferred Western states. It is generally argued, especially in the South that most of the Tamils who seek political asylum were not political refugees but seekers of greener pasture. However, it is imperative to note that although economic calculations were certainly part of the scheme, most Tamils, especially from the North were desperate to leave the country for lack of security and the threat emanated from both the armed forces and the LTTE. Suspects who were picked up by the armed forces faced the prospect of long detention assisted by the PTA and the ER. A large number of suspected Tamil militants are still in prisons without trial. Moreover, the LTTE in the later stages began to force almost all able men and women to join force and others to work for them in different capacities. The LTTE was also recruiting child soldiers. Consequently, parents in the North and East were sometimes selling all their properties including symbolically significant cultural markers in order to send their children to one or another Western country.

Consequently, in the recent past the number of Tamils in Western Europe, Australia and North America multiplied making the Tamil Diaspora a force to reckon with. One of the salient features of the Tamil Diaspora politics in the West is that it was staunchly pro-LTTE. LTTE agenda was fully backed up and it was supported financially as well. The Diaspora however lacked capacity to influence decision making process within the LTTE. It was like an Automatic Teller Machine (ATM), which provided cash when the LTTE was in need. The Tamil Diaspora in the

West was to a great extent disoriented and confused by the sudden and unexpected collapse of the LTTE. In the immediate aftermath of the collapse, there was confusion about the future direction and even leadership. Kumaran Pathmanathan, who once acted as the LTTE's chief international procurement agent declared himself as the leader of the organization following the killing of Velupillai Prabhakaran. In a surprising development however he was caught by the Sri Lankan authorities in Malaysia and was brought back to Sri Lanka. In a news interview Pathmanathan maintained that he was brought to Sri Lanka in Business class and has developed an understanding with the present Government.[27] It is speculated that the self proclaimed new leader of the almost non-existent LTTE, is currently working with the Sri Lankan authorities in the international campaign of the Government to crush the international network of the rebels.

Meanwhile, the other major international figure of the LTTE, V. Rudrakumaran, has been elected by the Diaspora as the Prime Minister of what is called the Transnational Government of Tamil Eelam followed by the appointment of a cabinet of ministers. The so called Transnational Government will hardly have any impact in the absence of an effective local movement except assisting the state to keep a keen watch on the Tamil community in Sri Lanka. Prejudicial or even oppressive policies could be justified by the continuing threat to national security.

Foreign Policy

As a small state and a state that was to a large extent dependent on foreign assistance for economic development, Sri Lanka generally followed a friendly foreign policy in relation to major states and key international organizations. It is indeed interesting to note that in the first fifty years of its post colonial existence, the country managed to strike friendly relations with almost all the states that are connected to the region, except of

---

[27] "KP speaks out: An interview with former Tiger Chief How Prabhakaran met his death" available online at http://www .lankanewstoday.com/%E2%80%9CKp%E2%80%9D-speaks-out-an-interview-with-former-tiger-chiefhow-prabhakaran-met-his-death-kp-speaks-out

course India. Sri Lanka had strained relations with India largely due to the big neighbor's involvement in the ethnic conflict. Even in this case, Sri Lanka attempted to resolve the issues through diplomacy and accommodative policies. The point here is that Sri Lanka in general managed to preserve friendly relations with major international actors. In general Sri Lanka also adopted friendly relations with the West largely due to the colonial past and the economic development assistance, which flowed from the Western states.

This general trend however, had changed radically in the recent past largely due to the conduct of the civil war. In the early 2000s, the Western states enthusiastically supported the peace process and in order to pressurize the LTTE, most of the states especially the member states of the European Union legally proscribed the LTTE as a terrorist organization. However, when the peace process collapsed and the parties returned to the battle field leading to a humanitarian crisis, the West began to question the Sri Lankan Government on the human rights situation in the country and introduced steps to pressurize the Government to halt the strategy of war and return to the negotiating table. The Sri Lankan Government on the other hand was determined to finish off the LTTE regardless of the humanitarian consequences and the Western pressure.

Assistance from the West, economic or otherwise was attached to conditionalities connected to human rights, democracy and good governance. Meanwhile, most of the non-Western states came forward to support the Sri Lankan Government in its attempt to crush the LTTE without preconditions. For instance, India, China, Pakistan, Russia, and Iran extended support in terms of arms and ammunition, and economic assistance; no conditions attached. Some of these states were even willing to defend Sri Lanka on human rights issues. For instance, Sri Lanka came under severe fire from some of the Western states and human rights organizations during the final stage of the war and an attempt was made to pass a resolution condemning Sri Lanka for human rights violations in the UN Human Rights Commission in 2009. However, due to the intervention of India and China, the commission ended up adopting a resolution commending Sri Lanka for successfully defeating terrorism.

Currently, Western states and human rights watch dog institutions are calling for an international investigation to establish accountability for the human rights violation that took place during the final stage of the civil war. The new friends of Sri Lanka on the other hand, have been transformed into the major donor countries. For instance, currently China and Iran have become the major contributors making the assistance of the Western states inconsequential. Therefore, the present Government has been leaning heavily towards non-western states like China, Iran and Russia.

Implications for the Future

Analysis of the ethno-political conflict in Sri Lanka, to a great extent, was undertaken on the conjuncture that the conflict cannot be resolved through military means as the parties to the armed conflict, namely the Government of Sri Lanka and the LTTE did not have the military capacity to overcome the other in the battle field. Especially, the demand for a peaceful resolution was justified on this basis. Stable peace requires a peaceful approach was the assumption. A small segment of the radical Sinhala nationalists however for a long time argued that it is possible to militarily crush the LTTE. The argument had less to do with battle field calculations and more with the desire to promote total war. The conventional wisdom however was that a military solution to the conflict is impossible. It is this belief that motivated the LTTE to pull out from the recent peace process and claymore the present President into war. What the LTTE failed to understand was that the international politico-military milieu this time around had changed radically against violent non-state armed groups largely in response to the September 11 attack on the USA. In Sri Lanka, the combined effect of determination of the political leadership, military assistance of friendly states such as China, the USA, and especially India, and the international campaign against terrorism led to the certain defeat of the LTTE. The war was concluded with the killing of the top leadership of the LTTE including its supreme leader Velupillai Prabhakaran in May 2009. Termination of violence has shifted Sri Lanka into a post-war scenario where a systematic scheme is required to transform the community into an environment of sustainable peace, which obviously entails addressing not only the causes but also the consequences of the conflict.

As aforementioned, one of the first causalities of the conflict is the erosion of democracy as a value and practice. Compromising of democratic values and practices was justified by the need to win the war. The end of the war however has not arrested the trend towards more authoritarianism. For instance the 18th Amendment which was introduced to the constitution in September 2010 further centralized political power and consolidated the presidency. Ideally however, the constitution needs to be reformed to make it more democratic by de-centralizing political power through for instance re-establishing the Westminster mode of Government. Authoritarianism is not in fact a problem of constitution and governance alone; it is a problem of attitude and political culture. Projects especially by non-Governmental and civil society organizations need to be introduced for attitudinal change. The problem of political culture may be addressed through educational mechanisms and media.

Constitutional reform should certainly entail measures for devolution of power. The demand for devolution of power is at the heart of the ethnic conflict. The provincial councils system, which was established in response to the Tamil demand for devolution of power, however, failed to resolve the conflict. Powers given to the councils were taken back gradually by the central Government making the provincial councils a meaningless institution. The provincial councils experience amply demonstrated that devolution within the existing unitary structure will not help effectively resolve the conflict. Powers devolved by one Government could be taken by another Government in the future. In a federal setup, both the central Government and the federal units are sovereign and one cannot eliminate the other. Therefore, a federal structure in Sri Lanka would provide minorities the confidence that the center cannot undermine their interest and serve as an alternative for a separate state.

As a consequence of the conflict, ethnic politics have intensified and infiltrated into all the communities. This has proved detrimental to the formation of a national identity and slowed progress as politics in general lacks ideas and projects based on national interest. Political parties and communities work on parochial ethnic and or regional interests. As a solution, especially in the post-LTTE period, suggestions have been made, mostly by Sinhala nationalist elements, to ban what is called "ethnic parties." In reality this cannot be done because, almost all political parties, including the two largest parties, are "ethnic" in nature. What is possible, however, is the banning of parties with ethnic or religious labels. This would however, prove to be detrimental as minorities would find it difficult to play a leadership role in what is now called 'national parties' leading to further disintegration within minority communities and even new tensions in the future. Therefore, solution to ethnic politics in Sri Lanka lies in the transformation of larger parties and politics into truly national and accommodative of the minority concerns.

The prevailing anti-terrorism laws especially the Prevention of Terrorism Act has been proved to be detrimental to national integration and peace. However, the tool has assisted the state to deal with militancy firmly and the LTTE has been terminated successfully. The Tamils currently do not have the psychological strength or the capacity to even think about another phase of violent campaign, let alone carrying on one. In fact no community, be it the Sinhalese or the Tamils can challenge state violently. It has been proved effectively that non-state violence against the state will not work in Sri Lanka for a long time to come. This reality makes a tough anti-terrorism law such as the PTA irrelevant. The PTA therefore should be repealed. Repealing the PTA should not be a major problem because, if necessary, it could be reintroduced in the future.

Politicization of the military and militarization of politics have been a problem generated by the conflict. The size and the role of the military in politics have increased many fold in the recent past. In terms of democracy and democratic governance this could become a serious question. Ideally, the armed forces should be right-sized, and the military's role in politics and civil administration should be curtailed. The general insecurity constructed by the conflict could be addressed through demilitarization and for instance through strengthening the judiciary and the police force. Replacing the military with an effective and civilian friendly police force would prove to be valuable in terms of establishing trust among the people who live in the conflict affected regions. Another issue that requires the immediate attention of the Government is the resettlement of the war displaced. An assisted and rapid resettlement of the people, including the Muslims, in the North-East would buttress ethnic reconciliation. Several internment camps that were setup by the Government to house about 300,000 displaced Tamils have been closed down. Currently, about 50,000 people still remain in these camps. Releasing these people into their own villages and shrinking of the high security zones would speed up the normalization and resettlement process.

The problem of external intervention especially from India has been handled successfully and India has turned a staunch ally of the Sri Lankan state. As long as Sri Lanka remains pro-India or at least neutral, India will not attempt to influence the domestic politics in Sri Lanka. However, leaning too radically towards powers that are not too friendly with India might upset the equation. Increasing Chinese involvement in Sri Lanka may make policy makers in Delhi nervous. For the moment the balancing act seems to be working in favor of the Sri Lankan state. The Tamil Diaspora has become the new enemy of the Sri Lankan state. The Diasporas' projects and activities are based on the image of Sri Lankan state as an oppressor. As long as this image remains strong, the anti-Sri Lanka projects of the Diaspora will also remain robust. Accommodative policies and minority friendly attitude of the Sri Lankan state and the Sinhala people will have the potential to weaken the Tamil Diaspora. In terms of foreign policy directions, Sri Lanka in the post war period should seek to be in the league of democracies rather than leaning too radically towards countries like Russia, China and Iran.

Conclusion

The Sri Lankan ethnic conflict between the majority Sinhala community and the Tamils, who form the second largest ethnic group in the country, originated with the split in the Ceylon National Congress in

1921. Ethnic polarization and the contestation that were intensifying in the following years led to the apparent conflict and civil war in the later years. Obviously the long drawn conflict led to severe consequences, some of which may have long lasting impact on the current and future direction of the society. One of the interesting dimensions of consequences of the conflict is that it is difficult to distinguish between the causes and consequences as causes had been reproduced as consequences. With this limitation in mind this chapter identifies two major types of consequences: (1) domestic impact, and (2) impacts with international dimensions. In terms of domestic impacts there is political, security, and demography related consequences. Politically for instance, the conflict caused severe damage to the democratic tradition and values of the society and it also led to over-centralization of political power. The conflict also led to establishment of ethnically oriented political parties, especially among the minority communities and the adoption of racially motivated policies and strategies. Major aim behind ethnic politics practiced largely by political parties and their leaders was to win votes. One can therefore, argue that it was not only the ethnic grievances that deepened the conflict but also the competition for political power.

The escalation of violence and the assault on the state paved the way for stringent anti-terrorism laws. The Prevention of Terrorism Act was introduced in 1979, implementation of which led to serious questions of human rights violations in the country. Consequent to the violent challenge posed by the Tamil militant organizations, status of the armed forces increased considerably. This led to the politicization of the military and militarization of the politics and the civil services. The conflict also caused serious changes in the demographic composition of some the regions that were closely linked to the war. Jaffna peninsula, Colombo and Puttalam district are some of the areas where drastic changes have taken place.

Some of the consequences have international dimensions. For instance, the involvement of India in the ethnic conflict, first as a mediator and then as negotiator, and the eventual deployment of the Indian armed forces in Sri Lanka under the banner of the Indian Peace Keeping Force are consequences of the conflict that had a certain international aspect. Impact of the conflict however was noticed in the Indian soil as well. For instance, ethnic nationalism in Tamil Nadu was boosted to a certain extend and currently being expressed through the Sri Lankan Tamil cause. Activities of the Tamil militants also created law and order problems in Tamil Nadu. Moreover, many Tamils chose to leave the country over time and seek refuge in mainly Western states. This chapter argues that although economy plays a role in the decision to migrate, lack of security was the fundamental reason for many Tamils to settle not only in the Western states but also in other states like India. However, the Tamil Diaspora eventually transformed into a major financial contributor for the struggle, which in turn sustained the war machinery of the LTTE.

A shift occurred in the Sri Lankan foreign policy in response to the needs created by the present Government's decision to terminate the LTTE through military means. Despite its friendly relations with most of the other states, Sri Lanka generally managed to preserve a cordial link with most of the Western states. Western states on the other hand supported Sri Lanka economically and extended their cooperation for the peace process. On the request of the Sri Lankan Government, many of them proscribed the LTTE as a terrorist organization. These states however, grew increasingly concerned about the state of human rights when the peace process collapsed and the parties returned to the battle field. Serious human rights questions were raised during the final stage of the war. Also the Western assistance for the war efforts of the present Government was attached to human rights, democracy and good governance related conditionalities. Some of the non-traditional allies of Sri Lanka were willing to extend support and defend Sri Lanka in international human rights forums unconditionally. Since this worked very well for the Sri Lanka, the present Government is detaching itself from the pro-western foreign policy fundamentals and leaning more towards non-western states like, China, Russia and Iran.

The end of the war however has offered an opportunity to address the negative consequences of the conflict. For instance, the problem of erosion of democracy could be addressed through reforming the constitution to make it more democratic. Constitutional reform should also entail measures for devolution of power. A federal structure in Sri Lanka would provide minorities the confidence that the center cannot undermine their interest and serve as an alternative for the demand of a separate state. In order to minimize the impact of ethnic politics, the larger parties should become truly national and accommodative of the minority concerns. The end of the war has made the PTA irrelevant. The PTA therefore should be repealed. The armed forces should be right-sized and military's role in politics and civil administration should be curtailed. The general insecurity constructed by the conflict could be addressed through demilitarization and for instance through strengthening the judiciary and the police.

The problem of external intervention especially from India has been handled successfully as India has turned a staunch ally of the Sri Lankan state. The Tamil Diaspora has become the new enemy of the Sri Lankan state. The Diasporas' projects and activities are based on the image of Sri Lankan state as an oppressor. As long as this image remains strong within the Diaspora, the anti-Sri Lanka projects of the Tamils abroad will continue. Accommodative policies and minority friendly attitude of the Sri Lanka state and the Sinhala people on the other hand will have the potential to weaken the activities of the Tamil Diaspora. In terms of foreign policy directions, Sri Lanka in the post war period should seek to be in the league of democracies.

PURSUIT OF SUSTAINABLE PEACE AFTER THE MILITARY DEFEAT OF THE LTTE: INSIGHTS INTO POST-WAR SCENARIOS

Gamini Keerawella

A new dawn broke over Sri Lanka last year. There is new promise of a new era of peace and stability over the island. There is optimism in the air; optimism that the time has come to address all outstanding issues in a sprit of understanding and mutual accommodation. There is expectation that the recent election will sow the seeds for genuine reconciliation between the various communities. At the same time, there is also apprehension that things may not quite work out the way it should and yet another opportunity may slip away. But, one thing is evident there is now a historic opportunity to shape the destiny of Sri Lanka and its people. [1]

Nirupama Rao

It is usually difficult to reach conformity on matters of contemporary historical development. However, all tend to agree regarding one event in recent history, that Sri Lanka has entered a decisive phase in its post-colonial historical development after the military collapse of the Liberation Tigers of Tamil Eelam (LTTE) in May 2009. The LTTE that carried out an armed struggle for nearly 30 years was long considered the most ferocious and well-organized terrorist group in the world, with a sizable

---

[1] Speech delivered by Nirupama Rao, Foreign Secretary, Government of India at the inaugural session of the International conference on Sri Lanka organized by the Observer Research Foundation in New Delhi on May 10 2010.

suicide squad of its own, in addition to having naval and air arms. Having defeated the LTTE in 2009, Sri Lanka presently stands at a crucial historical juncture with many opportunities and possibilities as well as problems and challenges before it. The prospects for peace and stability of post-LTTE Sri Lanka depend on the manner in which the Mahinda Rajapaksa regime and other stake-holders address these problems and challenges. The immediate issue in this context is how to utilize the political space opened up by the ending of the separatist war to move from conflict to post-conflict society.

The transition from conflict to post-conflict society is not a simple shift or a *fait accompli* with the silencing of the guns. It is a long and multi-track process that needs to be carried out assiduously with a clear vision. Apart from other deep social and political implications of the war, some pressing residual issues such as the resettlement of a large number of internally displaced people (IDPs) make the process of transition from conflict to post-conflict society more challenging. However, the fundamental issue is how to transform the military defeat of the LTTE into a foundation for a sustainable and positive peace in the country by offering a solution to the ethnic problem of the country. This chapter intends to address some issues involved with the process of transition of Sri Lanka from a conflict to post-conflict society.

With the demise of the LTTE, it is now high time to have a plan with short, medium and long term targets to fully utilize the political space opened up by the military defeat to lay a foundation for a sustainable peace in the country. It is no doubt that ethnic reconciliation is a priority in the context of psychological distancing and seeing the other in terms of the enemy image. However, the main challenge before the government is to embark on a long–term post-war peace building process with a clear vision. In order to achieve this objective the government has to address many issues from transitional security to political reforms.

Transitional Security

One of the key concerns that should receive priority attention in the transition from conflict to post-conflict environment is how to reframe security concerns and security building mechanisms to suit the changed environment. After three decades of war, it is natural for the government to consider that all other concerns are secondary to the security concerns in the North and East. In view of the enormous pain and destruction caused by the war, the government's main preoccupation would be to leave no room for the reemergence of the LTTE. The key issue in transitional security is how to ensure security intelligently in the North and the East in the post-LTTE environment. It is necessary to move gradually from the earlier framework, where dealing with the LTTE in the war context was the prime concern, to a new environment where security is ensured through a successful peace building process. It is no doubt a challenging task. The precise role and the extent of deployment of the security forces need to be decided carefully. Well trained, elitist units capable of attending emerging security concerns in a peace-building environment could be utilized. As Dayan Jayatilleka pointed out, "the security concerns can be taken care of by maintaining a sufficiently strong but 'smart' (not 'heavy') military presence in the province, on its perimeters and embedded in small deployment within the community (as recommended by David Petraeus' COIN doctrine)"[2]. At the same time, while deviating from more coercive practices, new operational mechanisms relating to security need to be introduced as part of post-conflict reconstruction and reconciliation. A more subtle mechanism for security surveillance and intelligence gathering, which should not appear offensive, is needed. The analysis of security intelligence needs more sophistication. The difference between dissent and subversion should be clearly identified. Dissent needs to be accepted and allowed as a healthy safety valve embedded in democracy and subversion needs to be dealt with appropriately. Putting dissent and subversion in one basket would definitely be counterproductive politically and strategically in the long run. The execution of security functions must be regulated in terms of rule of law to win the trust and confidence of the people. In this context, healthy civil military relations will be a crucial factor in peace and stability in the

---

[2] Dayan Jayatilleka, "Sri Lanka; Emer ging Encirclement, Slow Siege, " *The Nation*, May 30, 2010.

region for some time to come. A well thought out and clearly planned security mechanism is to be set in motion which would assign a new role for the military as part of post-conflict reconciliation to build civil military relations in the North. It is imperative to develop a comprehensive phenomenon of national security in which the security of the state is integrated with the security of the individual and their collective identities. In the post-LTTE context, the Sri Lankan state cannot afford to consider a section of its citizenry a security threat. Accordingly, the Sri Lankan Government has to adjust itself from a conflict environment to a post-conflict environment. By moving away from the constraints faced in the conflict frame with emphasis more on security than freedom it is necessary to have a forward-looking policy frame of partnership and devolution of power. In the last analysis, sustainable security and stability can be achieved by ensuring individual security of Tamil people as well as their collective identity. A security building process with individual and collective identities as the main units is a multi dimensional process with political, economic and social aspects. Hence, transitional security constitutes an important aspect of post-conflict peace and reconciliation.

How to Deal with Sri Lankan Tamil Nationalism

Another crucial but complex issue in the present situation is how deal with Tamil nationalism in the post-LTTE context. As a point of departure in the formulation of a proper response to Tamil nationalism is coming to grips with the reality and accepting its existence and also its diversity. What was manifested in LTTE activities was one facet of Tamil nationalism which D.B.S. Jeyaraj termed "Tamil Ultra-nationalism"[3]. In the conflict environment, the LTTE political agenda and activities had overdetermined Tamil nationalism and through the activities of the LTTE it saw it's most violent and exclusivist presentation. It is a reality that, in view of the fact that Sri Lanka is a multi-ethnic country where ethnic groups are dispersed throughout the island with some geographical concentrations, government will not be able to come to any compromise

[3] D.B.S. Jeyaraj, "The Politics of Transnational Tamil Eelam Government", 28 May 2010, available online at http://dbsjeyaraj.com/dbsj/archives/1450

with the ultra Tamil nationalism of LTTE based on an exclusive Tamil homeland. However, the issue here is how to deal with the Tamil nationalism in the broader sense of the word. In the context of ethnic resurgence in many parts of the world, the acid test for solid statesmanship in multi-ethnic societies is the manner in which the challenge of ethno-nationalism is managed by accommodating and diverting it in order to give strength to the multiethnic polity. Looked at from the historical perspective, we need to admit that, as Anthony Smith observed, "It is still nationalist high noon, and the owl of Minerva has not stirred."[4] In this context, the formulation of a policy framework for dealing with post-LTTE Tamil nationalism needs careful attention. There are three possible policy options in this regard. The first is to ignore it as if there is no such thing called Tamil nationalism. In this line of thinking, Tamils are not a nation in the early Modern European 'nation state' sense of the word. Without a nation there cannot be nationalism. The thirty years of war and the movement for Tamil Eelam was the product of a personal dream of a megalomaniac. As long as the leadership of the LTTE is annihilated and all avenues to military reemergence are successfully blocked, the issue will be over. However, we have to admit the existence of a 'Tamil national movement', and its weaknesses and potency. As long as we do not recognize it and accommodate and divert it with appropriate responses, once again extremist and terrorist elements would come forward to lead it and direct it on a suicide course. The second option is to consider Tamil nationalism as a monolithic body and put all the variations in one basket and go for a head on confrontation in order to defeat it politically and ideologically. In the short run, it may appear successful in dealing with Tamil nationalism, but in long rum it is doomed to fail as it would create a situation for all the variants of Tamil nationalism to form a united front. The internal divisions and controversies in the Tamil Diaspora cropped up in connection with the Transnational Government of Tamil Eelam (TGTE), illustrating the divisions between the pro-LTTE 'ultra-Tamil nationalist' and others who also want to identify themselves as

---

[4] Anthony D. Smith, *The Nation in History- Historiographical Debates about Ethnicity and Nationalism*, (Cambridge: Polity Press, 2000), p.76.

representatives of Sri Lankan Tamil interests. The third approach is to recognize the diversity of Tamil nationalism and, while ideologically confronting ultra-Tamil nationalism, to engage in a constructive dialogue with the other elements of Tamil nationalism. The role that credible and democratic Tamil political and civil leadership can play in this regard is also very important. Labeling all the Tamils who are not with the Government as traitors or LTTE agents would not create conducive conditions for peace and stability. Instead of projecting Sinhala and Tamil nationalisms in a zero-sum frame, it is essential to find a frame and mechanisms which allow projecting both from a multi-sum perspective. Both the government and the democratic Tamil leadership must not once again allow the extremist element to lead and guide a Tamil national movement by default. Political space must be created and widened to integrate it as vital part of civic nationalism and incorporate it as an urge for democracy and justice for the entire country.

Re-settlement of IDPs

The two elements discussed above need a fundamental policy shift and a long term programme. However, the immediate and pressing issue in the post-conflict situation is definitely the resettlement of Internally Displaced Persons (IDPs). The IDP issue is not new to Sri Lanka and, since the commencement of the armed conflict; Sri Lanka had to grapple with the problems of people displaced by the conflict. In terms of their origin, these IDPs can be identified into three categories: (1) the Tamil IDPs who fled their home due to pre-2005 armed confrontation or those who were forced to leave their ancestral homes with the expansion of high security zones by the government forces; (2) the Muslims who were forcefully evicted by the LTTE, mainly in Jaffna and Mannar Districts; (3) a comparatively small number of Sinhalese who fled their ancestral homes located in or close to battle lines[5]. What is unique in the post-2006 situation was the sheer magnitude and quick influx of IDPs. The government had to face this challenge in two stages

---

[5] Gamini Keerawella, *Evolving Security Discourse in Sri Lanka from National Security to Human Security*, (Dhaka, BIIS , 2008), p.115.

- first in the East and then in the Wanni. In the wake of the Government military offensive against the LTTE, people in the LTTE controlled area sought refuge in the Government controlled area. In the Batticaloa District where the LTTE had more control, one-fourth of the entire population of the District became internally displaced. It was a really formidable challenge. In the face of the influx of IDPs, the first urgent task was to establish safe gathering centres. It was followed by a transitional step with the establishment of welfare centres, which was a more systematic arrangement by the Ministry of Resettlement. The main concern was to avoid a humanitarian crisis situation by immediate accommodation and the provision of day to day basic needs and other facilities. The manner in which the institutional apparatus of the state was mobilized with the help of international agencies, to meet this challenge revealed that Sri Lanka may be a 'weak' state but definitely not a failed state. In the East, the Sri Lankan government relatively successfully absorbed the initial shock of avoiding a 'grave humanitarian crisis' with the sudden influx of IDPs.

Table 1

Internally Displaced Persons in the Eastern Province prior to the Eelam War IV [6]

	District	Families within Dist.	Families Outside Dist	Persons within Dist	Persons Outside Dist	Total families	Total Persons
1.	Trincomalee	2401	167	10523	408	2568	10931
2.	Batticaloa	1836	0	6872	0	1836	6872
3	Ampara	5	49	17	180	54	197

[6] Compiled by the author using materials collected from the Dept. Statistics, Katchcheri, Batticaloa, Statistical Handbook 2006-2007, District Planning Secretariat, Batticaloa, Ministry of Resettlement and Disaster Relief Services.

The second and third steps are more crucial in post-conflict reconstruction and rehabilitation. Having attended to the immediate humanitarian needs of the IDPs, the next task is to launch a systematic resettlement programme. The success of resettlement depended on the provision of essential facilities required for the IDPs to go and settle down in their habitual villages.

Table-2

Number of IDPs in Relief Villages by May 2010

Relief Village	No. of IDP Families	No of IDPs
Kathirgamar Relief Village (Zone - 0)	3302	10800
Ananda Kumarasamy Relief Village (Zone - I)	4903	15980
Ramanathan Relief Village (Zone - II)	3988	13054
Arunachalam Relief Village (Z one - III)	3877	13017
(Zone - IV)	2118	6814
(Zone - V)	243	857
Total	**18431**	**60522**

The IDP challenge in the Wanni was more difficult than in the East and the destruction and land mine problem was more extensive there. As of September 2009, according to the statistics prepared by the Rehabilitation and Disaster Relief Services Ministry, there were a total number of 247,186 IDPs in Vavuniya 'Welfare Centres' while 7,379 persons were housed in Jaffna and 7,712 persons in Trincomalee[7]. The provision of accommodation for over fifteen hundred thousand people

---

[7] Mohammed Naalir, "IDP resettled and North developed despite criticism" *Sunday Observer*, 4 October 2009 a vailable online at ht tp://www.sundayobserver.lk/2009/10/04/new20.asp

within a couple of days was a monumental task. While attending to essential requirements of food and medicine, other administrative procedures such as identification, the registration of IDPs and their security clearance had to be completed soon. The initial shock was absorbed with the experience gained from the same situation in the East. However, compared to the situation in the East, moving to the next stage became far from easy and the resettlement of IDPs in Wanni could not be commenced for months due to a number of practical problems. This created an impression that the IDPs were flocked into 'concentration camps' in the Wanni. The long stay in transitional arrangement at the welfare centres, waiting to be resettled without a clear time frame has generated some concerns nationally and internationally. Restrictions on movement out of the centres for IDPs and the highly-controlled visiting access to the centres fueled these concerns. In addition to security related considerations, the government had to attend to the reinstallation of basic infrastructural facilities which were totally damaged due to the intense fighting. Furthermore, clearing land mines remains a time consuming task as the area had been densely mined. Under international pressure, the government lifted certain restrictions in the IDP centres and expedited the resettlement process. According to the *Reliefweb* of the United Nations, "The Government of Sri Lanka had taken steps to resettle approximately 6,000 Internally Displaced Persons (IDPs) during the first two weeks of March 2010, in Kilinochchi and Mullaitivu districts, bringing down the total number of IDPs living in government-run welfare centres to 65,591. All IDPs have been given the option to return to their original villages or to relocate to areas of their choice. Those who wanted to remain in the welfare centres are permitted to stay at these centres"[8].

As of 8 March 2010, 24,292 IDPs returned to the welfare centres. Simultaneously the de-mining programme was accelerated with the addition of 29 mine sweeping machines imported from the Czech

---

[8] Relief Web "Government Expedites Resettlement of IDPs", 15 March 2010, available online at http://www.reliefweb.int/rw/rwb.nsf/db900sid/AZHU-83KMF2?OpenDocument&query =Sri%20Lanka accessed on 27 January 2011

Republic with assistance from UNHCR and Australia[9]. It should be noted that re-settlement is an integrated process and it is not simply the provision of a makeshift dwelling and sending them to their original places. Its economic and social dimensions must be taken into account. The full gravity of one who was earlier an organic unit of a dignified social and cultural milieu and is now an internally displaced person has to be understood. The social and economic wellbeing of the people goes beyond the mere provision of emergency relief and the restoration of essential services. A well integrated capacity building programme is required to promote sustained livelihood and restore their dignity. This will invariably be a long-term venture. Hence, the success of the resettlement of IDPs is ultimately linked with the progress of rehabilitation and reconstruction of the war-torn region and its people.

Rehabilitation and Reconstruction

Another crucial aspect in post-conflict scenarios is proper guidance and direction of post-conflict rehabilitation and reconstruction. It is useful to record here that systematic discussion with the participation of government agencies and other non-governmental stake-holders commenced in order to develop a comprehensive programme for Relief, Rehabilitation and Reconstruction (Triple R) as far back as the 1998-9. However, it was only after the total military defeat of LTTE in May 2009 that post-conflict rehabilitation and reconstruction became a priority. Earlier, after the flushing out of the LTTE from the East, the government launched '*Negenahira Navodaya*'. The entire Eastern province was never under the total control of the LTTE and the Government administrative apparatus functioned more or less similar to that in other parts of the country. In the Wanni area, the Kilinochchi and Mullaitivu districts were different as they were under LTTE control. In addition, the destruction of infra-structural facilities in these districts was almost total. In this context, the task of rehabilitation and reconstruction in the north

---

[9] During 2009 (from 01 January to 31 December) a total of 897 square km has been cleared of mines in the districts of Anur athapura, Jaffna, Kil inochichi, Mannar, Mul laitivu, Polonnaruwa, Trincomalee and V avuniya.

was a mammoth task. In June 2009, the Sri Lankan government launched the 'triple R' programme named Uthuru *Wasanthaya* with much media hype. A Presidential Task force chaired by Basil Rajapaksa (M.P.), Senior Advisor to the President, was established for Northern development– *Uthuru Wasanthaya*. It was meant to coordinate all the government ministries and agencies, international agencies, inter-governmental organizations and non-governmental organizations. First of all, it announced a 180 day plan to resettle the IDPs. The process of implementation involved building up basic infrastructure like houses, roads, schools, energy grid, telecommunication etc. The government was able to mobilize a wide range of intergovernmental organizations in the post-conflict rehabilitation and reconstruction drive including the International Monetary Fund (IMF), the World Bank, the Asian Development Bank (ADB) and the various organs of the United Nations like United Nation High Commissioner for Refugees (UNHCR) and the World Food Programme (WFP). Principal state actors assisting Sri Lanka in the Triple 'R' include India, China, Japan, Libya, Pakistan, Iran, the United States, and the European Union[10]. Presently, comprehensive infra-structure development programmes are going on apace under the coordination of the Presidential Task Force[11].

However, the real success of post-conflict rehabilitation and reconstruction cannot be measured only in terms of construction of new roads, bridges and buildings. It is not simply a technical or economic venture. Post-conflict rehabilitation and reconstruction should be carried out with a clear political vision of the direction of post-conflict Sri Lanka.

---

[10] N Manoharan, "Where is the Northern Spring in Sri Lanka?" Institute of Peace and Conflict Studies (IPCS), Article No 2974, 23 September 2009, available online at :http://www.ipcs.org/article/south-asia/where-is-the-northern-spring-in-sri-lanka-2974.html, Accessed on 24 January 2011

[11] These infrastructure development progammes under Uthuru Wsanthaya included permanent housing for IDPs with water and sanitary facilities, repair of public buildings such as schools, hospitals with adequate staff and equipment, functioning irrigation for agricultural development, upgrading and repairing roads , provision of electricity to all townships. As far as economic recovery is concerned it included the establishment of state banks in all townships, livelihood support in agriculture, livestock, fishing and cottage industries and reestablishment of public markets.

Hence, the guiding principle for post-conflict reconstruction must be a new vision of the nature of the post-conflict Sri Lankan state.

The constant vacillation and contradictory statements relating to the ethnic problem and the devolutionary arrangement of power illustrate that the Government lacks a clear vision in this regard. The need for a clear vision on how to restructure the system of power and governance in post-conflict Sri Lanka is particularly important when a comprehensive approach towards rehabilitation and reconstruction is adopted to include (1) security (2) justice and reconciliation (3) social and economic well-being and (4) governance and participation. As the joint Commission on Post-Conflict Reconstruction of the Centre of Strategic and International Studies (CSIS) and the Association of the U.S. Army (AUSA) observed "Security, which encompasses the provision of collective and individual security to the citizenry and to the assistors, is the foundation on which progress on the other issue areas rest"[12]. The fourth element, namely governance and participation required a clear broader vision of democracy and it should be directed to achieve four main objectives: (a) strengthening the rule of law and respect for human rights (b) developing more genuine and competitive political processes (c) fostering the development of a politically active civil society and (d) promoting more transparent and accountable government institutions[13]. Accordingly, in order to be successful in achieving a post-conflict society it is necessary to pay attention in the course of post-conflict rehabilitation and reconstruction to the four interrelated physical infrastructure, economic, social and political dimensions. As a result, an interconnected and balanced approach and a coherent single strategy are required. The entire process needs to be handled carefully with due consideration to political sensitivities. The issue of resettling of Muslim IDPs can be cited as a case in point. It is very crucial for peace and stability in the post-conflict order to handle it diligently.

---

[12] Post Conflict Reconstruction, (A Joint project of the Centre for Strategic and International Studies (CSIS) and the Association of the United States Army (AUS A), Task Framework. May 2002,

[13] Ibid.

Rehabilitation and reconstruction could be used as a tool for reconciliation. Hence it should not appear to be one imposed from above, mainly from Colombo. The people of the area must own the reconstruction process. In view of the ground situation, it is not possible at present. There should be a clear road map to transfer the ownership of the process once it is set in motion. Implementation of post-conflict rehabilitation and reconstruction projects could be used as avenues for economic, social and political empowerment of the people and local communities in the region and the construction of civil society in a post-conflict setting. Finally, if it is properly handled, post-conflict rehabilitation and reconstruction could develop a matrix of reconstruction, community resource building, and civil society and legitimacy reconstruction[14]. What is essential here is a clear vision and the political will.

How to Reach Out to the Tamil People and the Politics of Symbols

From the point of view of long-term peace, stability and the security of post-conflict Sri Lanka, another important issue that needs to be addressed in the present context is how to forge an organic relationship between the Sri Lankan state and the Sri Lankan Tamil people. The alienation of the Tamils and their political leaders from the system of power and governance due to a number of reasons ranging from systemic majoritarian practices in the political order to their voluntary withdrawal from the existing democratic parliamentary process and also their exclusion by various means had created conducive conditions for separatist political projects to present their course. In this back drop, it is a high priority for the Government to reach the Tamil people in the North and the East using the new political space opened up by the military defeat of the LTTE and the collapse of its political project. The protracted war and having lived under the military domination of the LTTE had a profound impact in these dignified people with deep rooted cultural traditions.

---

[14] Ian Macduff, "Capacity Building in Conflict Transformation: Integrating Responses to Internal Conflicts", *Journal of Humanitarian Assistance*, 15 October 2001 available online at http://www.jha.ac/articles/a073.htm

Living through violent and protracted inter-communal conflict, as Stephen Ryan observers, "can lead to immobilism and negativism: a belief that little can be done to change the situation because constructive action is so difficult…Alienation, hopelessness, resentment, and powerlessness may have profound impact on communities in conflict especially when it is combined with economic underdevelopment"[15]. In this situation, it is a high priority of the government to reach out to the people in the region to empower the people not only economically but also socially and politically, in the broad sense of the word and not in the definitely narrow party political sense. In order to 'reach out' to them, a clear vision, once again, and a coordinated action plan is required. First of all, the objective mapping of the ground situation and general perceptions of the people is essential for proper policy direction. The ethnic content of the conflict at least on the part of the LTTE should not be forgotten. The perception of an enemy image that the LTTE assiduously created of the Sri Lankan State and its institutional apparatus cannot be wiped out overnight. In this regard, two perceptions presently prevailing among the Tamil people should be noted: (a) the Sinhalese Army (b) the 'Occupied Territory'. As long as these perceptions are perpetuated among Tamil people it would be difficult for the Government to cultivate healthy relations with them. Practical and effective attempts are urgently needed to remove these perceptions and to convince them otherwise. There should be no room for perception of domination and subordination in social and political relations. The politics of symbols play a crucial role in the present situation. The government must be more conscious of the sensitivities of the Tamil psyche. The defeat of the LTTE was by no means a defeat of the Tamil people. Statements by the Government to that effect are not sufficient. To convince Tamil people of it, lots of practical measures have to be initiated including reactivation of the democratic political process and empowerment of civil society. The significance of the dialogue between the Government and the TNA could be viewed in this perspective. Constitutional and political reforms based

---

[15] Stephen Ryan, *Ethnic Conflict and International Relations*, (London: Dartmouth, 1995), p. 93-94.

on devolution to widen the democratic space to incorporate 'other' ethnic/political forces are needed more than ever today.

Reconciliation

Moving from conflict to post-conflict is not simple; many scars left by the war in the collective psyche of the people on both sides linger for some time and sustain mutual fear and suspicion in every step of accommodation. Any war, just or unjust, by nature is a brutish affair but it is especially so in a civil war that is fought on ethnic lines. Both parties believe that the character and behaviour of the adversary is the main cause of war and justify one's actions *vis-a-vis* the other. The people behind each party believe that their actions are defensive and others offensive. Even after the conflict, the tendency is to ponder over your scars and bruises and a tendency to overlook the scars of the 'other'. For ethnic harmony and national unity, it is necessary to get out of this syndrome. The importance of reconciliation in the post-conflict recovery and rebuilding process could be understood in this background. Reconciliation is of course a broader phenomenon that covers various aspects. The main element of reconciliation is healing hearts and minds and restoring healthy social relations in the post-conflict environment. The role of 'Truth' Commissions has been brought into focus by the high profile Truth Commissions in post-Apartheid South Africa, Chile and Argentina and especially the Iraq inquiry in Britain. It should also be noted that the TRC is only one tool of reconciliation. The issue here is what model of reconciliation Sri Lanka could follow. President Mahinda Rajapaksa expressed his intention to appoint a Post-conflict Study and Reconciliation Commission on 10 May 2010 when he addressed the Diplomatic Corps in Colombo. An eight member 'Lessons Learned and Reconciliation Commission'(LLRC) was formally constituted by President Mahinda Rajapkasa on 15 May 2010, a few days prior to the first anniversary of the 'V Day', with C.R. de Silva (former Attorney General) as its chairman[16]. The mandate of the Commission is to inquire and report

---

[16] Other members of the Commission include Dr . Rohan Perera, Prof. M.T. Jiffry, Prof. Karunaratna Hangawatta, C. Chanmugam, H.M.G.S. Palihakkara, M. Ramanathanand M.P. Paranagama.

on,

1. "the facts and circumstances which led to the failure of the Ceasefire Agreement operationalised on February 21, 2002 and the sequence of events that followed thereafter up to May 19, 2009;

2. whether any person, group or institutions directly or indirectly bear responsibility in this regard;

3. the lessons we would learn from those events and their attendant concerns, in order to ensure that there will be no recurrence;

4. the methodology whereby restitution to any person affected by these events or their dependents or heirs, can be effected;

5. the institutional administrative and legislative measures which need to be taken in order to prevent any recurrence of such concerns in the future, and to promote further national unity and reconciliation among all communities, and to make any such other".[17]

The establishment of the LLRC has not generated much enthusiasm in the domestic sphere. The mandate, timing and the composition of the Commission were partly responsible for this lukewarm response. There is no doubt that a truth commission is a welcome move if its real intention is true reconciliation. What is more important in such initiatives is that it must have credibility and legitimacy from the very outset in order to proceed on a rough terrain with wide acceptance. In Dayan Jayatileka's words, "Colombo is still to understand the words 'credibility' and 'legitimacy' and the link between them. To illustrate, had the panel been chaired by Justice Christie Weeramantry, it would have both"[18]. This is particularly important in view of the fact that the track record of Mahinda Rajapaksa Government on commissions is not particularly

---

[17] "President appoints 'Lessons Learnt and Reconciliation' Commission", *The Asian Tribune*, 18 May 2010 available online at http://www.asiantribune.com/news/2010/05/18/president-appoints-%E2%80%98lessons-learnt-and-reconciliation%E2%80%99-commission

[18] Dayan Jayatileke, "Sri Lanka: Emer ging Encirclement, Slow Siege", *The Island*, May 23 2010.

impressive[19]. The LLRC should not appear as a hurried response to Western pressures. No satisfactory explanation has been given for limiting it only to the post-Ceasefire Agreement phase either. The true intentions in constituting the LLRC Commission came to be questioned due to very timing of the Government move. In the face of mounting international calls for some action relating to alleged violations of International Humanitarian Law, the LLRC can be interpreted as just a safety valve vis-a-vis the growing international pressure. As R. Hariharan observed, "If local and international political expediency was behind the appointment of the Commission, it is a little too late as the issues have been ignored for over a year and the critics have gained considerable mileage"[20]. After the appointment of the LLRC, an editorial of *The Island* asked why we should expend our time and energy to reinvent the wheel; "Lessons that all of us have already learnt and have yet to learn from thirty years of fighting are fairly well known. Some of them are - no community can or must try to suppress another; violence does not pay; this country does not belong to any particular community; all communities belong to it; it is too small to be divided among different communities but certainly large enough for all communities to live in peacefully."[21] Yet, we have to learn many more lessons from the past in order to proceed in the direction of a post-conflict society. In the background of long years of traumatic experiences and deep, searing emotions, before reconciliation can be achieved, people must somehow come to terms with the past. It goes without saying that reconciliation is a broader process and restorative justice constitutes only one aspect of it[22]. Apology and forgiveness is the

---

[19] The circumstances that led to resignation of Justice Bhagwati of India who led the Group of Eminent Persons appointed by the President Mahinda Rajapaksa to inquire into the deaths of the NGO workers in Muttur contributed to erode the credibility of the government in contrast to intensions of the government. The role of the Attorney General in the proceedings seemed partly responsible for this situation.

[20] *The Island*, 2 June 2010.

[21] *The Island*, 18 May 2010.

[22] Restorative justice denotes an approach to justice which institutionalizes peaceful approaches to harm, problem-solving and violations of legal and human rights. The focus here is on the needs of victims and offenders rather than abstract principles of law. "Restorative Justice", available online at: http://en.wikipedia.org/wiki/Restorative-justice, Accessed on 24 January 2011.

main goal of a truth commission which may pave the way for attitudinal change. First of all, the initiative in that direction should be taken by the government and it should be reflected in its actions and behaviour. The government approach towards the issue of how to deal with the former combatants, and those who had links with the LTTE, are very important in this context. The rehabilitation of former LTTE combatants has already commenced. An enlightened approach, without compromising security concerns, towards the former LTTE combatants would promote stability and reconciliation. Another, important aspect that needs more emphasis is health programmes, including trauma healing, which could effectively be used as a tool of reconciliation, capacity building and construction of civil society in the post-conflict setting[23]. The WHO initiative, 'Health as a Bridge for Peace', provides a good example in this regard. It is an initiative that is "designed to integrate the health-oriented activities of medical agencies and personnel with community building and hopefully, peace building activities"[24]. This is also an area where the Government can develop a dialogue with the Tamil Diaspora.

Role of the Tamil Diaspora

In the post-LTTE political situation in Sri Lanka, another key issue that the government needs to address carefully, in order to transform a potential challenge and vulnerability to an actual resource base for post-conflict reconstruction, peace and stability, is the activities of the Sri Lankan Tamil Diaspora. In the changed political balance of forces after the phenomenal military collapse of the LTTE, the centre of Tamil nationalist political activism appeared to have shifted from inside Wanni to the outside Diaspora. For peace and stability in post-war Sri Lanka, it is very necessary to have a clearly designed realistic approach, rather than an emotional ad hoc response, towards the Tamil Diaspora scattered in Western Europe, the North America and Australia. A thorough understanding of internal dynamics, the strengths and weaknesses inherent in Tamil Diaspora politics

---

[23] Paula Gutlove, "Health Bridge for Peace: Integrating Health Care with Community Reconciliation", *Medicine, Conflict and Surviv al*, Vol.14, 1998, p 6-23.

[24] I an Macduff, "Capaci t y B uilding in Conflict T ransformation: Integr ating R esponses to Internal Confects" available online at http://www.jha.ac/articles/a073.htm#_edn1

and their modes of operation is very useful to chart a proper policy direction and a framework for a constructive dialogue with the Tamil Diaspora. It should not be forgotten that the Tamil Diaspora is operating on a different plane and the Sri Lankan government enjoys only little leverage to control their activities as long as they remain within the parameters of their host countries. The communication revolution in the present information age has effectively contracted the concept of space and the rapid expansion of telecommunication technologies has brought the Sri Lankan Tamil Diaspora communities dispersed in different parts of the world closer to each other. The prevalence of internet, e-mail, World Wide Web and YouTube has opened up many opportunities for the Diaspora and lent popularity to the term 'transnational community'. Long-distance nationalism is a stronger but cushioned poignantly and, till the end of the LTTE, the direction of the politics of the Tamil Diaspora was determined mainly by their responses to the political agenda decided in the LTTE high temple in the Wanni. The total demise of the LTTE high command in Wanni has brought Tamil Diaspora politics into a new era.

In the light of its power and influence, the Tamil Diaspora constitutes a very important aspect of the political equation in relation to the post-conflict peace-building process. There was a historical tradition of educated Sri Lankan Tamils migrating to Malaysia, Singapore or Britain, during British colonial rule and after. However, the present Tamil Diaspora is different and they are mainly made up of refugees and former refugees. As one of the direct aftermaths of the 1983 July riots, several Western countries readily accepted Tamil immigrants and asylum seekers by granting visas and implementing special programmes to help them settle in those countries. As R. Cheran estimated, presently "the Tamil Diaspora consists of an estimated 700,000 people settled in Canada, Europe, India and Australia. It is likely therefore that one in every four Sri Lankan Tamils now lives in the Diaspora"[25]. In the period from 1980 to 1999,

---

[25] R Cheran, "Diaspora Circulation and Transnationalism as Agents for Change in the Post Conflict Zones of Sri Lanka", (A paper submitted to the Berghof Foundation for Conflict Management, Berlin, Germany, 2004).

Sri Lankan Tamils remained one in top ten asylum seekers in Europe, amounting to 256,307. One of the main concentrations of the Sri Lankan Tamil Diaspora is in Canada. Sri Lankan Tamil migration to Canada saw a phenomenal increase after 1983 and many of them are refugees. In Canada, the acceptance rate for Tamil refugee claimants has been high and over 90 percent of them settled in two provinces—Ontario and Quebec. In Toronto, the epicenter of Sri Lankan Tamil Diaspora activities, there are ten weekly Tamil language newspapers and four radio stations broadcasting programmes 24 hours a day[26]. The LTTE had conveniently tapped this resource base. The LTTE was also to trawl international networks for equipment on the strength of remittance and network contacts provided by the Tamil Diaspora. As Chris Smith observed, "Although the LTTE has been known to resort to extortion, this is rarely necessary and expatriate Tamils have proved to be unerringly generous over the past 15 years. By some estimates, the LTTE manages to collect US$ 1 million a month from expatriates in Australia, Canada, Switzerland and the United Kingdom, but not the United States, where Tamils are prevented from raising money because the LTTE has been designated a terrorist organization"[27]. There were a number of front organizations of the LTTE in the Diaspora. The proscription of the LTTE as a terrorist organization in these countries and the confiscating of funds of noted pro-LTTE organizations disrupted their operations. However, there are many organizations such as the World Tamil Movement (WTM), The World Tamil Association (WTA), the Tamil Rehabilitation Organization (TRO), the Federation of Association of Canadian Tamils (FACT), the Coordinating Committee of Tamils in France (CCTF/TCC), the United Tamil Organization in the UK, the British Tamil Association who are active in the Tamil Diaspora communities. As long as they operate within legal boundaries they enjoy freedom of speech and association. It is in

---

[26] R Cheran "The Sixth Genre: Memory , History and T amil Diaspor a Imagination," No.7, *A History of Ethnic Conflict in Sri Lanka: Recollection, Reinterpretation and Reconciliation,* Marga Institute, Colombo, 2001.

[27] Chris Smith, "In the Shadow of a Cease-fire: The Impact of Small Arms Availability and Misuse in Sri Lanka", *Small Arms Survey–* Occasional Paper No.11, Graduate Institute of International Studies, Geneva, October 2003, p.8.

this context that Sri Lankan Government has to design its policy towards the Tamil Diaspora with a broader perspective in order to get them as organic partners in the post-war peace building process. From the point of view of the interests of the Tamil people who live in Sri Lanka the best thing that the Tamil Diaspora can do is to work towards broadening democratic space for fellow Tamils in Sri Lanka, instead of sweating any more for the pipe dream of a Tamil Eelam.

Against the background of the earlier image that had been assiduously created that the LTTE was an indomitable force, the dramatic military collapse of the LTTE sent shock waves through the Tamil Diaspora that helped the LTTE sustain the war in many ways for years. The impact of the collapse of the LTTE on the Tamil Diaspora should be studied carefully. It is important to note that even prior to the collapse of the LTTE, the earlier influence enjoyed by the LTTE in the Diaspora was gradually declining. The second generation of Tamil expatriates had become less interested in the ideology and activities of the LTTE.[28] It is not realistic to view the Sri Lankan Tamil Diaspora as a pro-LTTE entity and put them all in the same basket. Internal heterogeneity and divisions should be taken into account to understand the politics of the Tamil Diaspora. There are three broad categories; Pro-LTTE, Anti-LTTE and the non-committed or apolitical section. In the overall picture the LTTE was the dominating force but the differences between the LTTE activists, LTTE supporters, LTTE sympathizers and TNA supporters are important. Anti-LTTE activists are numerically small, but they are also active, and include followers of Anandasangaree (TULF), Devananda (EPDP) and remnants of the EPRLF and the PLOTE. At the same time those who are fed up with active politics and take care of their own affairs are also considerable. However, it goes without saying that all of them are concerned with the plight of their kinsmen in Sri Lanka. Even within the overseas LTTE networks, there were factions and conflicts but they did not surface in the face of the undisputed authority exercised by

---

[28] Dhananjayan Sriskandarajah, "The Migration-Development Nexus: Sri Lanka Case Study", Mimeo, Centre for Development Research, Oxford University, Feb. 2002.

Prabakaran. Indeed, the present internecine warfare within Diaspora tiger elements began during the ceasefire period. These divisions began to develop after the demise of the leader and the collapse of the LTTE military machine. After the total annihilation of LTTE leadership in May 2009, Selvarasa Pathmanathan alias KP, the international relations head of the organization assumed the leadership of the LTTE. The main challenge to the leadership of KP came from Perinbanayagam Sivaparann alias Nediyavan who was placed in charge of LTTE overseas administration by Veerakathy Manivannan alias Castro, who was in charge of LTTE overseas administration in the period 2003-January 2009[29]. The main initiative of the pro-LTTE Tamil Diaspora after the military collapse of the LTTE in Sri Lanka is the Transitional Government of Tamil Eelam (TGTE). The co-architects of the TGTE are Rudrakumaran and Selvarasa Pathmanathan (KP). As KP was arrested in Malaysia before it took off, Rudrakumaran took the initiative. The process clearly revealed the internal divisions and dynamics of the pro-LTTE section of the Tamil Diaspora in the post-war context. In the process leading up to the convening of the TGTE, three groupings among the LTTE/pro-LTTE networks are discernible:

1. Pathmanathan (KP) - Rudrakumaran faction

2. Tamil Eelam Peoples Assembly (Thamizh Eezha Makkal Peravai) or Nediyavan faction

3. Global Tamil Forum (GTF) or Fr. Emmanuel faction[30]

---

[29] According to D.B.S. Jeyaraj, convulsions within the LTTE after the ceasefire of 2002 had resulted in the wings of KP get ting cl ipped. Veerakathy Manivannan al ias Castr o w as placed in char ge of LTTE overseas administr ation. KP went into v oluntary retir ement in 2003. Castro transformed the LTTE overseas structure by reducing the functional autonomy enjoyed by branches under KP administration. They were brought under a structure of centralized control in the Wanni. He also removed KP loyalists and replaced them with his cronies. When the war escalated in 2006 and maintenance of regular contact with all branches became difficult Castro appointed the Norway-based Nediyavan to be the overseas LTTE Branches administrative co-ordinator. In late 2008 Pr abhakaran turned to KP again and appointed him as the International Relations chief in January 2009. D.B.S. Jeyaraj, "The P olitics of T ransnational Tamil Eelam Government", 28 Ma y, 2010,http://dbsjeyaraj.com/dbj/archives/1450

[30] Fiv e existing or ganizations in di fferent countries, including the B ritish Tamil F orum got together to form GTF Rev.Fr.S.J Emmanuel now based in Germany became the GTF President.

As DBS Jeyaraj observes "the TGTE in a sense is a re-branded manifestation of the LTTE overseas structure. A crucial difference between the earlier tiger or pro-tiger organizations of the old time within the Diaspora and the newly evolving entities such as the TGTE are the elements of democracy and transparency"[31].

The main issue that the government is to address in the present context would be how to get the Sri Lankan Tamil Diaspora to be partners in the post-war peace building process. For that, the government needs a clear perspective, direction and work plan with a realistic assessment of the strength as well as the limitations of the Tamil Diaspora. The Diaspora circulation during the ceasefire period provides some insights in this regard. It was estimated that 25-35 Tamils from the Diaspora circulated annually after the signing of the Ceasefire Agreement. As Cheran pointed out "there are three major areas where the circulating Diaspora can be involved: knowledge capital and knowledge transfer, capacity building and investment, and peace-building and strengthening civil society in the North East'[32]. At this point, the present role of KP, who is still technically under the detention of the government, is interesting to watch. *The Sunday Observer* on 20 June 2010 reported that a delegation of former militants domiciled in Canada, Switzerland, Germany, United Kingdom, France and Australia met Defence Secretary Gotabaya Rajapaksa and Minister of External Affairs Prof. G.L. Peiris in Colombo with regard to the Sri Lankan Government's peace building efforts". It further reported that "Pathmanathan (KP) who played a key role in bringing down the nine-member delegation to Colombo was also present at the meeting held with the Defence Secretary and the Minister of External Affairs. Pathmanathan said that an understanding has been reached to set up a NGO to streamline financial assistance for the post-conflict humanitarian programmes from abroad"[33]. This NGO is expected to be called North

---

[31] D.B.S. Jeyaraj, " The Politics of Transnational Tamil Eelam Government", 2010

[32] R Cher an, "Diaspora Circulation and T ransnationalism as Agents for Change in the P ost Conflict Zones of Sri Lanka", (A paper submi tted to the Berghof F oundation for Conflict Management, Be rlin, Germany, 2004).

[33] Ananth P alakidnar, "Tamil intel lectuals, ex- mil itant sympathizers to assist go vernment" Sunday Observ er, 20 June 2010 av ailable online at http://www .sundayobserver.lk/2010/ 06/20/sec01.asp accessed on 6 May 2011

and East Development Programme (NEDP). It would be interesting to observe the diverse future implications of the Government-KP link.

Handling International Actors and Situations

Within a year after the defeat of the LTTE, the Mahinda Rajapkasa regime was able to establish its hold firmly in domestic politics, reaping victories in both the Presidential and Parliamentary polls. In view of the internal squabbles and bickering in the main opposition party (UNP) and the disarray of opposition political forces, it is very unlikely that there would be any serious internal political challenges or policy alternatives emanating from the domestic political sphere to the Rajapaksa regime. The main challenges that the government is confronting presently are those coming from the international sphere. Immediately the government has to address carefully and confidently the issue of the demand for an international probe of the alleged misconduct of the war and other human rights issues. In the broader canvass the important issue is how to build a wider trust and confidence between the government and an array of international actors whose role is crucial in shaping international public opinion. International trust and confidence is also very important not only for averting unacceptable external probes, with very serious implications, but also for promoting the stability and progress of the post-war peace building process. In order to achieve this objective the government needs a different set of tools and language. In order to be equipped with these tools the policy-makers need to understand the link between trust and confidence and the legitimacy and credibility. The importance of having a clear vision and mechanism to handle international actors and situations should be understood against the background of two factors; first, the past internationalization of the Sri Lankan ethnic problem; second, the changes that have taken place in international politics where, in addition to the states, other non-state international actors have also come forward to play a key role.

In this context, the changes and developments, not only in structure and texture but also the range and mechanism of international actors in post-cold war politics, should be recognized. On the one hand, in the context of globalization, a qualitatively different process of interdependency resulting from the advances in communication and exchange of goods, services, information and ideas (multi-dimensional contacts) created an unprecedented interconnectedness among societies. On the other hand, the areas where the sovereign state enjoys its prerogative have increasingly contracted in international politics due to the emergence of international order of multi-dimensionally patterned interaction of a number of actors, in addition to the 'sovereign nation states. On the other hand, the 'resurgence of ethnic identities' and atrocities linked to neo-tribal warfare in many parts of the world and the 'human' rather than state focused approach to international political issues have contributed to change the role of the United Nations, especially under Kofi Annan. In 1994, the UNDP Annual Human Development Report presented the concept of 'Human Security'. In the background of crisis situations in Rwanda, Somalia, Bosnia and Kosovo, Kofi Annan initiated a dialogue at the United Nations General Assembly on 'the right of humanitarian intervention' which resulted in the appointment of the International Commission on Intervention and State Sovereignty[34]. With these developments the order of priority in international politics has also changed. With the emergence of the international order of multi-dimensional patterned interaction, a number of other actors acquired prominence in international politics that include inter-governmental organizations, UN instruments with new roles, International NGOs, interest groups and academic bodies. The role and significance of these non-state actors vary from one issue area to another. In issue areas such as the protection of International Humanitarian Law, human security and human rights, the non-state actors increasingly come forward to play a more proactive role.

The Sri Lankan foreign policy-making process has to take these changes in international politics into due consideration and design its approach accordingly. Foreign policy is not simply the management of

---

[34] The Commission was co-chaired by Gareth Evans and Mohamed Sahnoun and it produced the report – The Responsibility to Protect (R2P)

state to state relations. In the changed international political environment, a wide range of international actors must be taken into account in an understanding of the 'definitions of situation', to use the term in Foreign Policy Studies[35]. The same tools and mechanisms as in state to state relations may not be effective as far as other actors are concerned. The ground rules and the language of the game are very important in dealing with these international actors. The issue of credibility and legitimacy comes in this context. The argument that we are a sovereign and independent country and that no one has a right to interfere in our domestic maters is technically correct. The stark reality is that the Sri Lankan government has failed to convince the Secretary General of the United Nations to not appoint an expert panel to advise him on the situation in Sri Lanka. On 23 June 2010, Ban Ki-moon appointed a three member Panel of Experts comprising Marzuki Darusman as chair and Yasmin Sooka and Stevan Rattner as members of the panel[36]. In its news-release issued soon after the appointment of the panel, the Ministry of External Affairs declared "Sri Lanka regards the appointment of the Sri Lanka – Panel of Experts as an unwarranted and unnecessary intervention in a sovereign nation. This interference, moreover, has potential for exploitation by vested interests hostile to the process of reconciliation taking place in Sri Lanka"[37]. The Minister of External Affairs was reported to have stated that "We will not issue them with Visas; we will not allow them into this country". The Sri Lankan government cannot agree to any international investigation. It has been proved that mere resistance and in-house bravado would not be sufficient to check international moves. This is a very difficult situation and the government

---

[35] It is the definitions of the situation that form the reality and expectations upon which foreign policy decisions are formulated. See Kal Holsti, *International Politics- Framework for Analysis*, (Englewood Cliffs, N.J.. Prentice-Hall, Inc, 1983) p.113-17

[36] Marzuki Darusman is former Indonesian Attorney General and member of the United Nations Independent Commission, while Yasmin Sooka is a former member of the South African Truth and Reconciliation Commission and Stevan Rattner is a lawyer in USA.

[37] Ministry of Defence, Sri Lanka, "Government strongly opposes the appointment of the Sri Lanka - Panel of experts by the UNSG" available online at http//www.defence.lk/new.asp?fname=20100623_08

needs to handle it with sophistication and acumen. Sri Lanka may be able to stop the Panel of Experts visiting Sri Lanka, but it cannot afford to stop other UN visits. Two days prior to the appointment of the Panel, Lynn Pascoe, United Nations Under-Secretary General for Political Affairs, visited Sri Lanka for talks with the political leadership and senior government officials[38]. It is also important to note that US State Department Spokesman Mark Toner quoted US Ambassador to the UN, Susan Rice as saying "we urge the Sri Lankan government to take advantage of the team......take advantage of their offer"[39].

It seems that Sri Lankan foreign policy is still governed by the old thinking based on the assumption that as long as state to state relations in key capitals (New Delhi, Washington, Brussels, London, Beijing and Tokyo) are managed satisfactorily every thing would be all right. A notable development in foreign policy under Mahinda Rajapaksa is the turn towards Asian powers. The US Senate Foreign Relations Committee report titled Sri Lanka; Re-charting U.S. Strategy after the War, dated December 7, 2010, observed that "The United States is one of the largest donors of humanitarian aid to Sri Lanka, including food aid and de-mining assistance. Yet, in Colombo, the Government considers the bilateral relationship with Washington to be on a downward trajectory. Most US criticisms of Sri Lankan actions at the end of the war and of the treatment of IDPs have fallen on deaf ears. This growing rift in U.S.–Sri Lanka relations can be seen in Colombo's realignment towards non-Western countries, who offer an alternative model of development that places greater value on security over freedoms. Indeed, Sri Lanka's geopolitical position has evolved considerably".[40]   So far, Sri Lanka played this balancing game nicely in promoting national interests as far as state-to-

---

[38] Lynn Pascoe met President Mahinda Rajapaksa, External Affairs Minister Prof. G. L. Peiris, Economic Development Minister Basil Rajapaksa, Defence Secretary Basil Rajapaksa, and Attorney General Mohan Peiris during the visit which included Vavuniya and Mullativu also.

[39] U.S. asks Sri Lanka to welcome U.N. panel,   The Hindu, 25 June 2010, available online athttp://www.thehindu.com/news/international/article485014.ece?service=mobile accessed on 7 May 2011

[40] U.S., Senate, Committee on Foreign Relations, Sri Lanka: Recharting U.S. Strategy After the War, One Hundred Eleventh Congress, First Session. December 7, 2009.

state relations are concerned. The balancing strategy paid handsome dividends to Sri Lanka as Russia and China came forward to back Sri Lanka by blocking Western diplomatic maneouvering against Sri Lanka at the Security Council and other UN instruments. China prevented the UN Security Council from putting Sri Lanka on its agenda. "When the US ended direct military aid in 2007 over Sri Lanka's deteriorating human rights record, China leapt into the breach, increasing aid to nearly $1bn (£690m) to become the island's biggest donor, giving tens of millions of dollars' worth of sophisticated weapons, and making a gift of six F7 fighter jets to the Sri Lankan Air Force. China encouraged its ally Pakistan to sell more arms and to train pilots to fly the new planes"[41]. However, in view of the geo-political realities of Sri Lanka's location in South Asia and also of the ascendency of India as a global power in the changed constellation of world powers, the prime concern of Sri Lanka's foreign policy is how to handle the India factor. The importance of repeated undertakings given by Colombo to New Delhi relating to a political settlement to the ethnic problem lies in this backdrop.

By the same token, the importance of Sri Lanka's relations with the European powers cannot be underestimated. The network of LTTE overseas activities was concentrated mainly in the western world. It should be noted that after the proscription of the LTTE as a terrorist organization by the European Union in December 2008, European states have taken firm action against the LTTE activists operating on their soil. The clamp down on LTTE operations and operatives posed a severe blow to LTTE activities. According to Ravinatha Aryasinha, Sri Lanka's Ambassador to Belgium, Luxembourg and the EU, "The November 2009 action by a Paris court banning the CCTF [Coordinating Committee of Tamils in France] and the convicting of 21 LTTE activists for up to seven years was the most significant judicial action related to terrorist financing that has taken place in Europe. Additionally it must be noted that in March 2010 Germany arrested seven and, since then, two other individuals for pro-

---

[41] "How Beijing won Sri Lanka's civil war", *The Independent*, 23 May 2010, available online at http://www.independent.co.uk/news/world/asia/how-beijing-won-sri-lankas-civil-war-1980492.html accessed on 7 May 2011

LTTE activity, while in April 2010 the Netherlands arrested seven for the same reason."[42] In this context, the EU peace conditionality to the Sri Lankan government cannot be simply viewed as pro-LTTE moves.

Another key issue in international dimension is how to deal with the new actors in international politics, namely, advocacy groups and INGOs. The International Crisis Group Report is a case in point. In its report released on 17 May 2010, the Brussels-based advocacy group stated that "evidence also provides reasonable grounds to believe that the Sri Lankan security forces committed war crimes with top government and military leaders potentially responsible. There is evidence of war crimes committed by the LTTE and its leaders as well, but most of them were killed and will never face justice"[43]. The main issue is how to handle the situation. The US Senate Foreign Relations Committee report observation in this regard is striking: "the Government's paranoia about criticism and the way some government officials equate criticism with support for the LTTE complicates efforts to move forward. Strikingly, the whole Rajapaksa Government strategy seems to be still driven by security concerns"[44]. Moreover, the Rajapkasa Government is yet to learn the gravity of the impact of some domestic political moves taken to ensure short-term political stability in Sri Lanka's internal environment. In this context, the international implications of mishandling of the Sarath Fonseka factor by the Government should be noted. By portraying Sarath Fonseka as enemy number-one of the state, the Mahinda Rajapaksa regime would be able to discredit its main contestant in the domestic political sphere. What would be the international implications of charging him for revealing 'War Secrets'? What is important is that the Government

---

[42] Text of the speech made b y Ravinatha Aryasinha at the 'The 2010 Diplomatic Securi ty Conference on the T errorism Situation and T rends in the EU' held at Colonial P alace in Brussels on May 11, 2010.

[43] International Crisis Group, "War Crimes in Sri Lanka", Asia Report N 19, 17 May 2010. available online at http://www.crisisgroup.org/en/regions/asia/south-asia/sri-lanka/191-war-crimes-in-sri-lanka.aspx

[44] U.S. Senate, Committee on Foreign Relations, "Sri Lanka: Re-charting U.S. Strategy after the War", 7 December 2009 available online at http://www.boston.com/news/politics/politicalintelligence/tamil%20report.pdf accessed on 7 May 2011.

needs to address the real challenges smartly, such as the ICG report, with moral high ground, equipped with the same political language along with a different set of tools, not by bravado within the house. In order to achieve the moral high ground to deal with actual challenges and to enhance the credibility and legitimacy of the government, it is essential to take concrete steps in three spheres: firstly, strengthening independent national human rights agencies (such as the Human Rights Commission) and the practices and mechanisms promoting good governance and participation, secondly, speedy and satisfactory attention to the problems of IDPs, re-establishment of their livelihood, and promotion of their economic and social well being, and thirdly and more importantly, embarking on political reforms in the direction of establishing, inter alia, viable structures for devolution of power and regional autonomy that will make the people as partners in the post-war rebuilding process.

Political Reforms

Finally, the central element of the post-war peace building process that determines the long-term stability and peace of the country is political reforms and constitutional revision widening the democratic political space in the country. The ultimate success of post-war rehabilitation and reconciliation will be determined by the progress of the political process. It should be kept in mind that all programmes and activities linked with rehabilitation and reconciliation mainly address the consequences of the war. It is the political reforms and the necessary constitutional arrangement that address the root causes of the war. Therefore, the *piece de resistance* of the post-war peace building process must be political reforms. The ethnic conflict is mainly a manifestation of the political crisis of the post-colonial Sri Lankan state, a conflict over arrangement of power. The key issue is who owns the Sri Lankan state. The answer to this question should be reflected in the ideology of the state, in the constitution and the institutional apparatus of the state.

As Nirupama Rao correctly observed, with the end of the war "there is new promise of a new era of peace and stability over the island. There is optimism in the air"[45]. The end of war opens up enormous opportunities to move the country forward. In order to embark on a new historical mission towards achieving a strong and stable post-colonial country, the Sri Lankan state needs a new vision, that which would be capable of integrating all the identities into the ideology of the state which could be done on the basis of equality and partnership. This vision of the state should be reflected in concrete terms in the constitution, 'the grammar of politics', to borrow the term from Harold Laski.[46]

In the present context, far-reaching political reforms and constitutional revision is the requirement of the day. The Maninda Rajapaksa regime requested the people to give it a two-thirds majority in the legislature in order to effect constitutional change. The people responded positively to the government's plea at the parliamentary polls and the government was able to secure a near two-thirds majority, which is truly unprecedented under the proportional electoral system. Now, the Government does not need to invent the wheel once again. The concept of devolution of power was introduced to the Constitution by the 13th Amendment in 1987. The issue of how to improve the devolutionary arrangements has been one of the key elements of the political discourse in the country from the time the Chandrika Bandaranaike Kumaratunga Government presented the text of Government's "Devolution Proposals" on January 16, 1996[47]. The new initiative of the Mahinda Rajapaksa government to achieve a consensus among different political forces on constitutional revision was reflected in the All Party Representative Committee (APRC) chaired by Minister Tissa Witharana. After three years of exhaustive discussions, and of course with many constraints, the APRC presented a mere one page interim proposal to President Mahinda

---

[45] Speech delive red by Nirupama R ao, Foreign Secretary, Go vernment of I ndia at the Inaugural session of the international conference on Sri Lanka organized by the Observer Research Foundation in New Delhi on May 10 2010

[46] for more detai ls see Harold Laski, " A Gr ammar of P olitics", (London, George Allen and Unwin: 1938)

[47] For documents relating to the devolution debate see, ICES, "Sri Lanka: The Devolution Debate", International Centre for Ethnic Studies, Colombo , 1996.

Rajapaksa in February 2009. Since then, the APRC seems defunct.

In order to move the post-war peace building process forward in a wider democratic space, it is necessary to embark on political reforms and constitutional revision with a clear vision and commitment to strengthen good governance and devolution of power. In identifying the parameters of the re-arrangement of power in the form of devolution, one needs to pay due attention to the geo-political unity of Sri Lanka as an island, the pattern of water resources and distribution of natural wealth and also to other geo-political and geo-strategic imperatives of Sri Lanka's location in South Asia which demands a strong centre too. At the same time, devolution of power which is one of the proven political safeguards against separatist political projects must be the focus. Devolution of power offers democratic space for diversity and plurality and facilitates inclusion, not exclusion, of diverse forces. Further more, true devolution makes democracy meaningful, real and effective by bringing the decision-making process closer to the people and more responsive to the needs of the people. The synergy of two principles, a strong centre and true devolution would inject vitality to the post-war Sri Lankan state. The principle of devolution of power has now become an organic element of our political life. Going forward from this point, what is needed is a constitutional arrangement to ensure clarity and consistency in the distribution of power between the centre and the provinces. It will definitely strengthen the centre. Such a devolutionary arrangement could be utilized as a channel to ensure participation of all communities fully, whether it may be at the national, regional, or local levels, thereby encouraging the provinces and the communities to become constructive partners in a stable pluralistic society. In a multi-ethnic society with regional ethnic concentrations, devolution of power offers a constitutional framework and constituent political mechanisms within which all the ethnic groups can work together while maintaining group specific collective identities. This would provide the basis for reconciliation between ethnic groups.

The objective of structural reforms in a post-war context should be the widespread distribution of political power among the people. Devolution is not a panacea for all the political ills. To be viable and effective, devolution should be accompanied by other elements of good governance such as accountability and transparency. Such a broader approach to structural initiatives needs to cover another three public policy spheres in addition to the constitutional sphere. Closely related to the constitutional sphere are the political and administrative spheres. In order to deviate from the existing ultra-centralized administrative practices, a devolution-friendly administrative culture capable of responding to the requirements of a multi-ethnic social order should be promoted. The resource allocation sphere has a very crucial dimension in the reconciliation and peace-building process. The distribution of physical and human resources and development planning must ensure 'balanced development' and equal distribution of resources. Any failure in this sphere would definitely sow the seeds of social and political discontent and unrest. Finally, in the social-cultural sphere, a systematic initiative needs to be launched to promote the culture of peace and tolerance to eradicate culture of violence and intolerance through education and media.

There is now a growing acceptance by the people in general of a long-term political solution to the ethnic problem in the form of constitutional arrangement to devolve power. As a result of the grass-root level peace promotion campaign initiated after Chandrika Bandaranaike Kumaratunga Government came to power in 1994, support for devolution as a political solution to the ethnic problem among people increased. Two opinion surveys conducted in late 1994 and early 1998 revealed that support for devolution of power increased from 23.2% to 68%. Again, the support for devolution and political settlement declined sharply after 2002. The recent surveys conducted by Colin Irwin of the Liverpool University revealed that "the support for constitutional revision embodying devolution among Sinhalese increased after the military defeat of the LTTE, 67% of Sinhalese and 86% of Tamils support the reforms proposed by the President's All Party Representative Committee (APRC)". Furthermore "the top priorities for the Tamils are 'Language Rights' at 85% 'essential or desirable' and 'Fundamental Rights' at 76%. The Sinhalese also welcome these reforms at 71% 'essential or desirable' for 'Fundamental Rights' and 68% for 'Language Rights'. With only

9% of the Sinhala opposed to 'Language Rights', there should be little political difficultly with their implementation"[48]. Still there are lonely voices in some quarters in Colombo that 'grievance first, devolution later (if at all)'[49]. The stark reality is that the common sense of the ordinary masses is more realistic and progressive; the problem always lies with the political leadership which has become imprisoned in its own self-proclaimed prophesies.

It is not possible to avoid the issue anymore. The credibility and legitimacy of the government is closely linked with its willingness to go forward with the devolution of power and widespread distribution of political power. It should not be forgotten that the Sri Lankan government has repeatedly given firm assurances to India regarding this matter. During President Mahinda Rajapaksa's four day state visit to India in June 2010, the Indian prime minister harped on a meaningful devolution package and that building on the 13th amendment would provide suitable conditions for reconciliation. In view of the enormous trust and confidence that President Mahinda Rajapaksa is presently enjoying, especially among Sinhala people, it is now high time for him to take the initiative. Those 'paper lions' that were earlier very vocal against devolution of power are now caged in ministerial cells or in the corridors of power. It is the duty of the political leadership not to allow another opportunity to slip away. If the main objective of constitutional reform is to get rid of the constitutional barrier for the incumbent President to hold office more then twice, and other revisions are mere cosmetic, the entire constitutional revision would become a farce. The observations of the US Senate Foreign Relations Committee are worthy of mention. "Indeed, the end of Sri Lanka's long-running separatist war opens up enormous opportunity to move the country forward on multiple fronts:

---

[48] Colin Irwin, *The APRC Proposals and 'Winning the Peace* ", Institute of Irish Studies, University of Liverpool, 9 July 2009, available online at http://ict4peace.files.wordpress.com/ 2009/07/aprcarticle.pdf accessed on 7 May 2011

[49] Malinda Seneviratne, "Grievance first, devolution later (if at all), *Sunday Island Online*, May 30, 2010 available online at http://www.island.lk/2010/05/30/features9.html accessed on 7 May 2011.

political reform, economic revival and the internal re-engagement. For the country to make the transition from a post War to post-conflict environment, Sri Lankan leaders must be prepared to take difficult steps to bring the country together and resolve the underlying political and socio-economic tensions that led to the conflict"[50].

Conclusion: Political Will

In the last twenty five years Sri Lanka suffered enormously in many respects due to the war. Sri Lanka does not have to go through the same experience once again in order to come to grips with the realities of post-colonial state-formation and the national integration processes. The bleeding of war has now come to an end and the period of sweating in peace has begun. Sri Lankan people have an enormous capacity and inner resilience to bounce back after calamities. The long history of Sri Lanka is replete with such examples of bouncing back after dire calamities under the direction of sound leadership with a clear vision and commitment. The historical task before the country is to go forward in the direction of achieving reconciliation and positive peace with a clear vision and commitment. The challenges and problems that Sri Lanka faces in the post-war peace building process would also be enormous. The Archimedean screw of the entire post-war peace building process in the true sense of the word is political will. Nelson Mandela in his *Long Walk to Freedom* stated that "there are times when a leader must move ahead of the flock, go off in a new direction, feeling sure that he is leading his people down the right road"[51].

---

[50] U.S. Senate, Committee on Foreign Relations, Sri Lanka: Re-charting U.S. Strategy After the War, 2009.

[51] Nelson Mandela, Long Walk to Freedom (80th Birthday abridged Edition), (London: Little, Brown and Co. Ltd, 1996), p.120.

ECONOMIC DIMENSIONS OF THE CONFLICT

Deshal de Mel[1]

The majority of literature and debate on the conflict in Sri Lanka between the government and the Liberation Tigers of Tamil Eelam (LTTE) revolves around the political dimensions of the conflict. However there are substantial economic factors that have shaped the conflict and at the same time the conflict has to an extent shaped the economy. In this context, economic policy measures become important when formulating a post conflict policy structure, both in terms of addressing the adverse impacts of conflict, and in terms of using the economic lever to lock in peace and prevent resurrection of conflict. At the same time, the conflict has shaped macroeconomic structures in the country, particularly with regard to fiscal policy formulation which has in turn driven monetary policy, affecting overall macroeconomic stability. The post conflict situation opens several avenues for reforming macroeconomic structures and also calls for various macroeconomic policy measures to facilitate the post conflict reconstruction process.

This chapter is organized in four sections. The first deals with the economic roots of the conflict which have been largely overshadowed by the political dimensions. Policy priorities in terms of averting conflict resurgence are examined through this lens. The section also considers the

---

[1] The views expressed in the chapter are those of the author and do not necessarily reflect the position of the Institute of Policy Studies of Sri Lanka. The excellent research inputs of Anneka de Silva are gratefully acknowledged, whilst any errors or omissions are the responsibility of the author alone.

economic policy lessons that arise from the peace process between 2002 and 2004. Section two addresses the economic costs of the conflict both at a national and regional level, providing an indication of the degree of economic reconstruction that would be required and the potential areas which could rebound once conflict has ended. Section three outlines the impacts of conflict on macroeconomic policy and Section four deals with the policy requirements for sustainable post conflict economic resurrection.

Economic Policy Dimensions Influencing the Conflict

Violent conflict in Sri Lanka is often traced back to 1976 with the formation of the LTTE along with several other militant Tamil youth groups. Much of the literature on the conflict in Sri Lanka is focused on political dimensions of the conflict including issues such as language, tertiary education and the devolution of power to the regions. In this chapter, we examine the economic aspects that influenced conflict in Sri Lanka. To understand the economic roots of the conflict it is necessary to provide some background of Sri Lanka's economy in the post independence era. Immediately following independence in 1948, Sri Lanka maintained the open economic colonial structures with reliance on plantation agriculture exports (tea and rubber in particular) until 1956. With a change of government the focus shifted towards mild import substitution in an effort to de-link from colonial economic ties and to rejuvenate the domestic economy. Between 1965 and 1970 another regime change saw a reversion to some degree, of economic liberalization but within the framework of overall import substitution. This period coincided with a general shift by developing economies towards import substitution industrialization (ISI) as dependency theory postulated the impossibility of export oriented development. In 1970, Sri Lanka turned to a full blown import substitution industrialization effort as the economy all but completely closed. This situation continued until 1977 when another change of regime saw economic liberalization as Sri Lanka became the first South Asian economy to liberalize its economy.

The period 1960-1977 saw Sri Lanka's growth performance stagnate to a great extent compared to other developing nations, particularly East Asian economies. Between 1960-1977 economic growth averaged 3.9 per cent whilst between 1970 and 1977 growth averaged 3 per cent[2]. Given Sri Lanka's small island economy, the domestic market was never going to be sufficient to create the requisite economies of scale for large scale import substitution industrialization. Furthermore, economic production in Sri Lanka has relied on imported inputs and with the restrictive trade regime it was difficult for industrial production to take place. Manufacturing came to a near halt during this period, and the boom in production soon after liberalization underscores the extent of stagnation during the import substitution period. Between 1978 and 2003, manufacturing output grew at 8.2 per cent compared to 4.8 per cent in the period preceding reforms[3]. The ability of the Sri Lankan economy to create jobs was very limited in this period as a result of stagnant growth. The Central Bank's Consumer Finance Survey of 1973[4] indicated that unemployment had reached 24 per cent of the labour force in that year, whilst the same survey of 1978 showed that unemployment was 14.8 per cent, a reduction, but still unacceptably high. The inability of the economy to create wealth and employment resulted in the exclusion of certain segments of society from economic activity and the benefits thereof. The youth in particular were excluded from economic activity as is evident in the abnormally high rates of youth unemployment in the country. In 1978 when total unemployment was 14.8 per cent, youth (ages 19-25) unemployment had reached 31.1 per cent according to the Central Bank Consumer Finance and Socio Economic Survey.

Even in 1981 when economic liberalization had taken place and

---

[2] M.P. Peiris, "Economic Growth and Structural – Institutional Change since Independence", in W D Lakshman ed. *Dilemmas of Developments: Fifty years of Economic Changes in Sri Lanka*, (Colombo: Sri Lanka Association of Economists, 1997).

[3] Perma- Chandra Atukorala, "Outward-oriented Policy Reforms and Industrialsation: The Sri Lankan Experience" Journal of South Asian Development 1:1, (New Delhi/ Thousand Oaks/London: Sage publications: 2006).

[4] Central Bank of Sri Lanka Annual Report, Various Editions; Other labour surveys indicated high unemployment throughout the 1970s – for instance the 1971 census (19%), 1975 Land and Labour utilization survey (19.9%).

economic activity had been enhanced and total unemployment had fallen to 11.7 per cent, youth unemployment remained high at 28.8 per cent. This is explained by several factors. The absorption of employment by new industries was limited, and several rural informal sectors such as the handloom and cottage sector were adversely affected by liberalization of trade, and employment creation in formal industries failed to compensate for this[5]. In fact the adverse (largely unaddressed) negative impacts of trade liberalization in 1977 had substantial impacts on the Northern Province in particular as the agricultural produce of this region was faced by increased competition from imported products – undermining livelihoods in the region[6].

At the same time, youth unemployment is to some extent explained by the contradictions between Sri Lanka's labour market and the higher and tertiary education sector. Education at higher and tertiary level is free of charge and creates expectations of high end employment, which the economy has failed to deliver[7]. At the same time new entrants to the Sri Lankan labour market have lacked the relevant skills in demand by employers[8]. As a result youth unemployment has led to brewing frustrations amongst Sri Lanka's youth since the 1970s. The ethnic dimension to this issue was fuelled by the government policy in the early 1970s which standardized university admission examinations by language. As a result Tamil language students had to score higher marks to obtain university admission. This was supplemented by a district quota which made it more difficult for students from more privileged districts such as Colombo and Jaffna (which is a Tamil majority district) to obtain university entry. These policies, though reversed within the decade, had

---

[5] Saman Kelegama, "Development under Stress: Sri Lankan Econom y in Transition", (New Delhi/ Thousand Oaks/London: Sage publications: 2006).

[6] David Dunham and Sisira Jayasuriya, "Equity, Growth and Insurrection: Liberalization and the Welfare Debate in Contemporary Sri Lanka", *Oxford Development Studies*, Volume 28, Issue 1, 2000, Pages 97 – 110.

[7] Sirimal Abeyratne, "Economic Roots of Political Conflict: the Case of Sri Lanka",   *World Economy*, Vol 27, Number 8, August 2004

[8] Ibid.

significant implications on perceptions of discrimination[9] and were seen as a deliberate move to inhibit the upward social mobility of Tamil youth.

The Role of Economic Exclusion

Abeyratne argues that the economic exclusion of youth of all ethnicities has shaped conflict in Sri Lanka.[10] The JVP[11] uprisings of 1987 and 1971 were largely the result of the economic exclusion of rural Sinhalese youth. Abeyratne argues that both the LTTE and the JVP were made up of largely marginalized, unemployed rural youth and the LTTE is arguably an ethnic manifestation of the frustrations of rural youth. [12] Abeyratne in a separate work[13] goes on to illustrate the significance of the economic dimension through a comparison between Sri Lanka and Malaysia. The two countries began on similar socioeconomic platforms (multiethnic countries reliant on plantation exports). Malays made up the majority in Malaysia but ethnic Chinese dominated the economic spheres. Economic inequity was countered by the "Malaysian Malaysia" policy which entailed "Special Malay Rights". Malaysia experienced growing communal resentment and riots in 1969. The New Economic Policy (NEP) of 1970 institutionalized affirmative action for Malays, covering spheres of education, training, business ownership, business opportunities, access to credit and employment. Furthermore, public discussion and criticism of "sensitive issues" was prohibited by constitutional amendment. Snodgrass (1995) stated that Malaysia's affirmative action was probably the most ambitious amongst any developing country.

---

[9] The actual impact on Tamil student university admissions, particularly in the science medium was limited – the percentage of Tamil students entering the science stream dropped from 35.3% to 33.3%.

[10] S Abeyratne, Economic Roots of Political conflict: The case of Sri Lanka, 2004

[11] Janatha Vimukthi Peramuna: A violent Southern Sinhalese uprising made up of rural youth.

[12] S Abeyratne, "Economic Roots of Political conflict: The case of Sri Lanka". 2004

[13] S Abeyratne, "Economic Development and Political Conflict: A Comparative Study of Sri Lanka and Malaysia" *South Asia Economic Journal*, Volume 9, Number 2, 2008, Pages 393-417.

Sri Lanka had a similar situation in terms of economic and political distribution of power in the immediate post colonial era. In fact, even as of 1970 Tamil university students made up 49 per cent of medical students, 48 per cent in engineering and 40 per cent in science. In 1963 mean income in Tamil communities was LKR 327, low country Sinhalese was LKR 292 and Kandyan Sinhalese was LKR 218. Unemployment and underemployment of Tamils was also much less than that of Sinhalese.[14] However the "corrective" measures taken by the Sri Lankan government (language policy 1956 and university admissions on language basis 1971-1974) were far less ambitious than those undertaken in Malaysia. Abeyratne argues that the reason for the lack of violent conflict in Malaysia was the economic expansion that resulted in increased opportunities for all communities.[15]

Malaysia did not follow an ISI program and export led growth facilitated 7.9 per cent average growth between 1970 and 1995. During the same period average growth in Sri Lanka was 4.4 per cent. Successful industrialization in Malaysia enabled employment creation which reduced surplus labour resulting in increased wages and poverty reduction. Sri Lanka's failure to follow a similar process resulted in a stagnant economy that created a frustrated pool of unemployed youth – a situation conducive for violent conflict. Whilst economic exclusion is one of many causative factors that resulted in the violent manifestation of Tamil nationalism, it provided the requisite conditions for violent conflict and is clearly important in terms of understanding the roots of conflict. Youth unemployment remains a concern in Sri Lanka even today. By the second quarter in 2009, unemployment in the 20-24 age category was 21.6 per cent whilst national unemployment was 6.2 per cent. It is essential that post conflict economic reconstruction activities prioritize the generation of employment for youth. There are also implications for access to education in the region, particularly in terms of ensuring better matching between demand and supply of skills. Education in the conflict areas will be discussed in greater detail later in the chapter.

[14] Sirimal Abeyratne, *Economic Change and Political Conflict in Developing Countries with Special Reference to Sri Lanka*, (Amsterdam: VU University Press, 1998)

[15] Sirimal Abeyratne, "Economic Development and Political Conflict: A Comparative Study of Sri Lanka and Malaysia", 2008

Land Re-distribution

The Mahaweli[16] Development Project was fully established in the 1970s and intended to utilise surplus land within the dry zones of the North-Central, North and East Provinces so as to relieve overcrowding and provide land to the landless. The project aimed to re-house approximately 18,500 families allocating 0.2ha of newly irrigated land to each for the cultivation of paddy and other crops.[17] The high costs of implementing the project meant that there was heavy reliance on the provision of foreign aid[18] and so in 1977 the government established the Accelerated Mahaweli Development Project (AMDP) in an attempt to increase progress and reduce long term costs. The project was successful in terms of easing population pressures and providing incomes for poor families. However, there were a number of economic, social and political shortcomings that may have acted as a catalyst in the subsequent conflict experienced in the north and east.

The government projected that the high costs of the AMDP would be recovered through the increase in domestic paddy production (estimated at 186,000 additional tons) and the future ability of farmers to buy their allocated plots of land from the government. Whilst the scheme was successful in increasing paddy production, it coincided with the decline in domestic rice prices, which dramatically hindered its economic success. Furthermore, the poor augmentation of farmers' incomes resulted in the majority of farmers choosing not to buy their land, thus increasing the continued costs to the government.

With the mass migration of people into the dry zones came a number of social impediments which played a role in dampening the project's performance. There are many arguments surrounding the mass movement

---

[16] The Mahaweli is the longest river in Sri Lanka.

[17] The World Bank Group, "Sri Lanka : Mahaweli Ganga Development" available online at http://lnweb90.worldbank.org/oed/oeddoclib.nsf/DocUNIDViewForJavaSearch/ 0D869807701D1EEE 852567 F5005D8903

[18] Donations came from the W orld Bank, Britain, Germany, Sweden and Canada.

of largely Sinhalese populations into the Eastern and Northern Provinces. Shastri claims that much of the controversy surrounding the AMDP was caused by the shift in ethnic ratios within the Eastern Province: the Trincomalee district saw the Sinhalese and Tamil populations shift from 21 per cent and 40 per cent respectively in 1946, to 34 per cent each by the 1970s[19]. Similarly, the split of the Batticaloa district, wherein the Tamil community held a majority at 51 per cent, resulted in the reduction of Tamils in the new district of Amparai to a minority of 24 per cent with both Sinhalese and Muslim communities forming the majority, whilst the bulk of Tamil inhabitants concentrated in the smaller Batticaloa district wherein they represented the majority at 71 per cent. This apparent encroachment of land may have acted to heighten tensions between the Sinhalese and the Tamils. Furthermore, critics noted that the greatest development within the AMDP occurred in the Sinhalese-dominated areas of the Northern-Central Provinces. However, as highlighted by Peiris the highly emotive nature of this discussion can often lead to a one dimensional portrayal of government policies. Peiris's critique of Shastri's argument points to the mis-interpretation of data and the coincidental occurrence of greater development within Sinhalese-dominated regions of the AMDP, as opposed to the pursuit of Sinhalese-elitism.[20]

What can be drawn from the past experience of the AMDP is the vulnerability of land redistribution and development schemes within the post-conflict regions to race-related criticism. Whilst a degree of criticism is unavoidable, the government must ensure that polices are not, or cannot be misconstrued as, favouring any one ethnic group. Such portrayal will only work against efforts for redevelopment in the area, causing unrest and threatening the new found peace. In order to maximize the efficiency with which development can ensue, the restructuring of social capital is a vital adjunct to land redistribution. Therefore, social equity should be at the forefront of all land development projects.

---

[19] Amita Shastri, "The Material Basis ór Separatism: The Tamil Eelam Movement in Sri Lanka", Journal of Asian Studies, 49(1): F eb 1990, pp 56-77.

[20] G H Peiris, "Irrigation, Land Distribution and Ethnic Conflict in Sri Lanka: An Evaluation of Criticisms", Ethnic Studies R eport, Vol XII, No. 1, I nternational Centre f or Ethnic Studies (ICES), Colombo.994

Economic Lessons from the 2001-2003 Peace Process

In November 2001, the United National Front (a UNP[21] led coalition) came into power and declared a ceasefire in the wake of a deteriorating economic situation (Sri Lanka recorded negative GDP growth of -1.5 per cent for the first time in its post colonial history in 2001) and successive strategic losses on the military front. The LTTE was also in a compromised position following substantial cadre losses following major military engagements and also faced difficulties on the international front in the wake of the terrorist attacks on America on 11 September 2001. The new government envisaged a plan to create rapid development in the conflict provinces and thereby lock in the peace process through an economic dividend[22]. Several measures were undertaken including the removal of the goods embargo to the North-East, the re-opening of the A9 highway connecting the Jaffna Peninsula with the rest of the country and extensive de-mining activities. However the bulk of the economic dividend was expected through the trickle down impact of macroeconomic reforms which were undertaken simultaneously. These reforms included consolidation of the fiscal position including enacting the Fiscal Management Responsibility Act, a freeze on new public sector hiring, reforms of loss making state owned enterprises and reforms to labour and foreign exchange markets[23]. The economic results were initially rapid. Following the -1.5 per cent contraction in 2001, economic growth in 2002 reached 4 per cent and increased to 5.9 per cent in 2006, above Sri Lanka's trend growth rate of around 5 per cent since the 1990s. The number of tourists increased to 500,000 for the first time in 2003, fishing output in the North-East doubled and paddy output increased five fold. FDI increased from US$ 82 Million in 2001 to US$ 230 Million in 2002. A substantial inflow of portfolio investment resulted in the Colombo Stock Exchange reaching a new

---

[21] United National Party – The current opposition part y, associated with a liber al economic policy stance.

[22] Kelegama, "Development under Stress", (2006)

[23] Ibid.

peak since 1994.

However, with the emphasis on the macroeconomic front, there were limited efforts in terms of direct poverty reduction measures and other social issues. Furthermore, the missing markets and institutional weaknesses (such as perceived weaknesses in SIHRN[24] – the institution charged with immediate rehabilitation needs) in the North-East made it difficult for the economic dividend to filter down effectively. Largely due to fiscal constraints, the government relied more on external donor support for the social and immediate livelihood generation activities. The World Bank spearheaded the NERF[25] which was due to focus on resettlement, special needs of women and children, income generating opportunities for the war affected, small scale infrastructure and basic health and education facility development. However the weaknesses in absorption by institutional mechanisms in the North East undermined the efficacy of these measures[26]. Furthermore, not all the aid that was pledged by donors was disbursed. For instance, out of the US$ 567 Million IMF PRGF, only US$ 80 Million was disbursed as economic reforms did not proceed at the pace the donors envisaged. The economic dividend was not sufficiently rapid to lock in peace as there was increasing discontent with the peace process in the South of the country as the LTTE attempted to focus discussion on the basis of forming an interim fully autonomous administration, and did not fully cooperate with rehabilitation activities which were not fully under their control[27]. By April 2003 the LTTE withdrew from the negotiations and the peace process deteriorated as violations of the cease fire by LTTE increased substantially until the government eventually withdrew from the ceasefire in early 2008 – after full scale war had already broken out. The government's plan of locking in the peace process and undermining

---

[24] Sub-Committee on Immediate Humanitarian and Rehabilitation Needs in the North and East.

[25] North East Reconstruction Fund.

[26] Kelegama, " Development under Str ess", (2006).

[27] Ibid.

support for the LTTE through the economic lever was not successful as the other dimensions of the conflict took greater significance within the limited time span. This situation is unlikely to arise in current efforts since the LTTE has been militarily defeated, and there will be more time for economic measures to have a meaningful impact. However the importance of delivery institutions in the post-conflict areas and fiscal space become important issues. The importance of addressing grass roots level economic issues, both in conflict regions and the rest of the country are also highlighted from this experience – the failure to do so is arguably one factor that influenced the reversion to conflict. Finally, the lack of political stability of the incumbent regime (whilst parliament was controlled by the UNF through a delicate coalition, the presidency was held by the opposition party) resulted in low credibility of any promised constitutional changes, and thereby undermined the economic levers of driving peace in Sri Lanka.

Economic Impacts of the Conflict

Estimating costs of conflict is notoriously difficult. A few papers have estimated the various macroeconomic and other impacts of the conflict. However none of these are sufficiently recent to take into account the impacts of the final military conflict that took place between 2007 and 2009. Therefore, whilst the broad coverage of the impacts of conflict remains valid, the magnitude will be greater in the Northern Province given the most recent fighting.

Direct Costs

The direct economic costs of the conflict include destruction of physical and human capital, military expenditure, exclusion of natural resources and resources required for refugee care. Arunatilake estimates that the cost of government expenditure on the conflict between 1983 and 1996 was LKR 288 Billion (present compound value which is equivalent to 41 per cent of 1996 GDP). Defense expenditure in 1982 was 1.1 per cent of GDP whilst it reached 4.4 per cent of GDP in 1988 and ranged between 4.2-4.5 per cent in 1990-1994 and in 1996 reached 6 per cent of GDP. Comparing with other developing countries, in 1985 developing countries defense expenditure averaged 7.1 per cent and in 1995 averaged 3.1 per cent - whereas in SL 1985 expenditure was 3.5 per cent and in 1995 it was 5.4 per cent. [28]In 2008 defense expenditure was 3.8 per cent of GDP or 17.1 per cent of total government expenditure. At the same time it needs to be kept in mind that defense expenditure has acted as an important stimulus to the economy, particularly in terms of rural employment and livelihoods and the multiplier impacts that result. However, expenditure on military wages contributes to current consumption but crowds out investment and increases future repayment obligations, thereby undermining future consumption. Kelegama estimates that a 1 per cent increase in defense expenditure causes a 2.4 per cent decline in public investment.[29]

The North and East is also home to many major industries, all of which either halted production or substantially cut down on production. This includes the cement factory in Kankasanthurei, the chemical factory in Paranthan, the salterns in Elephant Pass and Nilaweli, limestone in Pulmoddai, ceramics and Odduchuddan and Amparai and the paper mill in Valachenai. The North East region also accounted for 64 per cent of fish production in Sri Lanka prior to the conflict and was a major source of agricultural output. The loss of this output due to military (both sides) occupation of land and mining activities, adversely affected livelihoods in the North-East and also prices and availability of these products in markets across the country.

---

[28] Nisha Arunatilake, Sisira Jayasuriya and Saman Kelegama, "The economic cost of the war in Sri Lanka", *World Development*, Vol 29, No 9, 2001, pp 1483-1500.

[29] Kelegama, "Development Under Stress", 2006.

Table 1: Agriculture Production Share of N/E

Crop	1980 (%)	2005 (%)
Paddy	33	30
Chillies	25	11
Red Onions	62	23
Potato	13	0.6
Livestock (eggs)	13	12.6
Fish	64	34

Source: M Sarvananthan, 2006

It is estimated that US$ 1 billion (LKR 56.5 Billion) worth of damage to physical and social infrastructure had occurred up to 1995[30]. Damage was particularly severe in irrigation, roads and bridges, railways, industrial damage and housing – both in the conflict areas and in the South of the country as a result of terrorist attacks. The LTTE targeted economically significant institutions in order to curtail the ability of the government to finance the military effort. Attacks on the oil refinery (1995), Central Bank (1996), Colombo Stock Market/Galadari Hotel (1997), Island-wide Transformers (1999), Airport (2001) are among the main incidents which caused great damage both in money and human terms. For example, the cost of the Airport attack was estimated as US $ 30 million which was more than what the government received from privatization of the national airline (US $ 25 million). In the conflict areas extensive mining will pose a major challenge even in the post conflict period. There are approximately 1.8 million landmines laid both by the LTTE and government armed forces, spread over 640 villages in the

---

[30] Arunatilake, Jayasuriya, Kelegama, "The economic cost of the war in Sri Lanka", 2001.

North and the East. Nearly 500-700 people per year became victims of landmines during 1995-2000, which was a major deterrent to economic activity, particularly agriculture[31].

Social infrastructure has also been adversely affected due to the conflict, with potentially damaging impacts on long term economic performance, particularly in the conflict zones. Close to 2000 schools have been completely destroyed during the fighting. 360,000 housing units have sustained varying degrees of damage. Out of 400 health institutions, 55 were totally destroyed, 49 are not functioning, and 115 centres are damaged where these assets undergo minimum or no maintenance at all. Due to security fears, 4,522 posts were vacant in the health care sector mainly in the skilled and professional category in the North and East[32].

In the most recent needs assessment undertaken during the previous ceasefire, the estimated cost of reconstruction was US$ 2.5 billion (US $ 522 immediate, US $ 946 medium term, US $ 1031 long term)[33]. However as mentioned earlier, the damage that occurred in the final bout of fighting would have substantially increased this cost.

The human cost of the war in terms of deaths is estimated to be around 70,000. A large number of displaced individuals have accumulated since the 1980s, including the Muslims expelled from Jaffna by the LTTE in the 1990s who settled on the Western coast and the recent IDPs from the final stages of the war who numbered close to 100,000 at the time of writing. Furthermore the war resulted in the migration of several people from the country, particularly to Europe and North America.

---

[31] Saman K elegama, "Socio-Economic Cost of the War", presented at the *International Conference on Countering Terrorism*, at Bandaranaike Memorial International Conference Hall (BMICH) in Colombo from 18-20 October 2007.

[32] Ibid.

[33] World Bank, Background paper "Assessment of Needs in the Conflict Affected Areas" submitted to the Tokyo Donor Conference in 2003.

Indirect Costs

The indirect costs of conflict are numerous but harder to estimate quantitatively. Among the most important indirect costs of terrorism in Sri Lanka include the reduced Foreign Direct Investment (FDI) and domestic investment due to insecurity and instability, tourism losses again due to insecurity and the inaccessibility of tourist sites in the conflict zone, brain drain due to refugees leaving the country (this needs to be considered separately from economic migrants), increased taxation (to fund the military effort) and its adverse impacts on business competitiveness, the delays to economic reform processes and the adverse macroeconomic impacts of high fiscal deficits that were influenced by high military expenditure.

In terms of foreign direct investment, for instance, it is estimated that foregone investment cost 71 per cent of Sri Lanka's GDP in 1996[34]. Motorola and Harris Corporation abandoned plans to establish in SL, and the country lost a great chance to upgrade its industrial base. The risky investment climate has created a bias towards industries with limited fixed costs and high labour intensity, and as a result wages have been relatively low. Sri Lanka also had to offer special incentives for companies to compensate for the risk undertaken in investing. These incentives have been fiscally costly and the lack of competition has also been problematic. For instance Caltex was given exclusive market access until 2004 for lubricants, shell had the same for gas transactions from 1995-2000[35]. It was expected that in time other firms would also invest and provide the requisite competition, however this did not occur as planned, influenced by security considerations.

Similar estimations have been carried out for tourism and the foregone earnings are substantial, particularly when considering the fact that the multiplier effects of tourist revenue have an important impact on livelihoods.

---

[34] Kelegama, "Development Under Stress", 2006.

[35] Ibid.

Table 2: Loss of Tourism: 1983-2004[36]

Year	Estimated Tourist Arrivals	Actual Tourist Arrivals	Loss of Tourist Arrivals	Earnings per Tourist ($)	Loss of Earnings ($ Mn.)
1983	431,664	337,530	94,134	343.7	32.4
1990	649,063	297,888	351,175	433.0	152.1
1995	868,592	403,101	465,491	559.9	260.6
1996	920,708	302,265	618,443	550.5	340.5
1997	975,950	366,165	609,785	570.2	347.7
1981	1,034,507	381,063	653,444	604.4	394.9
1999	1,096,578	436,440	660,138	627.8	414.4
2000	1,162,373	400,414	761,959	631.3	481.0
2001	1,232,115	336,794	895,321	626.8	561.2
2002	1,306,042	393,171	912,871	643.5	587.4
2003	1,384,404	500,642	883,762	679.1	600.2
2004	1,467,469	566,202	901,267	729.4	657.4
Total loss					6,341.9

Source: Cost of the War in Sri Lanka, NPC, Cost of Conflict in Sri Lanka, Strategic Foresight Group

Note: The estimated tourist arrivals is calculated on the basis of 6 per cent growth as given in the Cost of the War in Sri Lanka, NPC report by Marga Institute

Numerous taxes and other levies were introduced over the conflict years in order to raise revenue for the military process. In May 1995, the defense levy was increased to 4.5 per cent from 3.5 per cent, and one intention of the privatization program was to free up resources for military expenditure.[37] The Save the Nation Fund was also introduced in 1996

---

[36] Kelegama, "Socio-Economic Cost of the War", 2007

[37] S Kelegama, " Sri Lankan Economy of war and peace", *Economic and Political Weekly*, Vol 37, No 7, November 23-29, 2002

which levied 3 per cent on income from those who earned above a particular threshold. The National Security Levy increased from 3 per cent in 1992 to 6.5 per cent in 2001 and financed 48 per cent of the defense expenditure in 2000. The cumulative impacts of these taxes were a burden on private sector activity and served to reduce competitiveness with respect to international competitors and to reduce margins, thereby discouraging investment and expansion of production.

As mentioned at the outset, the three decade long violent conflict has to a great extent shaped economic development in Sri Lanka. The economic costs of the war have been substantial, but at the same time the economy has become increasingly resilient and the performance of the economy particularly in recent years has been very creditable when taking into consideration the extremely adverse conditions in which it has found itself. In the next section we examine the recent trends in Sri Lanka's macroeconomic performance, taking a close look at the macroeconomic policy priorities that will arise in the post conflict situation.

Macroeconomic Implications of the Conflict

The conflict in Sri Lanka has to a great extent been geographically isolated to the Northern and Eastern Provinces of the country. Whilst intermittent terror attacks have taken place in Colombo and other parts of the country (Kandy (temple of the tooth), Galle (naval base), Anuradhapura (sacred Bo tree), the macroeconomic structures have by and large continued to function. Nonetheless, the high degree of government expenditure on the military effort and the revenue losses that have been associated with the conflict (particularly the fiscal concessions given to investors to compensate for the weak investment climate that has resulted from poor security and the below potential revenue collection due to sub-optimal economic activity) have had important macroeconomic implications. As we will argue in this section, Sri Lanka's poor fiscal performance has been a key economic challenge, and this has been influenced by the prolonged conflict in the country.

Impacts on Fiscal Policy

Management of fiscal policy has proved to be a major challenge for successive Sri Lankan governments. An important factor that has influenced this situation is the high expenditure on military activities. As is evident from Figure 1 below, military expenditure has accounted for on average 5 per cent of GDP and 20 per cent of Government expenditure over the last decade.

Figure 1:

Military Expenditure as a % of GDP and Government Expenditure

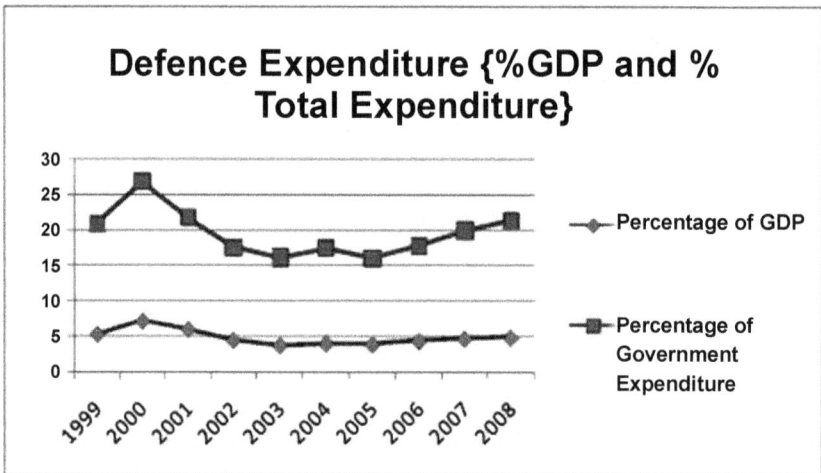

Source: Central Bank data

Sri Lanka has consistently maintained budget deficits. Since 1990, current expenditure has outweighed total revenues in every year. Therefore the entirety of capital expenditure (and part of current expenditure) has been financed by borrowing, resulting in a massive accumulated public debt that stood at 81.1 per cent of GDP in 2008.

Figure 2:

Government Fiscal Operations 1990-2008 (% of GDP)

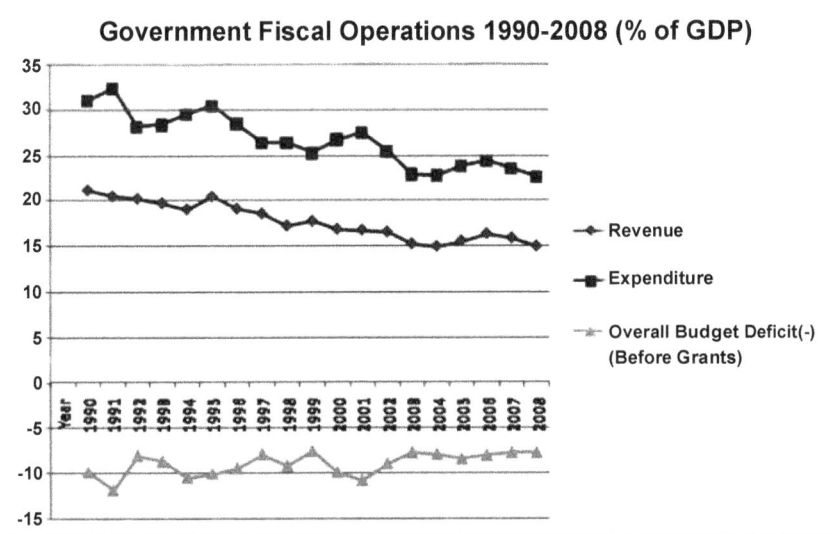

Legend:
- Revenue
- Expenditure
- Overall Budget Deficit(-) (Before Grants)

Source: Central Bank data

It is clear from figure 2 that budget deficits have ranged around 8 per cent of GDP in recent years and as of 2008 the budget deficit was 7.7 per cent of GDP.

Figure 3: Public Debt

Public Debt (% GDP)

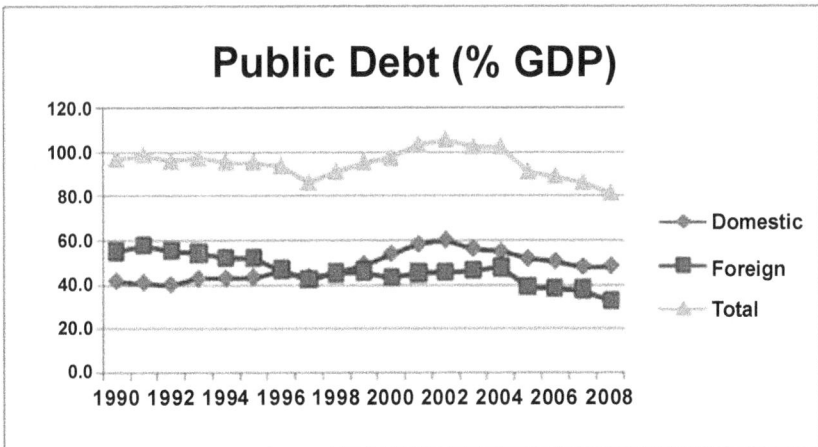

Legend:
- Domestic
- Foreign
- Total

Source: Central Bank data

Repayments of public debt continue to eat into a considerable portion of government expenditure (29 per cent of government expenditure was on debt repayments in 2008), crowding out alternative and more productive expenditure.

With the end of the military conflict there was initially some optimism that military expenditure could decline, thereby easing pressure on the budgetary position. However, given the significant share of expenditure allocated to defense wages and current procurement, and the policy of enhancing recruitment despite the end of the war, it is likely that defense expenditure will remain elevated in the short to medium term.

Figure 4:

Military Expenditure[38] (LKR Billion)

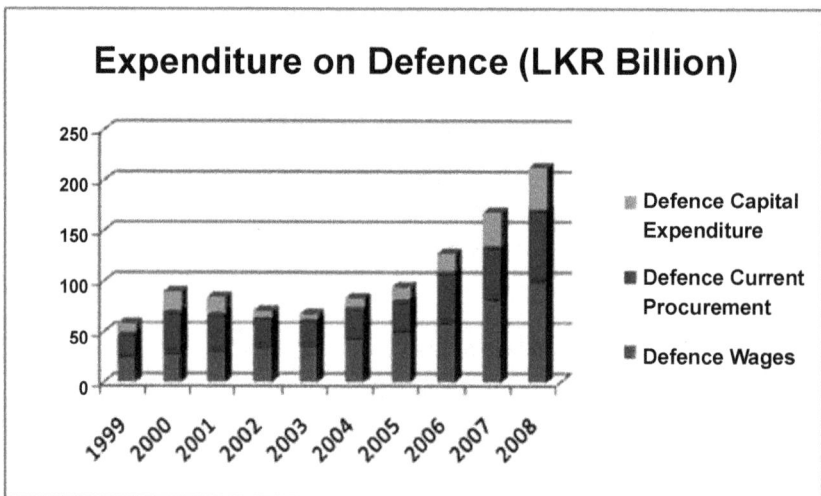

Source: Central Bank data

---

[38] Capital expenditure is obtained from the capital expenditure component of the Ministry of Defense whereas wages and recurrent procurement are derived from the economic classification of government expenditure of CBSLAR.

In 2009, the fiscal position deteriorated further with revenue declines associated with the global economic crisis and a domestic economic downturn coupled with higher than expected government expenditure. According to a pre-budget report released by the treasury in April 2010, the provisional budget deficit for 2009 is 9.7 per cent of GDP.

The persistently large share of military expenditure in government spending carries a number of indirect costs to the performance of the economy. One such cost is the negative effect that the spending may have upon the government's propensity to invest into the country's productive capacity. Empirical findings support the premise that military spending has dampened investment in Sri Lanka, thus hindering growth in the process. Examples of this include expenditure on infrastructure such as energy capacity (the failure to invest effectively in energy has resulted in Sri Lanka having to rely on expensive liquid thermal energy leading to the country having the highest electricity costs in South Asia), roads (the country does not have a single intercity expressway) and ports (the country has just one international airport and one major commercial international port). The government is at present attempting to make up for these shortcomings by investing in coal power plants in the North West of the country and in expressways between Colombo and the South and between Colombo and the airport along with a new international airport and sea port. It could also be argued that the military expenditure has eroded potential expenditure on education, health and other social services that contribute to the social capital of the economy. However, there are other countries which spend comparable or higher amounts on military expenditure but greater amounts on social services.

Table 3: Comparative Government Expenditure

Country	Government Expenditure on Defense (%GDP) 2008	Government Expenditure on Education (% of Government expenditure 2000-2007 average)
United States of America	4.1	13.7
India	2.8	10.7
Sri Lanka	2.8	9.9

Country	Government Expenditure on Defense (%GDP) 2008	Government Expenditure on Health (% of Government expenditure 2006)
Bahrain	3.4	9.5
Jordan	6.2	9.5
Sri Lanka	2.8	8.3

Sources: UNDP Human Development Report 2009, Stockholm International Peace Research Institute, Central Bank of Sri Lanka Statistical Abstract 2007

Whilst the case has been made that government expenditure on the conflict had a detrimental impact in terms of fiscal balances and productive investment, it must also be pointed out that military expenditure has also acted as a giant economic stimulus. As mentioned earlier, the bulk of expenditure has been in the form of wages. Considering the fact that many of the soldiers are from rural parts of the country, the salaries paid to them have contributed to economic activity through multiplier effects (due to high marginal propensity to consume). Over time with the gradual phase out of military expenditure, the negative income effects of the withdrawal of government expenditure on the military will be felt in the economy.

Effects on Monetary Policy and Exchange Rates

Given the rigidity of fiscal policy in recent years with budget deficits remaining constantly high around 8 per cent, the burden of macroeconomic stability has fallen upon monetary policy. In recent years monetary policy has lacked the stability and consistency to facilitate a smooth macroeconomic environment.

Figure 6: Monetary Policy Volatility

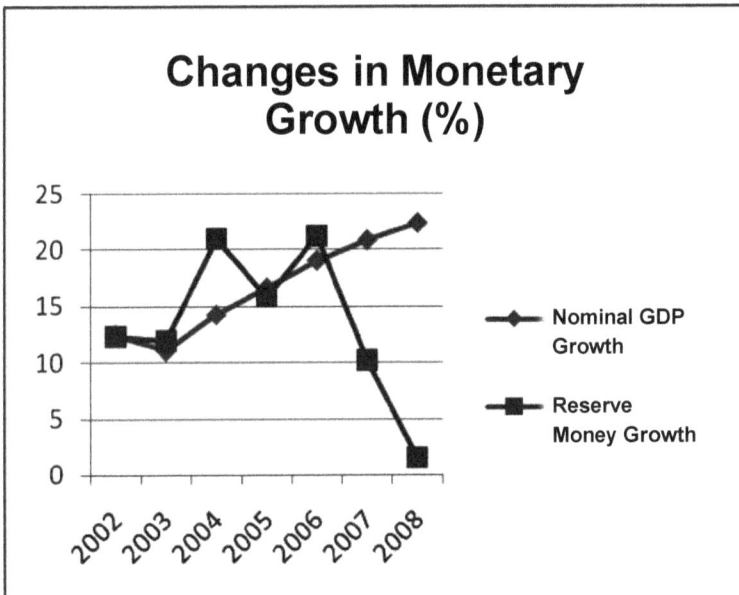

Source: Central Bank data

Real Interest Rates (%)

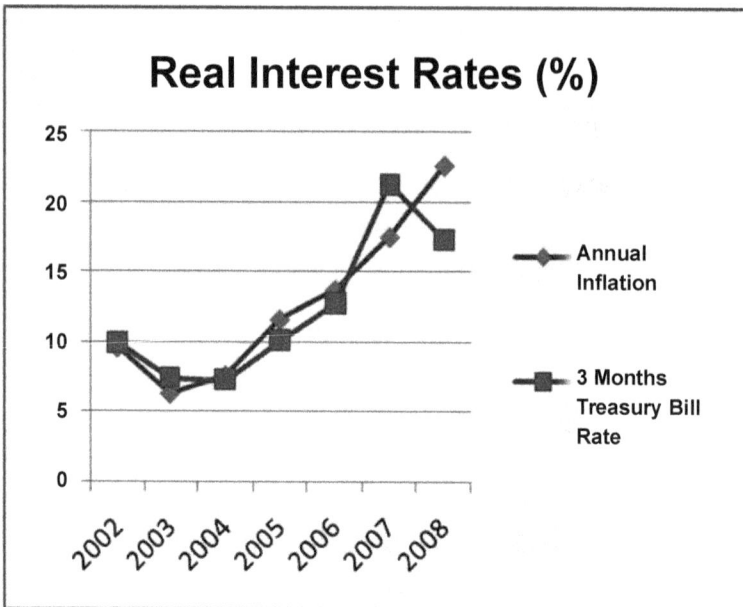

Source: Central Bank data

It can be seen that in 2004 and 2006 there were spikes in money growth and interest rates were negative between 2004 and 2006. One factor that created pressure to keep interest rates low was the extent of government debt service payments (due to accumulated fiscal deficits) that would be difficult to manage if interest rates became extremely high. As a result of this loose monetary policy[39], inflation increased rapidly in 2007 and 2008, reaching a peak of 28.2 per cent in July 2008. High inflation has been a feature of the Sri Lankan economy, and fiscal excesses have contributed to this. Net credit growth to the government is illustrated in figure 7[40].

---

[39] Together with the influence of increased prices of imported commodi ties such as oil and major food products

[40] The contraction in net credit growth to the government in 2007 is due to the utilization of part of a US$ 500 Mn sovereign bond by the Government of Sri Lanka to settle Central Bank payments.

Figure 7: Annual Average Inflation 1991-2008

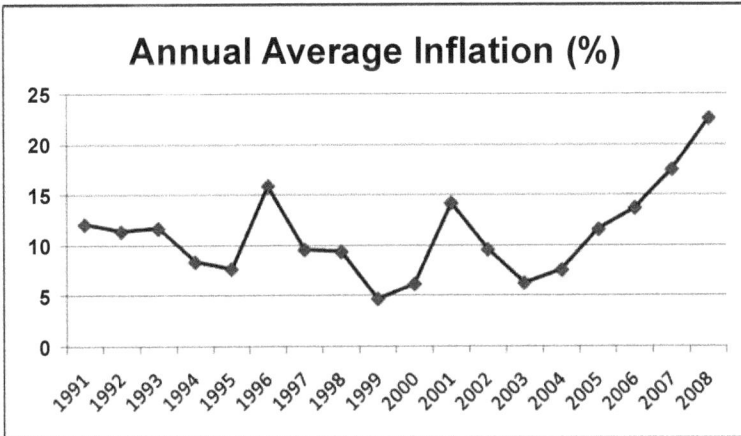

Annual Average Inflation (%)

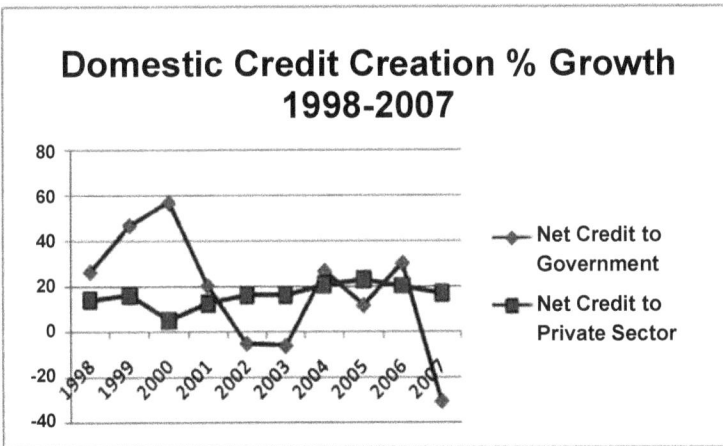

Domestic Credit Creation % Growth 1998-2007

Source: Central Bank Data

Exchange rate management was also influenced by fiscal considerations, particularly with regard to maintaining a soft peg between the Rupee and the US Dollar (LKR 108 to the US Dollar) between late 2007 and November 2008, without allowing the Rupee to depreciate, thereby curtailing growth of Dollar denominated repayments. However with inflation increasing rapidly at the same time, the situation was not sustainable. Between November 2007 (LKR 109.44) and November 2008 (LKR 109.91), the currency appreciated marginally against the US$ whilst annual average inflation in November 2008 was 23 per cent. This has an adverse impact on exporters since increases in domestic cost of production are not balanced by a depreciation of the currency – therefore the increased cost is passed on to buyers, reducing competitiveness. However given the resulting pressure on the balance of payments, the Rupee was allowed to depreciate until mid 2009, since then a new peg has been established at approximate LKR 115 to the US Dollar.

Impact of the Conflict on External Economic Policy

The Sri Lankan conflict has always had an important international dimension. This has been influenced by the large Diaspora of expatriate Sri Lankans of Tamil and Sinhalese origin who have lobbied governments in their host countries to influence the conflict in Sri Lanka. Furthermore, the reactions of the large Tamil community of Tamil Nadu in Southern India to the war in Sri Lanka have to an important extent influenced the role of the Indian government in Sri Lanka's conflict. However, it is relatively recently that the international dimension of the conflict has taken a commercial aspect[41]. The conflict in Sri Lanka has at various occasions influenced foreign government policy on Overseas Developmental Assistance (ODA) to Sri Lanka and trade policy.

Aid

Foreign governments have in the last decade attempted to use financial aid as a lever to influence outcomes of the conflict and peace processes in Sri Lanka. The Tokyo Conference on Reconstruction and Development of Sri Lanka in 2003 saw US$ 4.5 Billion pledged to the country by various donors. However, it was noted in the Declaration that the

---

[41] This is true at least from the perspective of the Sri Lankan government. The LTTE has long relied on a major international network to finance its activities –see S Jayekara, "Terrorist Fundraising and Money Laundering Operations", Centre for Policing, Intelligence & Counter Terrorism, Australia. Report Presented at the International Conference on Countering Terrorism, Colombo, Sri Lanka, 2007.

continued disbursement of this money was conditional on progress in the peace process. "In view of the linkage between donor support and progress in the peace process, the international community will monitor and review the progress in the peace process."[42] As things turned out, the peace process came to a stand-still as the LTTE unilaterally withdrew from the peace talks in April 2003 and direct talks did not resume and the bulk of the money was not disbursed. In 2006 and 2007, several countries including Germany and Britain temporarily froze aid to Sri Lanka in response to civilian casualties during the escalating conflict between the LTTE and the government. However the majority of aid received by Sri Lanka has been through multilateral donors – particularly the World Bank and the Asian Development Bank – and Japan, who together traditionally account for close to 80 per cent of Sri Lanka's official ODA[43]. Therefore the economic implications of bilateral aid freezes by a few countries were limited. Sri Lanka was also left out of the US Millennium Challenge beneficiaries because the resurgent civil strife made it problematic.[44] More recently, Sri Lanka requested a Stand-by Arrangement from the IMF in the wake of a balance of payments crisis in early 2009. There was a delay in the approval of the loan, creating serious concerns in Sri Lanka given the urgency of the economic downturn in early 2009[45]. It was widely speculated[46] that pressure was being applied by the United States and Western Europe to delay the loan. Eventually the Stand-by Arrangement was approved, but Britain, the US, France and Germany abstained from voting.

---

[42] "Tokyo Declaration on Reconstruction and Development of Sri Lanka" av ailable online at http://www.satp.org/satporgtp/countries/shrilanka/document/papers/tokyo_declaration.htm

[43] In recent years China has emerged as a major donor and was Sri Lanka's largest donor in 2009

[44] Curt Tarnoff, "Millennium Challenge Corporation", CRS Report to US Congress, June 2009 available onl ine at ht tp://www.fas.org/sgp/crs/row/RL32427.pdf

[45] Foreign reserves fell to approximately 5 weeks of imports in March 2009

[46] Arshad Mohamed, " US Acts to delay IMF loans to Sri Lanka"   , Reuters, 30 April 2009 available online at http://uk.reuters.com/article/idUKTRE53T0L420090430, and also see Peter Beaumont, " IMF under pressure to delay Sri Lanka'$ 1.9 bn aid loan,"The Guardian, 1 May 2009 available online at http://www.guardian.co.uk/world/2009/may/01/imf-aid-sri-lanka-tamil-tigers accessed on 7 May 2011.

Given Sri Lanka's constrained fiscal position, particularly in recent months, there will be an important role to be played by foreign aid in the post conflict situation, particularly with regard to reconstruction of the war affected provinces. There remains international pressure on Sri Lanka, given allegations of human rights violations during the final stages of the war in May 2009. Sri Lanka's receipts of aid from traditional donors has been on a downward trend, given increases in per capita income and along with declines in lending from bilateral donors, Sri Lanka has sought greater ODA from non-traditional donors such as China, which became Sri Lanka's highest donor as of 2009.

Trade Policy

In 2005, Sri Lanka became eligible to receive the European Union's Generalised System of Preferences Plus (GSP +). The GSP + is a non-reciprocal scheme of preferences that gave Sri Lankan exporters duty free access to approximately 7200 tariff lines entering the EU market. This facility was accorded to Sri Lanka to support the economy in emerging from the economic damage due to the tsunami of December 2004. Qualification for GSP + is contingent on the country ratifying and implementing 27 international conventions on core human rights[47], labour rights, environmental protection and good governance principles. The GSP + has been hugely beneficial to the Sri Lankan economy (particularly considering the fact that the EU is Sri Lanka's largest export market), enabling substantial growth in garments exports to the EU despite increased competition following the expiry of the Multi-Fibre Agreement in 2004, and declining market share in the US market in the wake of increased global competition. Other sectors such as fisheries have also benefited substantially from the facility. The GSP + facility expires after 3 years and was due to be renewed in Sri Lanka in 2008. The EU however did not renew the facility for Sri Lanka and conducted an investigation[48]

---

[47] The key human rights conventions include the International Convention on Civil and Political Rights (ICCPR) and the Convention Against Torture (CAT) and the Convention on the Rights of the Child (CRC)

[48] The government of Sri Lanka refused to allow the EU to conduct a formal investigation of the implementation of human rights laws in Sri Lanka– therefore the EU report was based on third party evidence.

into the implementation of the key conventions and based on the findings of the report of 19 October 2009 decided to suspend the GSP + preferences to Sri Lanka. Quoting from the proposal for the EU council regulation of 15 December 2009, *"The Report concluded that the national legislation of Sri Lanka incorporating the International Covenant on Civil and Political Rights, the Convention against Torture and other Cruel, Inhuman or Degrading Treatment or Punishment and the Convention on the Rights of the Child is not being effectively implemented. Temporary withdrawal of the additional tariff preferences under GSP+ with respect to all products originating in Sri Lanka is thus necessary."*

There has been concern expressed in Sri Lanka regarding the linkage of trade and political objectives in the EU's trade policy. The impacts of the withdrawal of GSP + will be felt by the approximately 250,000 employees (80 per cent of whom are women) in the garment sector. Furthermore, in terms of post-conflict development[49], duty free access to the EU market will provide significant potential benefits to post conflict provinces which have traditional strength in fisheries and agriculture – sectors that have benefited from GSP + in the last 3 years. Therefore GSP + could have played an important role in supporting post conflict development and livelihood creation in the North and East of Sri Lanka.

Policy Priorities for Post Conflict Economic Reconstruction

Economic growth of an inclusive and sustainable nature is essential for the long term viability of peace. According to the UNDP Crisis Prevention and Recovery Report 2008, countries with a weak economic performance are twice as likely to revert to conflict as those with a strong growth performance. Economic growth needs to be inclusive in that the benefits of economic activity are felt by as many individuals in the conflict area as possible. Therefore in the short term, labour intensive economic activity with substantial backward and forward linkages become important. In this context macroeconomic policy needs to support an environment that will encourage economic growth. Additional policy measures will

---

[49] See section five of this chapter

be needed to ensure that economic growth is indeed inclusive and sustainable.

Macroeconomic Policy

It is clear that the key impediment to stable economic performance in Sri Lanka has been the dominance of fiscal imbalances. The fiscal sector has influenced inflation and monetary measures to mitigate this have at times resulted in volatile interest rates and a misaligned exchange rate. Given the fact that fiscal revenue sources are being squeezed by the external economic downturn and a domestic economic slowdown, it becomes essential to curtail current government expenditure. Reductions in state sector employment and improved targeting of transfers have long been advocated as essential measures for improving fiscal stability. The Agreement entered into between the IMF and the government of Sri Lanka will also create some pressure for improved fiscal management – however the emphasis of the Agreement is on enhancing government revenue, and there is less emphasis on expenditure reduction. In the short term, post conflict situation government expenditure will have to address costs of rehabilitation and reconstruction. Whilst some finances can be expected from international sources in the form of overseas developmental assistance, given the current strains in the global economy, it would be necessary for a substantial contribution to be from the government.

If fiscal policy reform is successful the strains on monetary and exchange rate policy will be greatly eased. In the latter parts of 2009 Sri Lanka experienced low inflation but high market interest rates, but since the 2010 inflation has picked up (6.9 per cent in February) and interest rates continue to decline (three month Treasury bill rate being 8.4 per cent in the first week of March 2010). It is a matter of concern that the ability to obtain foreign financing of debt has declined in the wake of external credit tightening. Therefore there will likely be increased domestic borrowing by the government to finance the widening fiscal deficit – which will again put pressure on the Central Bank to retain loose monetary policy in the medium term.

In terms of exchange rate policy, it is encouraging to note that the Central Bank has allowed the Sri Lanka Rupee to depreciate against the US$ and subsequently prevented substantial appreciation of the LKR following capital inflows once the war came to an end in May 2009. In the short to medium term a competitive exchange rate will be important to develop export markets for the products (agricultural and fisheries in the early stages) and services (largely tourism) of the post conflict zones.

There is possibility of exchange rate appreciation following aid inflows. However many countries have not experienced substantial real exchange rate appreciation following post conflict aid flows. In fact, according to Elbadawi et al[50], 30 out of 36 countries studied did not suffer from substantial real exchange rate appreciation. However Sri Lanka experienced some real exchange rate appreciation following the December 2004 tsunami as money entered the country through increased remittances and foreign aid. This resulted in some standard Dutch Disease impacts on exports as well[51]. Sri Lanka experienced some appreciation of the Rupee as soon as the conflict ended as a result of foreign capital inflows. Remittances spiked during this period, along with foreign investment in equity and in the liberalized portion of government treasury bill and bond markets along with the capital inflows from the initial trench of IMF funding. The Central Bank has responded by stabilizing the Rupee at LKR 115 to the US$ (an appreciation from LKR 120 to the US$ in April), by purchasing US$s and mopping up the resulting excess liquidity. Furthermore, there was also some inflationary pressure that resulted from the post tsunami reconstruction as supply side constraints in the domestic non-tradable sector (particularly related to the construction industry) saw an increase in costs of raw materials and labour[52]. Similar impacts can be

---

[50] Ibrahim A Elbadawi, Linda Kaltani and Klaus Schmidt-Hebbel, " Post Conflict Aid, Real Exchange Rate Adjustment and catch –up Growth", World ABnk Policy Research Working Paper 4187, April 2007 available online at http://www.countrycompass.com/_docs/library/WB%20Working%20Paper%20-%20Post-conflict%20Aid%20Real%20Exchange%20Rate%20Adjustment%20and%20 Catch-up%20Growth.pdf

[51] Dushni Weerakoon, Sisira Jayasuriya, Nisha Arunatilake, and P Steele, *Economic Challenges of Post Tsunami Reconstruction in Sri Lanka* , (Tokyo: Asian Development B ank I nstitute, 2007)

[52] Ibid.

expected in post-conflict reconstruction, and cost estimates for reconstruction will need to take it into account.

Figure 11: Exchange Rate Appreciation Following the Tsunami

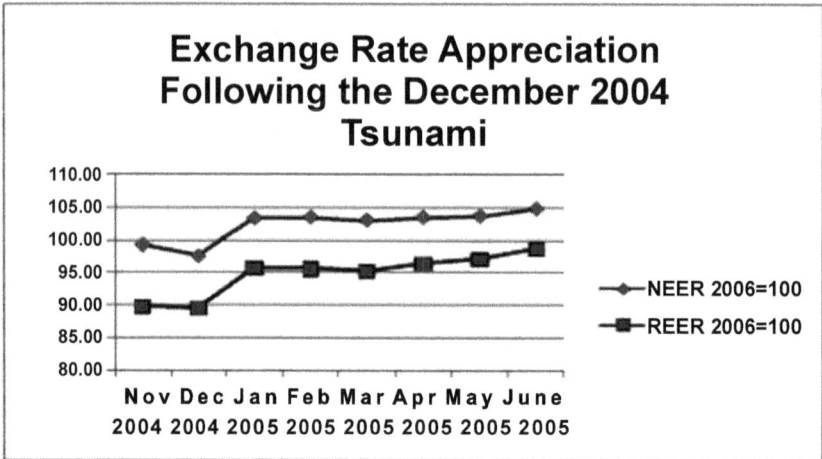

Source: Central Bank data

Microeconomic Policy Considerations

The conflict has very different impacts on the national economy and on the local economy that was exposed to the conflict. Whilst the national economy has not suffered large scale damage to productive and administrative infrastructure, the local economy of the North and East has suffered such damage. In this context it is important to assess the priorities in terms of rebuilding the local economies in the North and East that have been devastated by three decades of conflict. Earlier we addressed the macroeconomic policy requirements that would facilitate the regeneration of economic activity; in this section we consider the specific micro level policy issues in post conflict economic development.

It was made clear that unemployment, particularly youth unemployment, played a significant role in providing an environment conducive to armed conflict in Sri Lanka in the 1970s. Youth unemployment[53] in Sri Lanka in 2010 was 21.3 per cent whilst overall unemployment was 6.2 per cent in mid 2009. Official employment figures for the conflict provinces are unavailable. In this context the creation of employment opportunities becomes a priority in the post conflict scenario. This needs to be considered from different time frames – short and long term. In the long term, job creation requires the existence of a sound macroeconomic environment with low inflation, good investment policy, access to inputs and secure property rights. However in a post conflict situation job creation needs to be conducted on a more urgent basis. The most rapid measure is to maximize generation of local job opportunities through reconstruction activities.

Reconstruction should focus on the current impediments to employment creation. For instance, reconstruction of reservoirs and irrigation systems could assist the creation of employment in agricultural activities. It is important to keep in mind the fact that conflict does not necessarily wipe out economic activity in its entirety, some form of economic activity does occur but it usually falls into the informal sector or the subsistence sector rather than the formal economic sector. Therefore in the short term it is possible to build upon these existing economic structures, and encourage the creation of avenues for re-integration into the formal sector. In the case of Sri Lanka, agricultural production and fisheries have been the traditional strengths of the North and Eastern Provinces. Reconstruction activities should focus on attempting to address constraints to the functionality and economic viability of these activities.

Agriculture and fisheries are both labour intensive and will provide employment in the short term to a number of people. However in the medium term it is important that policy is directed towards creation of higher end employment. One of the reasons that youth unemployment has been a problem is the fact that younger generations are less inclined to work in traditional sectors and desire opportunities in white collar

---

[53] 15-24 years of age

occupations. In order to fulfill these aspirations education and training becomes essential. Access to education (and performance) at all levels in conflict zones has been greatly hampered by the war. It has not been possible to implement many of the educational quality enhancement programs that have been implemented in other regions, teacher training programs and so on in the conflict provinces. Furthermore parents have been reluctant at times to send children to schools in fear of abduction or forced recruitment. Education activities have frequently been disrupted by military operations.

Therefore enhanced investment in educational facilities and vocational training, both in terms of ensuring quality and access, is of paramount importance. Private provision of education services at certain levels (professional qualifications such as CIMA) becomes a useful tool (in terms of connection to market demand and in terms of freeing up government resources for investment in educational sectors that will not be handled by the private sector). At present however private provision of education services is not legal. In the longer term perspective, employment generation could be enhanced by macro level national labour policy reforms, particularly with regard to the costs of hiring and firing workers.

Another important factor that would need to be addressed is the creation of gainful employment opportunities for soldiers and ex-LTTE combatants. Sri Lanka's military manpower strength is substantial – close to 180,000 in the army, navy and air force, equivalent to 2 per cent of the national labour force (8.15 Million) and it is estimated by the Ministry of Defense that there are 10,000 surrendered LTTE cadres in IDP camps at present. The long term policy in this regard should be geared towards enhancement of the investment climate in the country to maximize the creation of jobs in the private sector. Vocational training would be important to equip former combatants with the requisite skills for such employment – however it is essential that these skills are those that would be in demand in the private sector. English language and information technology training would provide a good starting point in this regard.

Apprenticeship programs in the private sector and incentives for firms hiring former combatants could be considered. In the short term however the most viable prospect of employment is for the involvement of ex-combatants in reconstruction activities – both in manual work and in administrative work wherever possible. Employment prospects in the medium term would largely arise in rural markets in traditional sectors such as fishing, agriculture and small scale retail. In the longer term, training should focus on the aspirations of ex-combatants, particularly in terms of upward social mobility and equipping them with the requisite tools to do so. All training programs should be informed by a thorough evaluation of the available skills, strengths and desires of ex-combatants – but at the same time management of expectations with regard to actual future job prospects needs to be kept in mind as well.

Conclusion

The post conflict macroeconomic policy priorities are largely in line with the general macroeconomic policy priorities that have characterized the Sri Lankan economy in recent decades. The dominance of fiscal excesses has greatly undermined macroeconomic stability by passing on the burden of macroeconomic stabilization to monetary policy, which in turn has resulted in inflationary and balance of payments pressure. The recent global economic crisis has had negative impacts on the Sri Lankan economy in terms of export performance and on the revenue side of fiscal policy. However it has helped bring down inflation rapidly as prices of global commodities have declined sharply. This has also contributed to an easing of the balance of payments position. This will support post conflict economic development. What has been more worrying is the slower transmission of monetary policy as commercial interest rates remain high (prime lending rates remained at 10.52 per cent in March 2010). The government recently ordered state banks to cut lending rates to 7 per cent, in an attempt to bring down market interest rates. Whilst interest rates remain sticky downwards, they have been declining, albeit at a slow pace. The Central Bank has also continued to aggressively loosen monetary policy with a rate cut on November 19th, bringing policy rates down to

7.5 per cent. Monetary policy remains in a delicate position as inflation has begun to pick up but at the same time commercial interest rates remain comparatively high.

There are several microeconomic policy issues that would require attention in order to support post-conflict economic regeneration. The most critical of these include the rehabilitation of employment generating activities, particularly fisheries and agriculture in the post-conflict provinces. Potential measures have been highlighted in earlier sections. Many of these activities will also require substantial investment of resources by the government and foreign assistance sources, particularly in terms of reconstruction of infrastructure. The latter will be challenging in the present context of the global financial crunch, and this will pose a challenge to a government already facing fiscal constraints. Sri Lanka's key donors such as the World Bank and the Asian Development Bank have supported some of the relevant infrastructure projects, particularly with regard to connective infrastructure such as road development. It would be important for such support to continue in the short to medium term in the context of supporting economic rehabilitation in the post-conflict regions. At the same time the government must endeavour to improve the prioritization of expenditure to create the necessary fiscal space to effectively respond to the needs of reconstruction in the post conflict areas.

References

Abeyratne, S "Economic Roots of Political Conflict the Case of Sri Lanka", World Economy Vol 27, Number 8, August 2004.

Abeyratne, S "Economic Development and Political Conflict: A Comparative Study of Sri Lanka and Malaysia" South Asia Economic Journal, Volume 9, Number 2, 2008.

Arunatilake N, Jayasuriya, S, Kelegama, S "The economic cost of the war in Sri Lanka", World Development, Vol 29, No 9, pp 1483-1500, 2001

Athukorala, P. (2006), "Outward oriented policy reforms and industrialisation: The Sri Lankan experience", *Journal of South Asian Development* 1:1 2006.

Bhatt Semu & Mistry Devika (2006). *Cost of Conflict in Sri Lanka*. Strategic Foresight Group.

Central Bank of Sri Lanka Annual Report, Various Editions.

Dunham, D. and S. Jayasuriya (2000), 'Equity, Growth and Insurrection: Liberalization and the Welfare Debate in Contemporary Sri Lanka', *Oxford Development Studies*, 28, 1.

Jayasekara, S (2007). *Terrorist Fundraising and Money Laundering Operations*. Centre for Policing, Intelligence & Counter Terrorism, Australia. Report Presented at the International Conference on Countering Terrorism. Colombo. Sri Lanka.

Kelegama, S, (2006) "Development under Stress", Sage Publications, 2006.

Kelegama, S (2007), "Socio-Economic Cost of the War", presented at the International Conference on Countering Terrorism, BMICH.

Kelegama S and de Mel D, (2007), "Sri Lankan Perspectives on Reform of the International Aid Architecture", Report for the North-South Institute, Canada.

Peiris G.H (1994), "Irrigation, Land Distribution and Ethnic Conflict in Sri Lanka: An Evaluation of Criticisms", Ethnic Studies Report, Vol XII, No. 1, ICES, Colombo.

Peiris M.P, "Economic Growth and Structural – Institutional Change since Independence", in W.D Lakshman ed. Dilemmas of Development, 1997.

Sarvananthan, M "Economy of the Conflict Region in Sri Lanka: From Economic Embargo to Economic Repression", East West Centre, Washington D.C, 2001.

Shastri, Amita (1990), "The Material Basis for Separatism: The Tamil Eelam Movement in Sri Lanka"; Journal of Asian Studies, 49(1): pp 56-77

State of the Economy 2006, Institute of Policy Studies, page 83.

State of the Economy 2005, Institute of Policy Studies.

Tarnoff, C (2009) "Millennium Challenge Corporation", CRS Report to US Congress, June 2009.

Weerakoon, D (2009), Presentation at the Seminar "Global Economic Crisis and its impacts on Sri Lanka" organized by IPS and World Bank, Colombo, 2009.

Weerakoon, D, Jayasuriya, S, Arunatilake, N, Steele, P 2007 "Economic Challenges of Post Tsunami Reconstruction in Sri Lanka", Tokyo, Asian Development Bank Institute.

World Bank, Background paper "Assessment of Needs in the Conflict Affected Areas" submitted to the Tokyo Donor Conference in 2003.

THE PLIGHT OF FISHERMEN OF SRI LANKA AND INDIA: THE LEGACY OF THE CIVIL WAR

V. Vivekanandan

The civil war in Sri Lanka (1983-2009) had undoubtedly touched the lives of all citizens of Sri Lanka, both in the war zone and outside it. Its impact on the economy, polity and society was considerable, with many long term and permanent changes taking place. This chapter explores the impacts it had on fishing and the fishing communities of Sri Lanka. It also discusses the impacts it had on the fishermen of the Indian state of Tamil Nadu, Sri Lanka's immediate neighbour across the sea. It highlights how changes in fisheries both in Sri Lanka and Tamil Nadu, triggered by the war, represent a serious problem in peace time and need urgent resolution. The well being of the fishing communities on both sides depend on this resolution.

In terms of the coastal areas and fishing communities that were affected by the civil war in Sri Lanka and India, it may be useful to specify upfront the areas and the communities that were affected by the war directly or indirectly. On the Sri Lankan side, the fishermen of the north and east were obviously the ones directly affected. Even among them, it is the fishermen of the north who were the most affected. However, the war also had indirect effects on the fishing communities in the west and south of Sri Lanka, both positive and negative.

On the Indian side, the fishing communities affected belong to the Palk Bay and adjoining areas of the state of Tamil Nadu. In particular, the districts of Ramnad, Pudukottai, Tanjavur and Nagapattinam are affected.

Sri Lankan Fisheries—Pre-1983

Sri Lanka, like India, had a traditional small-scale fishery at the time of independence with the entire marine fisheries conducted by sailing and rowing boats. It also had fishing communities across its 1600 km coastline with a long history of fishing. All fishing was concentrated in the coastal waters near the shore. Shore seine fishing or *Madel* fishing was very prominent. If the Tamil fishermen of the Northern Province[1] used *Kattumarams*, the Sinhala fishermen in the south and west used canoes, especially the *Orus*, which are out-rigger fitted canoes. Though Sri Lanka is hampered by a narrow continental shelf where most of the fish resources are concentrated, fishing capacity and intensity was low enough for major expansion programmes to be contemplated.

The 1950s, 60s and the 70s saw the continuous expansion of the fisheries with major state interventions through cooperatives, promotion of new technologies and subsidies for fishing equipment. Much to the envy of the Tamil Nadu fishermen, the Sri Lankan fishermen were the first to acquire nylon nets. They then graduated to small fibreglass boats with Out Board Motors (OBMs). Improvements in transport systems and availability of ice gave a boost to these changes.

The Sri Lankan market for fish and fishery products was also an important driver for fisheries development. Fish has always been an important item of diet in Sri Lanka, and fish prices have always been higher than in neighbouring India. This explains the long standing export of dry fish from India to Sri Lanka and the absence of fish trade in the opposite direction. Tuticorin in Tamil Nadu was a major base for seafood exporters in India with dry fish to Sri Lanka being their mainstay.

Bottom trawling, particularly for export oriented shrimp, also made an entry in Sri Lanka, soon after it started in India. However, it ran foul of the existing set up very soon and was abandoned in most of Sri Lanka.

---

[1] Provinces came into being much later but for convenience I am using the term to designate the group districts that are contained in them. The Northern Province includes the coastal districts of Mannar, Killinochichi, Jaffna and Mullaithivu. Vavuniya, the fifth district of the province, is not on the coast.

That Sri Lanka has a very narrow continental shelf played no mean role in this. Very early on, the conflict between the artisanal fishermen and the trawlers erupted and it was obvious that both could not co-exist. However, a relatively small fleet of trawlers got established and entrenched in the Northern Province, both at Mannar and Jaffna. This can be explained as the consequence of the wider continental shelf that the Northern Province enjoyed.

The Palk Bay between India and Sri Lanka is a shallow water body with a depth not exceeding 50 meters. North of Jaffna is the Pedro banks, a shallow area with rich fishing grounds. The greater scope for the trawlers to co-exist with small boats made it possible for a small trawl fleet to emerge and survive till date in the Northern Province. However, this fleet was never allowed to develop into a large one and was always kept on a strong leash by the local community[2]. Sri Lanka provides the only instance of a country in the tropics that escaped creating the trawl-non trawl dichotomy in fisheries, a source of permanent conflict and resource degradation.

The generally higher level of human development in Sri Lanka—the result of the economic model that put human development above economic growth—meant that the fishing community in Sri Lanka were also far ahead of their counterparts in India/Tamil Nadu by a wide margin before the start of the civil war[3]. Standards of education, health and hygiene in fishing villages of Sri Lanka were far superior compared to most of India.

Something worth noting was the importance of the Northern

---

[2] This problem has resurfaced after the civil war with the small trawl fleet in the Northern Province insisting that they be allowed to operate when there is no control on Indian trawlers.

[3] Kerala in India is also said to have followed a similar economic model with emphasis on redistribution of wealth through land reforms followed by investments in health and education. However, as John K urien in "Evolving towards unsustainably: A personal statement on Kerala's Marine fishery spanning three decades" *International Journal of Rural Management*, June 2005 1:73-96 has demonstrated, the "Kerala model" did not really apply to tribes and fishing communities who remained "out liers" in Kerala's society.

Province to the overall national fish production in Sri Lanka. Due to the availability of the rich resources of the Palk Bay and the Pedro Banks, the Northern Province was the leading fish producing region of Sri Lanka and played a significant role in catering to the nutritional security of the island nation.

Tamil Nadu Fisheries- Pre-1983

India, like Sri Lanka, started its fisheries development after independence without a single mechanised boat but with a large traditional fishing community. With the resource exploitation being low even in the shelf area, the prospects for fisheries expansion looked limitless.

The 1950s and 60s saw fisheries development in India largely driven by the domestic market demand and the availability of new materials like nylon. Fisheries started expanding with increasing benefits to the traditional fishermen. However, efforts by the state to introduce mechanisation were not very successful, except in the state of Maharashtra where the combination of a wider continental shelf, much larger country boats that went on multi-day sailing trips, the Bombay market and the emergence of genuine cooperatives made mechanisation a smooth and less contentious process.

The foreign exchange crisis of 1966, the devaluation of the rupee and the national shame over dependence on donated food articles created conditions for a major overhaul of national policies. Increase in food production as well as export oriented policies in certain designated sectors became high priority. Marine fisheries became a key sector to earn foreign exchange. This made India pre-disposed towards promotion of bottom trawling for shrimp. Starting in a small way in the mid-60s, trawling started making a big impact by the mid-70s across the entire coast, leading to conflicts between the small scale fishermen and the new mechanised trawlers. However, the Indian establishment, while making some regulations to protect the small fishermen from trawlers, continued to back trawling as a method.

Tamil Nadu, with its 1000 km coastline, has a large fishing

community, but a relatively narrow continental shelf (relative to rest of India, but wider than that of Sri Lanka). The fishing community in Tamil Nadu is also known for its high skills and dynamism. Tamil Nadu also followed this national pattern of development to the extent that it is the Indian province with the largest number of trawlers. However, it is important to recognise that the "big vs small", "trawler vs traditional" debates can be misleading at times.

The trawl sector in Tamil Nadu (and in most Indian states) does not represent big business. Though trawl owners do represent a new class within the fishing community, they are at best the equivalent of green revolution peasant farmers growing commercial crops. The trawlers are owned mainly by those belonging to the fishing community, mostly employing labour from the fishing communities. Even in Rameswaram, where a motley crowd of non-fishing communities got involved in trawling, the trawl owner is not a big businessman but just a small entrepreneur trying to make both ends meet.

An important event that occurred on the Tamil Nadu side of the Palk Bay in the late 70s is worth mentioning. There was a major clash between the gillnet *vallams* (solidly built wooden canoes) and the trawlers. The gillnets used are quite long and need considerable space at sea while the trawlers operating in the same sea are bound to destroy these gillnets. Both cannot co-exist at sea. This clash led to "peace-talks" between the two groups organised by the district administration of Ramnad and the emergence of the "three day-four day" rule. As per this, trawlers and gillnetters will fish on alternative days with gillnetters getting four days a week to fish and the trawlers the remaining three days of the week. This agreement continues to be in force in the Palk Bay districts of Ramnad, Pudukottai and Thanjavur even today.

Indo-Sri Lankan Fishing Interactions- Pre-1983

The Palk Bay and Palk Straits are where the Sri Lankan and Tamil Nadu fishermen had close interactions at sea due to the proximity of the two coastlines. In the Palk Bay, the distance between the two countries ranges from a mere 16 km to 40 km. Even without mechanical propulsion it was possible to cross over by rowing boats at the extremities of the Palk Bay and with sail in the remaining parts of the Bay. Katchathivu in the centre of the Bay was an island where one could dry fish and nets and where fishermen from both sides met at the annual St.Antony's Church Festival. In addition to Tamil as a common language, the fishermen on both sides also had common origins.

It is said that there were tensions between the two groups on a couple of occasions when new technology made its entry. The Sri Lankan fishermen were the first to get nylon nets and some Indian fishermen were said to have stolen nets leading to a clash at sea. This got resolved shortly with the Indians also getting access to nylon nets at home. When the Indian fishermen obtained trawlers in 1967, there was again a clash but was resolved shortly when the Sri Lankans also obtained the same technology.

If one ignores these two blips in the relationship, there was considerable brotherhood at sea and a lot of give and take. It is said that whenever a new MGR film was released, Mannar fishermen would go across, anchor their boat in Rameswaram and see the film and this went on till 1983, well after the maritime boundary was drawn up in 1974.

The maritime boundary in the Palk Bay and Palk Straits was fixed as per an agreement in 1974, popularly known in India as the Katchathivu Agreement, (on account of the boundary being drawn to include the island in Sri Lankan waters). This was a politically contentious issue in Tamil Nadu, but it did not seem to make any difference to the fishing activities and the fishermen. It was business as usual for them till the civil war started in 1983.

Thus the pre-1983 relationship was one of free movement of fishing boats all over the Bay, something that did not stop with the formal demarcation of the boundary in 1974. There were occasional conflicts at sea, but these were much less severe than those between different groups of Indian fishermen. The civil war put an end to this idyllic situation when fishermen were the masters of the Palk Bay and sorted out their problems irrespective of nationality.

The Civil War and its Impact on the North and East of Sri Lanka

The 26 year civil war impacted fishing and fishermen in many ways. In the war affected north and east, these were the impacts:

- Displacement due to war; sometimes more than once for particular villages and communities.

- Forcible fleeing as refugees to India or to other parts of Sri Lanka (IDPs or Internally Displaced Persons).

- Destruction of fishing equipment time and again due to the war.

- Severe restrictions on fishing operations—on time of operations, area of operations, use of motors, etc.

- Deprivation of livelihood due to high security zones near military bases in the region.

- Deaths due to being in the wrong place at the wrong time

Some of these impacts are perhaps not unique to fishing communities but were common to many other communities in the north and east. It must also be mentioned that many rounds of rehabilitation took place only for war to destroy all that was done during periods of truce. The tsunami added to the woes of the war affected, especially in the northeast and east when the fishing communities took the brunt of the tsunami.

What must have been demoralising for fishermen of the north in particular was the loss of their premier position in Sri Lankan fisheries. While the south and west progressed with new technologies, development of deep sea fishing, etc., the northern fishermen regressed to a level well below their 1983 status. Jaffna, which used to be the district with the highest fish landings, declined from around 20,000 to 5,000 tonnes per annum.

Indian Fishermen—Fishing in the Midst of War

On the Indian side of the Palk Bay, the war did not stop fishing activities. With fishing being their sole occupation, fishermen saw no reason to stop fishing and continued to fish across the border, as they had been doing earlier. Straightaway, there were tragic incidents. The first incident took place in 1983 when three Rameswaram fishermen were shot dead by the Sri Lankan Navy. The entire community erupted in anger, blocking the rail transport to the island of Rameswaram. This was just the beginning of many such incidents.

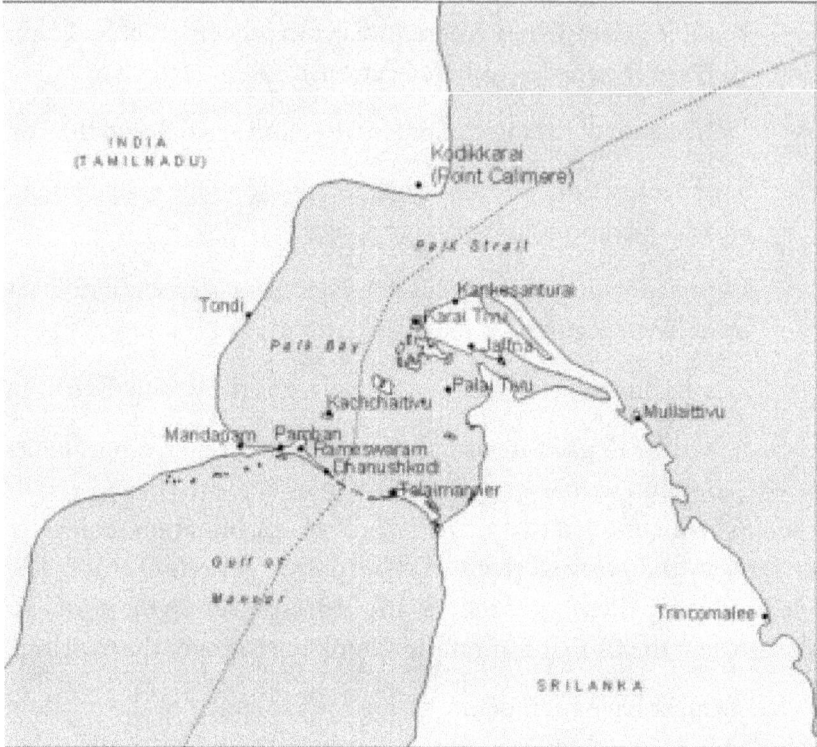

Source: india-forum.com

Things settled to an uneasy equilibrium with Indian boats routinely fishing across the border. Periodically, there would be incidents of shooting or physical harassment. These incidents would highlight the risks involved and scare the community. However, after a short gap, it would be business as usual. The area most affected by the war was Rameswaram Island with its 1000 mechanised boats and few hundred country boats that crossed regularly into Sri Lankan waters. A quick look at the map will provide an explanation. The maritime border is just 7-8 km from Dhanushkodi, the eastern tip of the Rameswaram Island. With fishing prohibited within 5 km from the shore to protect small boats, the trawlers would start operations after this limit. The very first fishing haul would automatically take them beyond the maritime border.

However, it was not just the trawlers who would fish beyond the borders. The gillnet *vallam*s go chasing after the shoals on both sides of the border. Even *kattumarams* would cross the border with their sail. Many a time, these traditional small scale units also paid the penalty with some of their crew losing lives.

Moving up the coast from Rameswaram, the extent of border crossing reduces significantly as the distance to the border increases. While the Rameswaram boats go towards Mannar and Delfts Island, the Jagadapattinam boats from the middle of the Palk Bay coast, go towards Delft Island and Jaffna. Further up the coast, it is more often than not that the country boats cross the border to go and fish on the other side. In the Palk Straits, the Nagapattinam boats, which migrate to Kodikarai or Pt.Calimere during the lean seasn, cross over to fish in the rich Pedro bank vacated by the Sri Lankan fishermen due to the war.

The actual casualties of Indian fishermen during the war are reported differently in different sources[4]. According to information collected from the Rameswaram fisheries office, 85 fishermen were killed between 1983 and 2000 from Rameswaram alone. Around 14 were missing and presumed dead. Around 276 had sustained serious injuries. A recent computation by Alliance for Release of Innocent Fishermen (ARIF) indicates that 226 fishermen have died (including 81 who went missing and are presumed dead) and 335 have sustained injuries.

As a piece of statistics, the casualty figures from the Indian side are not very large when compared with the death toll on the Sri Lankan side. No statistics exist on how many Sri Lankan fishermen lost their lives, not necessarily while fishing, but as civilian victims in the war. It would definitely be much higher than the casualties of Indian fishermen. However,

---

[4] A figure of 500 deaths is quoted routinely but there is no proper list substantiating this yet.

for a non-combatant country, such levels of casualties were completely unacceptable and every incident would trigger anger and anguish on the Indian side. It also showed the risks that the Indian fishermen took during the war to pursue their livelihood.

Another aspect of the risk was the arrests and detention. In some ways, this risk was statistically more significant than the risk to life. While Indian boats were routinely allowed to cross the border, on many occasions and during certain periods of the war, there were arrests and detentions of some of the boats and the fishermen. Till 2000, those arrested would spend months (and occasionally a year or two) in jail and return after a lot of hardship. An associated risk was the loss of the boat and fishing equipment. Some boats were destroyed in the midst of the action. Most would be confiscated and remain in custody till they were beyond salvage.

Diplomatic efforts and work of NGOs on both sides helped early release of fishermen and boats. By and large, the Sri Lankan civilian authorities and courts were sympathetic to the Indian fishermen and the release would take place once it was ascertained that no crime was involved other than that of poaching. However, physical roughing up, severe beatings and mental harassment were reported in many instances during the initial arrest and detention before handing over to civilian authorities.

Understanding the Sri Lankan Response

Despite the large number of incidents of shootings and arrests that took place, it is worth mentioning that statistically these fade into insignificance if one looks at the total picture. It needs to be understood that over 1000 Indian trawlers crossed into Sri Lankan waters three days a week for over 25 years. Add to this the few hundred country boats that would cross over on the remaining four days of the week. Obviously the Sri Lankan Navy did not arrest or shoot at Indian fishermen for crossing over to Sri Lankan waters. If they had taken such a position, the figures would have been astronomical and it would have been a geo-political disaster.

The reality was that the Sri Lankan Navy was merely concerned about security issues and not about poaching. Most incidents of shooting took place at night when it is difficult to distinguish between friend and foe. It often took place when Indian fishermen were perceived by the Navy to have been behaving "suspiciously". It is acknowledged by the Indian fishermen that for most of the time, the Sri Lankan Navy enjoyed a cordial relationship with Indian fishermen. Many a time naval vessels would provide drinking water to Indian boats. At times the Navy personnel would ask for fish in exchange for some provisions. So, despite the many tragic incidents, the relationship at sea was actually very good most of the time.

The Katchathivu Myth

Is should be clear from the above that border crossing by Indian vessels was accepted as unavoidable by Sri Lankan authorities during the entire course of the war. The same can be said about the Indian authorities. It is only during the IPKF operations that the Indian military proposed that fishing be completely stopped in the Palk Bay to enable it to do an effective job of controlling the sea. This was found to be politically infeasible and the idea was given up. The Fisheries Department, in between, tried to impose a fine on those crossing the border. This also could not be enforced.

However, a clear pattern developed around the way incidents involving shooting or arrests were reported. Finding that the insurance companies would not pay for loss of life or injury if the incident took place outside Indian waters, fishermen started reporting that they were fishing in Indian waters when the incident took place. Given that Katchathivu is close to the border (just 2 nautical miles inside Sri Lankan waters), it became a convenient excuse to say that they were fishing "near Katchathivu" when the incident took place. It was easy for all concerned to believe that the poor fishermen, who do not have modern gadgets, would not know where the border was exactly located and hence might have "accidentally" crossed over.

However, for political parties in Tamil Nadu, these reports reinforced their belief that Katchathivu was wrongly handed over to Sri Lanka and it is important to get it back. Every incident at sea would trigger a wave of indignation over the injustice done to fishermen on account of the Katchathivu Agreement. The media gleefully gave good coverage and the Katchathivu myth was born. The fishermen finding that the Katchathivu story gave them good mileage, stuck to it.

When I met the Fisheries Secretary of Tamil Nadu in 1997, soon after the formation of the ARIF[5], I found that he and the senior officials in the TN Government were blissfully unaware that the Indian fishermen fished right up to the Sri Lankan shore and that there are no good fishing grounds left near Katchathivu. While the local officials and the police knew about the ground realities, the higher ups were often in the dark.

Fishing Fleet Expansion despite the War

Another feature of fisheries during the war was the expansion of the Indian fleet in the Palk Bay, especially the trawlers. This can be attributed to the absence of competition from the Sri Lankan side. The Tamil Nadu trawler fleet expanded in other regions also during this period, though to a lesser extent[6]. Tamil Nadu, as every other coastal state in India, has no effective fisheries management system in place. While there are a number of rules and regulations governing fishing, with some of them enforced and the others not[7], there is no effective "limited entry" into fishing. Fishing, for all practical purposes, remains "open access". This is true to a large extent in Sri Lanka as well.

---

[5] ARIF is a network of trade unions, fishermen associations and NGOs that came together in December 1996 to form a common platform to take up the issue of arrests and detention, provide humanitarian and legal assistance to those arrested and to find a long term solution to the problem.

[6] Tamil Nadu trawlers are the scourge of all neighbours. If the Palk Bay fleet fishes in Sri Lankan waters, the Chennai fleet fishes in Andhra waters while the Colachel fleet fishing almost entirely in Kerala waters.

[7] A six week ban on mechanised boats every year is being effectively enforced in all states of India. However, the various restrictions on fishing gears and the 3 mile zone for artisanal fishing are effective only where the local communities themselves accept the need for these and take their own measures to enforce them or force the officials to enforce them.

The failures in fisheries management can be attributed to poor governance, but it also needs to be recognised that most fisheries management regimes that talk about "limited access", licences, "property rights", "quota systems" etc. have come up in developed countries and often in temperate waters where species based fisheries management is more applicable. For practical purposes, there are no real life examples of how to manage fisheries in countries like India and Sri Lanka where fishing is largely informal, a large and dispersed population depends on it and the scientific information needed for stock based or species based management does not exist.

So, during the war, the trawl fleet of the Palk Bay in Tamil Nadu literally doubled. However, this expansion came to a halt around 2000 when diminishing returns to fishing as a result of excess capacity, increased operational costs and decreasing price for shrimp combined to make trawling a less attractive proposition. It is only in Nagapattinam that the trawl fleet has expanded after that. This was on account of the tsunami largesse it received in 2005 and 2006.

War Impacts on Other Parts of Sri Lanka—Emergence of the "multi-day" Fleet

The fishermen of western Sri Lanka (Chilaw, Puttalam and Negombo) had a long tradition of migrating to the northern coast, especially Mannar, during their lean months. They used to take their shore seines with them and later on the FRP-OBM[8] combination as well. The war put an end to this migration. The inability to pursue seasonal migration forced the fishermen to intensify their fishing operations in their own coastal waters. Predictably, this resulted in higher horsepower, longer distances and increases in gear. There was obviously a limit to this type of intensification of fishing in the same area.

The late 1980s saw the introduction of "multi-day" boats to go beyond the shelf and fish in the deep sea for tuna and shark. The Negombo fishermen, under pressure to find new fishing grounds, jumped at the

---

[8] FRP is Fibre Reinforced Plastic and OBM is On-Board Motors.

opportunity and took to multi-day fishing. The Sri Lankan Government, also concerned by the increasing fishing pressure in coastal waters came up with subsidies and liberal bank finance for multi-day boats. By early 1990s, this became a rapidly growing sector.

The Sri Lankan multi-day boats are a unique phenomenon. By international standards, these are small boats which are normally not expected to indulge in oceanic fishing involving long voyages. Initially, they were just around 40 feet long and went for week-long voyages. The design was clever and provided for storing large volumes of fuel and water needed for voyage-fishing. The fishing gear used is also somewhat unusual and innovative. It is a "combination gear": a gillnet[9] used in combination with a long line[10]. The long line is tied to the gillnet so that both gears are simultaneously fishing. Skipjack tuna is mostly caught by gillnet while the long line is targeted at yellow fin tuna and sharks. Smoked and dried skipjack tuna is a delicacy in Sri Lanka and the multi-day boats had no problem in marketing their catch and compensating the cost of traversing the ocean.

As the number of multi-day boats increased and the fishermen gained confidence in going farther, the boat size steadily increased. Today most boats are in the 50-60 foot range and have the capacity to go for 2-3 month voyages. The entire Indian Ocean has become their terrain. Almost overnight, fishermen operating 18-foot fibre glass boats with OBMs for short trips of a few hours had become deep sea fishermen traversing the entire Indian Ocean. In many ways, this first deep sea fleet in South Asia

---

[9] Gillnets are the most common form of fishing nets. A gillnet is nothing but a rectangular piece of net that is set v ertically in the w ater. The multi-day boats use "drift gi llnets" wherein one end is tied to the boat and the other end drifts with the water current. Fish are normally caught at the gills in the mesh of the net, giving the gear its name. The thickness of the twine, the size of the mesh, length and width of the net varies according to the type of fish that is caught and the scale of the operation.

[10] Long lines are nothing but long lines (mostly made of nylon) to which hooks are attached through branch lines. The thickness of the main line, the size of the hook and the length of the mainline will vary according to fishing requirements. The hooks will need to be baited to catch the target fish. The bait is likely to be small fish caught en-route to the main fishing grounds.

has disproved the conventional wisdom that only industrial vessels operated by large corporate houses can undertake oceanic fishing. Most industrial fishing has its origins in temperate waters where the size of the vessel is huge in view of the rough seas as well as the need to protect the fishermen from the weather. In the tropics, all it needs is adequate storage facilities for fuel, water and the fish caught. The multi-day boats are also well equipped with communication facilities and GPS. Radio telephones are used and the Fisheries Department has set up base stations to receive messages from the multi-day fishing boats at sea. This ability to communicate easily with the shore and each other at sea has contributed immensely to the confidence and sense of security felt by the deep sea fishermen.

Trans-border fishing by multi-day Boats

With the oceanic Tunas, travelling thousands of miles in shoals, it is but natural that the fishing fleet targeting them also move long distances. Strictly speaking, the oceanic tunas do not belong to any country's EEZ[11] and are "highly migratory and straddling stocks" that move from EEZ to EEZ and from EEZ to the high seas[12]. Given the vastness of the ocean and the limited fish stocks in them, it is difficult to contain a deep sea fleet to one's own EEZ, especially that of a small island nation like Sri Lanka which has virtually no EEZ on its western side due to proximity with India.

---

[11] Exclusive Economic Zone. This includes the sea area that is 200 nautical miles from the shore.

[12] High Seas are the international waters beyond the EEZ and hence do not belong to any country.

Source: *Sri Lanka Dept. of Fisheries & Aquatic Resources*

No wonder, when the Sri Lankan fishermen increased their boat capacity for long voyages, they ended up in the EEZ of other countries in the Indian Ocean. India, the neighbouring country with a large EEZ, is naturally the number one destination for these boats. They also end up in the EEZs of Myanmar in the north, Indonesia in the east, Maldives in the west and even Diego Garcia in the south west[13].

---

[13] Occasionally these boats have been used for nefarious purposes, carrying people illegally to distant countries. Some boats have been spotted in the Mediterranean carrying persons to Italy. In 2003, the author came across a Sri Lankan multi-day boat str   anded in East Timor when it developed engine trouble while attempting to reach Australia with a group of people.

As far as India is concerned, the Sri Lankan multi-day boats visit both the east and west coasts and are often found in the Lakshadweep and Andaman Islands. With small islands acting as "tuna aggregating devices" in the ocean, the multi-day boats often end up near island chains. India is a doubly attractive destination as it has not been able to exploit its deep sea resource and its local fleet is more or less bound to the continental shelf. The "trawlerisation" of Indian fisheries has acted as a hurdle for the development of genuine deep sea fishing. It is only around the end of the 1990s that the shark fishermen of Thoothoor (Kanyakumari District) started moving into oceanic fishing (initially for pelagic shark and subsequently for tunas)[14].

The consequences of fishing in other country waters have been varied. Maldives is the strictest of the lot. With tourism and fishing as its main sectors of the economy, it cannot afford to be liberal. Once caught in Maldives waters, one can only bring back the fishermen and boat after paying a hefty fine that will bankrupt the owner. With India, the situation can be variable. Perhaps, one can escape detection as the Indian EEZ is large[15]. This may be the reason why the multi-day boats are willing to take their chances in Indian waters. Once caught, however, the Coast Guard is strict in enforcing the law—they seize the vessel and arrest the fishermen and hand over both to the civilian authorities on shore. Normally, the arrested fishermen are charged under the Maritime Zones of India Act 1981 (MZI) and tried in one of the seven designated courts enforcing the MZI Act. This process can be long and tedious taking over a year. The result is also certain as there is no escape route in law. The end result is a stiff fine and seizure of the boat.

Arrest and detention in India can be very traumatic. Even though the system treats them well, in the sense that there is no harassment, the

---

[14] The Thoothoor shark fleet is another extraordinary example of native ingenuity in South Asia. Unknown to the Govt, this fleet developed into a deep sea fleet. The Thoothoor boats are nowadays even bigger than the Sri Lankan multi-day boats, but voyage only for a maximum of four weeks. This seems to suit them fine.

[15] 2 million square kilometres.

long months in Indian jails going through the grind of the Indian legal system is hard for the ordinary fisherman. The families back home become desperate and send friends or relatives to India to check out the status of the arrested fishermen. Paying for lawyers is done but can be a waste as they only delay the inevitable. However, since 1997, as a result of ARIF's advocacy, the Tamil Nadu Government has been releasing the Sri Lankan fishermen without trial. This is clearly with a view to ensure reciprocal release of Tamil Nadu fishermen who also used to languish earlier in Sri Lankan jails. In other states, getting the release of the Sri Lankan fishermen can be quite difficult.

Thus, it is not a bed of roses for the multi-day boat fishermen who spend long months away from their families at sea and take huge risks in fishing in the EEZ of other Indian Ocean countries.

The significance of the multi-day boats is that they bring a certain balance to Indo-Sri Lankan fisheries relationship. Without them, trans-border fishing would be a one-sided affair with Indian trawlers fishing in Sri Lankan waters using the logic of historical rights. With both countries having their own "naughty boys", it is difficult for either of them to take the high moral ground or become totally legalistic in this matter. However, this does not mean that the trawler problem in the Palk Bay is cancelled out by the multi-day fishing boats fishing in the Indian EEZ. As will be shown, each is a distinct problem and has to be resolved satisfactorily for the well being of fish and fishermen[16].

Fishermen of the Northern Province—Biggest Victims of War and Peace

Throughout the war, the fishermen of the Northern Province had their livelihoods curbed severely and were barely able to pursue fishing. This varied considerably from area to area and from time to time. There were obviously long periods when there was a break in fighting and an

---

[16] I had argued in my first paper on this subject in 2000 for a system of reciprocal licensing of Indian trawlers in the Palk Bay in exchange for licensing of the multi-day boats in India's EEZ. While this might have made sense when the Sri Lankan fishermen were unable to fish in the Palk Bay, it makes no sense when they are back in action.

uncertain peace prevailed. Even during these times, the curbs on fishing continued and the fishermen of the Northern Province operated almost on a subsistence basis. Fishermen of some areas were a bit better off as they could get fuel for the OBMs while others could only undertake non-motorised fishing.

It was an irony that the Indian fishermen had a free run of Sri Lankan waters right throughout the war period while their Sri Lankan brothers were severely curbed from pursuing their livelihood. Over time, the Indian fishermen became more and more aggressive, operating their trawl nets within hand shaking distance from the Sri Lankan shore. Even when operating their small nets within the prescribed distances, the Sri Lankan fishermen would often lose their nets to the marauding Indian trawlers. In the Palk Bay where the Indian fishermen followed the three day-four day rule, the three days of the week when Indian trawlers came calling were days of uncertainty when only the desperate or foolhardy Sri Lankan fishermen would dare to go fishing. The following days when they would not be disturbed by the Indian trawlers would also become useless quite often as the Indian trawlers left behind a turbid sea unsuitable for the operations of their small gillnets.

Most of the period, the Sri Lankan took this treatment from their Indian brothers stoically. The strong sense of brotherhood prevented them from making a public issue of the matter. Moreover, in different phases of the war, many of them had been refugees in India and could not rule out the need to go back to India as refugees. The warmth and hospitality shown by the Indian fishermen to the refugees had also created a deep sense of obligation.

In any case, to whom could they complain? Both the Sri Lankan Government and the LTTE had their own reasons not to make an issue out of the Indian trawler operations in Sri Lankan waters. For Colombo, taking up the trawler issue would create a political turmoil in Tamil Nadu and potentially alienate New Delhi whose moral support for the war against LTTE was vital. The LTTE, whose support base in Tamil Nadu declined after the Rajiv Gandhi assassination, did not wish the fishermen issue to become a cause for further decline in support among the people and politicians of Tamil Nadu.

If the lull between periods of active warfare was fraught with uncertainties and hence prevented the fishermen of the Northern Province from taking up the issue of Indian trawlers, the end to the civil war in May 2009 has brought no respite to them. With recovery from war taking place slowly and reinvestment taking place in fishing equipment, the Indian trawlers have become a major threat to the recovery and rehabilitation of the fishermen of the Northern Province.

If the Indian media has constantly projected the Indian fishermen as the victims of the three decades of civil war, the fishermen of the Northern Province have been the real victims of the war. They continue to be victims in peace as well.

The 2004 Dialogue between Fishermen

The Norway brokered truce of 2002 created stable conditions for fishing activities to resume in many parts of the Northern Province, though still hampered by severe restrictions and the "high security zones" that cordoned off long stretches of the coast. By early 2003, some kind of a recovery had started. Not surprisingly, the Indian trawler problem surfaced as a block for this recovery. Clashes took place in Mannar and Wadamarachi between local fishermen and the Indian trawlers. As a result one fisherman died in Wadamarachi. Political leaders in the Northern Province became extremely concerned and started looking for solutions. Acutely aware of the geo-politics and the limitations of Governments on both sides, the idea of a fishermen-to-fishermen dialogue was mooted[17]. The idea also found favour on the Indian side with the trawler fishermen wanting to avoid clashes and fish in Sri Lankan waters with the full support of their Sri Lankan brothers.

---

[17] Selvam Adaikalanathan, the then M.P. from Mannar, was the first to propose this idea and it was welcomed by other political leaders from the Northern Province as well as civil society organisations.

As an organisation that maintained close relationship with fishermen on both sides of the Palk Bay, ARIF took the lead in organising this dialogue. A 21-member "Goodwill Mission" composed of 15 fishermen leaders and 6 supporters visited Sri Lanka in May 2004. The mission visited Mannar and had interactions with fishermen and others to get a grip on the field realities. A three-day meeting was held in Colombo for the Indian team to enter into dialogue with a delegation of Sri Lankan fishermen leaders from the Northern Province. The entire visit and dialogue was organised on the Sri Lankan side by a group of civil society organisations led by National Fisheries Solidarity (NAFSO) and Social and Economic Development Centre (Caritas, Sri Lanka). On the Indian side the ARIF mission was organised by the South Indian Federation of Fishermen Societies (SIFFS)[18].

The response of Governments on both sides was cautious. They did take note of the initiative but did not take it very seriously. Sri Lankan Fisheries Department sent an Assistant Director of Fisheries from Mannar as an observer while the Indian High Commission in Colombo also sent an observer. However, it opened the eyes of the two Governments to the role that such dialogues could play in resolving the issue. The Joint Declaration between India and Sri Lanka in October 2008 clearly states that such dialogues should be fostered and this has remained the policy, even though both Governments are yet to take steps to make this happen.

"The Border is not the Issue, it is Trawling"

The May 2004 dialogue was a path-breaker in many ways. For one, it changed the perception of the Indian fishermen about the issues involved. The Indian side has hoped to get an approval from their Sri Lankan counterparts for continuing their fishing operations in Sri Lankan waters, but with certain controls like the avoidance of more harmful forms of trawling like "pair trawling". However, the Sri Lankan response

---

[18] SIFFS, the apex body of India's largest network of fish marketing societies for small scale fishermen, has been the host organisation for ARIF ever since its formation in 1997 and has funded all ARIF activities.

was unexpected. They strongly condemned trawling and explained that they were taking steps to eliminate even their own nominal trawl fleet. They made it clear that they would not tolerate any trawling in Sri Lankan waters and wanted the Indians to stop trawling in three months. The message was clear: "We are brothers alright. The border is not an issue between us. But just stop trawling".

The Indian trawl association representatives were taken aback as they could not conceive of a life without trawling, as it has become so well entrenched in India and almost a way of life to a sizeable number of people. Despite confessions to the contrary in private, no trawler association in India had ever accepted till then that trawling was harmful to the environment and hence needed to be stopped. However, facing a determined Sri Lankan fishermen group, the Indian fishermen had to cave in and give a promise that they will work with their Government to develop a scheme to retire trawlers and to move on to alternative fishing methods or even totally new livelihoods. While no deadlines were given for this, they promised to be "good boys" in the interim, avoid "harmful nets" like pair trawls, ring seines, roller-trawl, chank-trawl, etc. They also promised not to come within three nautical miles from the Sri Lankan shore so that the small nets used by local fishermen would not be damaged[19].

There was no dramatic change in the situation after the fishermen "agreement". Attempts to reform the trawlers on the Indian side were only partially successful with many of them going back to their old ways after a while. However, the dialogue process had resulted in many of the trawler associations getting used to the idea of a "trawl buy-back" scheme and they started openly proposing it. What was inconceivable earlier became an open talking point. ARIF attempts to further the dialogue and to find a long term solution were abruptly halted by the tsunami of December 2004 with fishing coming to a virtual standstill in most parts

---

[19] A full report of the dialogue can be read in *Fishing For a Favour, Netting a Lesson* available in www.siffs.org or on www .icsf.org.

of Sri Lanka and Tamil Nadu[20]. By the time the fishermen recovered from the tsunami, Eelam War IV had started, making it difficult to focus on long term issues.

After the Civil War, Fishing Conflict Resurfaces and Intensifies

With the three decade-long civil war finally coming to an end in May 2009, the fishermen of the Northern Province have finally started thinking in terms of the long run and have started dreaming of their future once again. A whole generation that has not known normal fishing is hoping to get started and eventually catch up with the fishermen of the west and south who have gone on to conquer the Indian Ocean with their multi-day boats.

With resettlement of war affected fishing villages gradually taking place in the Northern Province, investment in fishing is slowly building up, partly with Government support and partly with merchant capital and own sources of funds. This process could take a while[21]. The various restrictions on fishing are being gradually dismantled and motorised fishing is picking up. The opening up of the A-9 highway and the resumption of normal fish transport systems is making fish prices attractive. However, straight away, the Indian trawlers have become the biggest hurdle to the revival or reconstruction of livelihoods. Fishermen all over the Northern Province are bitterly complaining about their inability to fish due to the invasion of the Indian trawlers. They have also been losing their new nets at regular intervals due to trawlers running over them.

Anger and frustration is building up and some fishermen have already started taking direct action despite the leadership advising patience. Pesalai fishermen in Mannar captured an Indian trawler in June 2010 and petrol

---

[20] Even in this, the Palk Bay fishermen on the Indian side were largely unaffected by the tsunami and could continue fishing after a short break. Ironically, the brunt of the tsunami was absorbed by Sri Lanka protecting the Indian coast line on the Palk Bay and Gulf of Mannar side. The Coromandel and the Arabian Sea coasts of Tamil Nadu were badly affected by the tsunami.

[21] Eelam War IV saw the internal displacement of population of all fishing villages in Killinochi and Mullaitivu. It also saw similar displacement in parts of the Mannar and Jaffna coasts.

bombed it after taking the crew ashore. Another trawler that came with permission to tow back the damaged trawler also met the same fate. In Jaffna, the fishermen have so far desisted from direct action due to the leadership advising patience and restraint. However, there have been stoppage of fishing and 'hartals'[22] in protest against Indian trawlers and the failure of the Sri Lankan Navy and Government to protect them.

Pressure is also building on local politicians to get the Sri Lankan Government to take action on the Indian trawlers. Very clearly things are heating up on the Sri Lankan side of the Palk Bay and a deep sense of crisis prevails.

Reviving the Dialogue Process

It is in this context that ARIF and National Fisheries Solidarity Movement (NAFSO) decided to revive the fishermen-to-fishermen dialogue process. In August 2010, a 24-member Sri Lankan team spent a week in Tamil Nadu, visiting Rameswaram, Jagadapattinam, Kottaipattinam, Mallipatinam and Nagapattinam en-route to Chennai for a three day dialogue with the Indian fishermen associations of the Palk Bay area.

This time the Government response was much more positive. The Sri Lankan Fisheries Minister himself approved of the idea and sent two fisheries officials as observers and the Sri Lankan Director General of Fisheries as Chief Guest for the valedictory session of the Chennai dialogue[23]. The response from the Indian side was also positive but a little less effusive. Three officials of the Tamil Nadu fisheries department participated in the Chennai dialogue as observers. The Indian Navy also sent an observer. However, no senior official participated in the valedictory session with the Director of Fisheries of Tamil Nadu present only as an observer without the mandate to speak. Clearly the multi-tiered Indian administration was unable to take a formal decision endorsing the dialogue,

---

[22] Closure of shops and establishments.

[23] It is worth noting that he was interested in personally attending the meeting but pulled out due to other commitments.

even though most of the people in power strongly supported the initiative in personal conversations.

The dialogue itself proved to be complicated with the Sri Lankan fishermen losing their patience with Indian fishermen and deciding unilaterally that trawling should stop within a one-year period even though the Indian fishermen have no clue how this is to be achieved without the Governments of India and Tamil Nadu coming up with a rehabilitation package. Strong restrictions on trawling were proposed during the one-year period. This "agreement" is subject to the two Governments approving it. However, both Governments have been slow to respond and the matter is still hanging fire as we go to press.

Some new issues have also cropped up. The Nagapattinam trawlers were only minor offenders in 2004 as they used to fish only for a short period every year in Sri Lankan waters, north and east of Jaffna. Now, they have become regulars in Sri Lankan waters[24]. Since the three day-four day rule does not apply to the Nagai trawlers; they fish all days in Sri Lankan waters making them a serious menace to local fishermen. Another issue is that the small motorised vessels of Tamil Nadu have started using long mono-filament gillnets in Sri Lankan waters. With Sri Lankan fishermen themselves banning mono-filament nets[25], this is becoming a new conflict. It has been decided to take this up when the Indian fishermen go to Sri Lanka on a "return visit".

The August 2010 dialogue has for the first time brought the plight of the Sri Lankan fishermen to the notice of the general public as well as the fishing communities themselves in Tamil Nadu. This is an important development that could create conditions for a realistic assessment of the issue and find a permanent solution.

---

[24] This is the unfortunate consequence of tsunami funding that allowed the Nagai fishermen to replace their damaged wooden trawlers with much larger steel trawlers. With this higher capacity, they cannot survive any more with just Indian resources but have to prey on Sri Lankan resources.

[25] They prefer multi-filament gillnets as they consider these to be less harmful to the eco-system.

Understanding it as a Fisheries Management Problem

The final solution to the Palk Bay problem (as well as the multi-day boat problem) requires that both countries start looking at it as a fisheries management problem caused by over-capacity and poor management systems. The de-facto open access system has caused this over-capacity in the trawl sector in India. Equally important has been India's failure to control trawling with all the ecological damage it does. This is an All-India problem not just a Palk Bay problem. Only, the fisheries problem in Palk Bay has got enmeshed in larger geo-politics due to the proximity of the international border and the long civil war that upset the balance that existed between the Indian and Sri Lankan fishermen before the war.

The Indian Government needs to realise that it is simply a problem of over-capacity and inappropriate technology. However, simple solutions do not exist for this simple problem. There are just too many people dependent on the trawl boats. If there are around 2000-2500 trawlers who depend on Sri Lankan waters for their fishing in the four districts of Ramnad, Pudukottai, Thanjavur and Nagapattinam, then there are around 15,000 owner and crew families directly dependent on the trawlers. If one assumes that for every one person directly dependent on trawling there is at least one more person indirectly dependent in the value chain, the total number of families that depend on trawling will be at least 30,000 families or a population of 1.5 lakhs. In addition, the trawl sector contributes immensely to the economy of the coastal areas in these districts and the consequences of closing it down is not easy to measure.

Obviously, it is not just a question of stopping the Indian trawlers from crossing the border. It requires a major initiative to restructure the fleet so that Indian trawlers do not need to go to Sri Lankan waters for their survival. This initiative will need a combination of many measures including, perhaps, a "buy-back" scheme. It will also require a complete revamping of the fisheries management system to enforce capacity limits and other regulations. This will not be possible without a fishing community buy-in. Some form of "co-management" with the fishermen associations taking responsibility for monitoring and enforcement is a must.

Instead of such tough decisions, if Governments of India and Tamil Nadu think that they can solve the problem by getting the Sri Lankan Government to continue tolerating Indian trawlers, they need to understand that it is not going to be a lasting solution. It will be unjust to the Sri Lankan fishermen in the Northern Province and lead to their alienation from their own Government and perhaps lead to strong anti-India sentiments that will harm India's cause in the long run. It is important to understand the enormity of the problem on the Sri Lankan side as a result of the Indian trawlers. If anything, a larger population is affected on the Sri Lankan side by Indian trawlers than what would be affected on the Indian side if trawling were to be stopped overnight.

On the Sri Lankan side, it is equally important to recognise that the multi-day boats are not just playing truant when they fish in Indian waters. It is inevitable given that the fleet goes after a highly migratory species like the Tuna. Fleet size and resource availability in Sri Lankan waters needs to be matched. Legal access to Indian waters needs to be negotiated. It is worth noting that the Sri Lankan multi-day boats fish far from the coast and that the Indian fishermen have rarely seen them as a problem[26]. India should seriously consider licensing the Sri Lankan multi-day boats and also promote joint ventures between the fishermen on both sides so that Indian fishermen also pick up the nuances of deep sea fishing.

Killing of Indian Fishermen—Inexplicable, Inexcusable

A problem that continues to haunt us and confuse the issues is the continuation of incidents involving Indian fishermen and the Sri Lankan Navy. As already mentioned, the Navy does not take action on Indian fishermen for poaching as it is reigned in by the Sri Lankan Government, anxious to avoid tension with India[27]. Most often, the relationships at sea between the Indian fishermen and the Sri Lankan Navy are actually cordial. However, inexplicably there are incidents of physical harassment

---

[26] It is also recognised that the multi-day boats use methods of fishing that are eco-friendly.

[27] The October 2008 Joint Declaration between India and Sri Lanka permits Indian vessels to fish in Sri Lankan waters with the exception of "high security zones". This was probably a war time concession, but is yet to be formally withdrawn at the time of writing this paper.

of Indian fishermen which occasionally (and tragically) leads to death. While these incidents of death are inexplicable, these are a couple of possible reasons:

- Caught between the instructions from the Government to ignore Indian boats and complaints from Sri Lankan fishermen about the damages done by the Indian boats, some Navy personnel take out their frustration by physically harassing some Indian fishermen. Such harassment at times gets out of hand leading to death of some fishermen.

- Night time shooting on Indian boats could be due to continuing fear of the LTTE and what is perceived as suspicious behaviour on the part of the Indian boat. The inability to distinguish between friend and foe from a distance at night due to an absence of suitable communication systems/protocols on Indian boats could be the problem in this case.

Whatever be the reasons, the killing of Indian fishermen is inexcusable and unjustifiable[28]. It is worrying that some of the recent deaths involve fishermen on small artisanal boats and not trawlers. The death of Indian fishermen also muddies the waters and reinforces the image of the Indian fisherman as a victim rather than aggressor. It raises the political temperature in Tamil Nadu and undermines attempts to find proper solutions.

Process is Crucial to the Solution

It is important to recognise that the problem of trans-border fishing is not just a question of experts or administrators or politicians working out a solution. It requires a deeper process involving fishermen on both sides and negotiating a settlement that is acceptable to them. Any number of "Joint Commission" meetings will not help resolve the problem unless there is a multi-tiered negotiation process. This will require Government-

---

[28] Sri Lanka has tended to deny the involvement of its Navy in such incidents. This could very well be because the Indian fishermen rarely report the correct location of the incident as part of the perpetuation of the myth of fishermen crossing the border inadvertently or fishing near Katchaitivu.

fishermen, fishermen-fishermen and Government-Government negotiations, all in parallel. In India, it may also involve Centre-State negotiations as well as inter-ministry negotiations.

It is important to recognise that without the fishermen there cannot be any solution. It is also important to recognise that the fishermen cannot solve the problem by themselves.

Conclusion

The civil war in Sri Lanka has had tragic consequences for the fishermen of the Northern Province with more than a generation losing out on fishing opportunities. It also triggered changes in fishing on the Indian side of the Palk Bay as well as in the Sri Lankan western and southern provinces. The Indian trawl fleet in the Palk Bay expanded enormously to make use of the vacuum created by the decline of fishing effort on the Sri Lankan side to such an extent that a large population on the Indian side now depends heavily on exploiting the fish resources on the Sri Lankan side. In the south and west of Sri Lanka, the emergence of multi-day fishing boats has resulted in a new dynamic fishery that often involves trans-border fishing in India's EEZ.

With the end of the civil war, the fishermen of the Northern Province have started to reclaim the space they had vacated as a result of the war. In doing this they find the Indian trawlers the biggest hurdle. Their fresh investments in fishing nets are proving disastrous as Indian trawlers continue to damage them during their operations. Any attempt at controlling the Indian trawlers leads to political repercussions in India with the potential to harm Indo-Sri Lankan ties. This is preventing the Sri Lankan Government from taking a hard stance on the issue. Moreover, incidents of Indian fishermen losing lives due to actions by the Sri Lankan Navy are muddying the waters and further confusing the issue.

It is time that the two Governments work on a long term solution taking into account that the problems of trans-border fishing are essentially arising from faulty fisheries management rather than viewing them as merely issues of sovereignty or to be dealt by Ministries of Foreign Affairs.

Any solution has to be just and mitigate the negative impacts on those who will lose by it. The onus is on India to resolve the trawl issue in the Palk Bay as continuation of trawling in Sri Lankan waters is not acceptable to the Sri Lankan fishermen. The multi-day boat problem requires careful assessment by Sri Lanka and an engagement with India to provide licences for their operations.

However, the process of finding solutions requires the strong involvement of fishermen from both countries for it to be just, workable and sustainable.

EXTERNAL CONSEQUENCES

IMPACT OF THE CONFLICT ON TAMIL NADU

A.X. Alexander

It can be said without any exaggeration that Tamil Nadu has been affected by the internal conflict almost as nearly as Sri Lanka. By its geographical contiguity, ethnic identity, linguistic similarity, cultural unity, long history, trade etc. Tamil Nadu is so closely connected with Sri Lanka that whatever has happened in the island has caused perceptible and tangible impact in Tamil Nadu. It has affected its politics, economy, society, demography, law and order and fishermen.

Although the impact has been on different fields, this chapter confines itself to the impact on repatriates and refugees, law and order, crime situation and fishermen. The chapter also looks into the impact of Eelam War IV and the current situation.

Linkages to Tamil Nadu and its Impact

It is necessary to highlight a few of the salient features of the linkages between Tamil Nadu and Sri Lanka.

The close relationship between Tamil Nadu and Sri Lanka can be traced even to the, Mahavamsa itself which speaks of the earliest King of Sri Lanka marrying a Pandyan princess and ancient history reveals that the, Sinhala kings had repeatedly sought the support and assistance of Chera, Chola and Pandya kings in wars in Sri Lanka. The fishermen of Mannar and the eastern coast of Tamil Nadu converted to faith by St. Francis Xavier and were close to each other and inter-married.

Modern history discloses that the British administered Ceylon from Madras from 1796 to 1812. The train to Dhanushkodi from Madras that connected the Indian Ferry to Talaimannar pier was called Indo-Ceylon express and one could buy a ticket to Colombo in Madras Egmore. The British coffee and tea planters imported Indian Tamils into Ceylon to work as estate labourers and they became permanent settlers sometimes exceeding the native Tamils in number.

Commercially, Tamil traders used to transport dry fish and onion from Tuticorin to Colombo by boats. From Jaffna, opium and nutmeg used to be smuggled to Vedaranyam and Kodikarai and *lungis* (sarongs) and plastic goods used to be exported in return.

Tamil cinemas and its songs fascinated people across the straits and nocturnal sailings to Tamil Nadu to see cinemas were a routine. Radio Ceylon was a house hold radio till 60s in Tamil Nadu.

The Anti Hindi agitation, the renaissance of Tamil brought about by DMK in 1940s, 50s and 60s in public oration and cinema, the demand for separation of Dravida Nadu from Indian union and fostering hatred for the North Indians had an impact on the thinking of Tamils in Sri Lanka.

No doubt the Sri Lankan Tamil holds that he has an umbilical connection with people of Tamil Nadu.

Repatriates

The first consequence of the conflict was the exodus of people from Sri Lanka, either as repatriates or as refugees. Whenever there has been rioting in Sri Lanka be it in 1958, 1977, 1981 or 1983, the Tamils have fled to Tamil Nadu seeking safe havens. Immediately after the 1958 clashes many Indian Tamils left the island and came to India leaving their property and jobs. Later in accordance with Sirimavo-Shastry Pact 1964 and Sirimavo- Indira Pact 1974, a total of 4,61,631 Indian citizens came to Tamil Nadu as repatriates. One must remember that this was a time (1963) repatriates from Burma were also coming in and the Tamil Nadu administration was busy settling them.

Repatriation of Sri Lankan Tamils started in 1968 and was suspended only in October 1984 at the height of clashes in Sri Lanka. Tamil repatriates who reached the shores of Tamil Nadu were initially stationed at Mandapam in Ramanathapuram District and Kottapattu in Trichirappalli and later were sent to Andhra, Kerala, Karnataka and different parts of Tamil Nadu. Most of them arrived without the all important family cards issued by the Indian Authorities in Sri Lanka without which the administration found it difficult to render any assistance to them immediately.

Some of them had left the island without collecting money due to them from their employers –the amount of money brought, determined the type of rehabilitation. On arrival the repatriates were given cash doles, rice at subsidized cost, free accommodation, free water and electricity. The bulk of repatriates were settled in Tamil Nadu; a few were sent to Andhra Pradesh, and a few others were sent to Kerala and Karnataka. Those who remained in Tamil Nadu were accommodated in tea plantations in the Nilgiris, in the converted cinchona plantations at Naduvattam, Valparai estates in Coimbatore district and in Kodaikanal in Madurai district. Those who did not choose to go to the plantations in the hills became transport drivers, mechanics, workers in spinning mills and clerks in the Government.

The Government organized state farm corporations to provide employment especially for the repatriates. However these corporations did not succeed as repatriates were novices in farm operations, most of state farm corporations had to be closed down and the repatriates in the farms had to be provided with other jobs. The Government also established colonies and provided three acres of agricultural land to each repatriate family in different parts of the state. They were given financial assistance to dig wells, buy farm equipments, and animals and build farm houses. However, the location of these colonies was not conducive and they suffered a slow death due to vagaries of nature and lack of expertise of the repatriates.

The Government provided business loans to the repatriates. Majority of the repatriates chose to apply for these loans. Each family was given Rs. 3000 initially to start a business. The beneficiary was sanctioned another Rs 5000 if he had been successful. Without adequate training and business acumen many floundered. Many repatriates utilized the amount sanctioned for daily expenses and became penniless over a period. The business loan scheme also turned out to be a failure.

Except those who had Government jobs and well settled in tea plantations, others lived a miserable life with little roof over their heads and hardly any thing good in their lives and moreover they added to the number of poor in Tamil Nadu. They bore a grudge against the Government that it was not looking after them while it continued to provide for the refugees though they are originally Indian Tamils.

According to statistics issued by the Government of Tamil Nadu, 77,475 families had been given business loans; 3,275 were settled in agricultural farms; 2,445 had found employment in tea plantations; 2,855 had been employed in rubber plantations; 125 were employed in cinchona plantations; 3,942 had been employed in spinning mills; 4,900 had found jobs with the assistance of Repco bank; 526 had settled in self employment and 57,461 had got housing loans.

Whereas, this is the picture of repatriates in Tamil Nadu those who went to Andhra Pradesh were given jobs in the spinning mills. Adverse weather conditions and the unknown language forced repatriates to return to the Tamil Nadu seeking employment from the Government of Tamil Nadu. Those who went to Kerala and Karnataka however had acclimatized themselves in rubber plantations and are doing well.

The generation that suffered in initial days is passing out. Of late the younger generation is mingling with the local population and has started living like locals. The politically savvy ones have become even members of local panchayats and at times are fighting for their rights. They occasionally indulge in disturbing law and order in the estates in the Nilgiri and in Kodaikanal demanding civic amenities. The Government no longer provides concessions to Sri Lankan repatriates.

Refugees

Whenever there had been clashes in Sri Lanka the Tamils came as refugees. In the first phase, from 1983 to 1987 a total of 1, 34,000 refugees came in. In the second spell, after June 1989 when the Eelam war was in full swing 1, 22,000 refugees came in. Between 1995 and 2002, 23,600 refugees came in. This reduced drastically after 2002. It is also reported that about 5000 have moved into Tamil Nadu by air after getting visa recently.

The refugees who came in droves by sea and air during the height of conflict in 1983 commanded initially the sympathy and support of local Tamil population and the Government, as they unfolded unvarnished tales of suffering of rapes, plunder, detention without enquiries and disappearances of youngsters. Sympathizing with them, the local people gave all support by providing them food, money and shelter. The Government installed nearly 150 camps in different places in the states for them and provided ration, utensils, educational facilities, medical facilities, employment opportunities, roof over their heads and cash doles for them permitting them to take up local jobs to support their livelihood. Many of the refugees also drew monetary support from friends and relatives in Western countries like Canada, Sweden, England, Switzerland, France, Norway and Australia and led comparatively comfortable lives, though shelter that was provided to them was not up to their expectation.

The refugees who came by sea, were received in Mandapam camp, photographed, fingerprinted and issued with a family card and later were sent to different camps mostly according to their wishes. One could see regional groupings in these camps. Those who were suspected to have leanings with militants were quarantined for some time and after due verifications were sent either to special camps or normal camps. The camp inmates were ordered to report for roll call initially daily and later thrice a week, and now once a month when they collect the dole. The attendance in the roll call was initially made stiff as some of the offences that occurred in the vicinity were traced to some refugees who were hard pressed for money. They were allowed to go out for local work to supplement their dole between 8 AM- 6 PM. Most of them resorted to masonry, carpentry, and driving motor vehicles.

The refugees are given Rs 400 for the family head; Rs 288 for other adults; Rs. 180 for the first child; and Rs. 90 for other children per month. The approximate burden on the exchequer is Rs.30 crores per year. They are given subsidized rice at the cost of 57 paise per kg where as the market price is Rs 30. Besides they are given utensils to cook, mats and since 2001, they are also given free clothes.

The camps organized in different parts of the state had temporary structures except in Mandapam and Kottapattu. Some of the cyclone shelters, vast grounds, and unused buildings were utilized for the purpose. Attempts are now made to refurbish and strengthen these structures. The Government of Tamil Nadu recently ordered its ministers to visit the camps and report conditions in the camp. In 2006 a similar exercise was carried out and Rs 5 crores was sanctioned to refurbish the camps.

On the basis of their reports:

- The Government had sanctioned Rs 100 crores for the welfare of Sri Lankan Tamils in camps.

- The Government had extended the medical insurance scheme to the Sri Lankan Tamil refugees living in camps. The inmates would benefit up to Rs one lakh in private hospitals and pay wards in Government hospitals.

- It has provided maternity assistance for poor Sri Lankan Tamils. Rs.6, 000/- is being given to the mother for every child born.

- It has provided T.V sets and sports equipments in the camps.

- Besides this it has increased the funeral expense grants from Rs 500 to Rs 2,500.

- It has provided bus passes to students in arts, science and engineering colleges.

- It has provided cycles to students of high school.

- In case of accidental deaths they are sanctioned Rs 15,000/-

There are 113 camps housing 73,250 refugees.

Non Camp Refugees

Apart from these who are housed in camps there are others who did not live in camps – these are refugees who came with travel documents into the country and settled on their own. These refugees had been asked to report to the police stations and register themselves. Such refugees number about 32,500. Though they had been ordered to register themselves in the police stations their compliance had been tardy. After 1987 accord, Government ordered non camp refugees to register themselves in police stations. But only 12,675 registered. In 1991 it again ordered them to register. It extended the deadline twice yet one can witness that even now Sri Lankan refugees desirous of going out of India come to police stations for clearance certificates to get exit permits or passports without registration.

Every individual refugee – whether in the camp or not – is being given a colour identity card which facilitates access to medical attention and educational facilities of free education, free books, free notebooks, free uniforms and free bus passes.

The non camp refugees because of the remittance they received from foreign countries had rented houses at higher charges than prevailing rates and this has caused considerable consternation among the native rent house seekers. Their extravagance was also a source of annoyance. Most of them violated foreign remittance rules. There had been tension in certain areas between the locals and the non camp refugees

Special Camps

Among the arrivals by sea or air who had connections or suspected to have connections with militant groups as ascertained at the time of arrival were segregated and quarantined. Likewise those who had been involved or suspected to be involved in offences and whose presence was required for trials etc were segregated and detained in special camps under

3(2)e of Foreigners Act. Two such camps are in existence now and there are 36 inmates. These inmates often clamour for release and the human rights groups are supporting them.

Militants among Refugees

Among the refugees who arrived by sea there were many youngsters who professed allegiance to different militant groups. Over a period they established different landing points in different villages on the shore and established recruiting centres at the landing points. They installed their own camps in different parts of the state and conducted their political propaganda activity claiming allegiance to one or other political party in the state. They established contact with different political parties and different Indian intelligence agencies and subtly played one against the other.

The Sri Lankan Tamil militant youngsters consistently spread rumours that Sri Lankan Intelligence, Mossad and CIA were very much active in Tamil Nadu collecting information on the groups and accused one another of being informers and indulged in clashes among themselves at times using firearms. They conducted public meetings and processions and exhibitions of photographs and video tapes of the ruins and destructions caused in the course of the conflict and invoked the sympathy of the local population and collected money to run their camps where they were training their cadres in weapons, and explosives and field craft.

They recruited cadres for their militant groups from the refugees camps also and these resulted in rival pamphleteering, skirmishes, kidnappings, abductions, tortures, murders, assaults, shootouts and assassinations. Hitherto unknown grenades and AK47's became common in the vocabulary of the press and public and were found freely. They procured their ware for their wars using Tamil Nadu as their base. They frequented the island on and off by boats which they called Eelam Boat Service and established ports of entry and exit at various locations in the eastern coast of Tamil Nadu sometimes supported by locals and sometimes by instilling fear in the local populace with the arms they had with them. The trips by these boats were so regular and routine that the

Indian immigration authorities could not help but stamp illegal ports as point of entries in travel documents.

They brought the injured for treatment in established hospitals and others, who wished to come into Tamil Nadu. A few of them with the money they brought, and with the money they collected as donations and by extortions, indulged in gunrunning, drug peddling, smuggling of medicines, petrol, oil, lubricants, fertilizers, explosives, motor cycles, cement, walkie talkies, uniforms, ammunition etc. They also established factories to produce grenades and depots to store them. They also extorted money from the well to do refugees and got into scuffles with local populations. They indulged in jail escapes too.

A series of misdeeds eventually turned the local people against them. These include the shootout at Pondy Bazar the planting of bombs at Meenambakkam Airport killing 39, the escapade from Tippu mahal by digging a tunnel, shooting and killing constables at Mamandur and Pattinamkathan, shooting and killing of Padmanaba and his friends, brandishing weapons and travelling as VIPs with armed escorts, resorting to firings at the smallest instance, donning uniforms while on move and finally, the assassination of PM Rajiv Gandhi.

The arrival of Sri Lankan Tamils either as refugees or as repatriates or long time visitors have an impact on the economy, public order and politics of Tamil Nadu.

Whereas these illegal activities were going on in the name of freedom fight, a miniscule section of refugees, indulged in thieving, chain snatching, robberies, dacoities, kidnapping and impersonation. A few others indulged in white collar crimes of forging passports and visas, cheating, establishing communication hubs, running long distance telephone exchanges etc.

Impact on Law and Order and Crime in Tamil Nadu

All these nefarious activities threw considerable strain on the law and order, crime machinery and judiciary. At times it was difficult to proceed against these criminals and law breakers due to the political patronage and common man's sympathy they enjoyed. At times the courts took a lenient view as the culprits happened to be refugees. Sometimes they got bails and jumped out of it and being not so easily identifiable went scot free of their offences and vanished back to the island. The leniency and inability to fix them up emboldened many to resort to more and more crimes. The culmination was the assassination of Rajiv Gandhi.

With this assassination the militants lost sympathy and they never regained it except with certain individuals and fringe political parties till the last phase of Eelam war 4.

Reaction of Tamil Nadu Police and Government

The militants were a strain on Tamil Nadu law and order. Time to time the Tamil Nadu police tried their best to cast away this albatross and registered cases on all violent incidents indulged by these militants.

In 1986, (8-11-1986) the police took a very bold and adventurous step of disarming weapons of all the groups including from Prabhakaran and did succeed in seizing their weapons, without firing a single shot. All the militant leaders, including Prabhakaran were rounded up, photographed and fingerprinted. Explosives, guns, machetes and *arruvals*, and communication sets were seized in lorry loads during this arrest search and seizure.

On 14 May 1992 the LTTE was banned. Tamil Nadu Police organized check on of all refugee camps and shifted camps away from the shores. Check posts were set up in the main high ways and arterial roads to detect and prevent movement of militants. By 1994 nearly 2000 LTTE suspects were held in various prisons and special camps

A Coastal Security Group was established as a part of the Tamil Nadu Police and set up shore check posts, marine police stations and provided them with speed boats. They received assistance of Indian Navy and Coast Guard, in the east coast.

Finding the activities of militants and recalcitrant refugees beyond bearing, the Government encouraged reverse flow of refugees from camps. In 1987 soon after the Indo-Sri Lanka Accord 25,600 refugees went back by chartered ships; between 1992 and 1995, 54,600 refugees went back to Sri Lanka. Besides these many on their own accord left Indian shores to countries in the west.

The Impact on Fishermen from Tamil Nadu

The most telling impact of the conflict in Sri Lanka is to be seen in the suffering of Indian fishermen in the Palk Bay and Gulf of Mannar when they fish around Katchativu, an island that India ceded to Sri Lanka in 1974. The fishermen consider the waters around Katchativu as their traditional and historic waters, and that they had been forfeited of their rights to fish in the waters where their forefathers had been fishing. They wonder why they should be attacked and shot at even after the war had ended. They feel that there was some justification in prevention of their perambulation in the sea during conflict period as it was alleged that the Indian fishermen were smuggling war wares and fuel. Though the shooting of fishermen has come down the fishermen now complain that they are apprehended and attacked - at times stripped naked, deprived of their catch, equipments, and made to face trials in Sri Lankan courts. Educated fishermen who go fishing these days in well equipped boats with walkie talkies, GPS etc. complain that their equipments and fish are plundered. Whenever there have been attacks and shootouts on the fishermen there has been a political and law and order echo in the state. The echo at times is violent. Political parties and common man feel that the remedy lies in getting Katchativu back but the Minister for External Affairs has ruled this out in the parliament itself. However a few political parties have gone to the Supreme Court to annul the Agreement of handing over of Katchativu but the proceedings in the court are slow. To get over the imbroglio a few academicians have suggested taking Katchativu Island on a lease in perpetuity or licensing the fishermen or allowing the fishermen of either country to discuss and arrive at a decision themselves. All the suggestions have not been given the required attention by the ruling powers on either side.

Eelam War IV and its Impact

The sympathy the refugees commanded in the initial days of their arrival wore out when they indulged in lawlessness, and it turned into hatred and contempt when they assassinated Rajiv Gandhi. For a long time, after the assassination, the common man did not evince any interest in the ongoing tussle in the island. However, there were political parties in Tamil Nadu who were harping on the LTTE. Many individuals also had secret sympathies for the Tamil Tigers but they were not bold enough to come out open as there was a ban.

Such secret sympathies came to the fore when the cease fire ended and clashes once again began with the Mavilaru issue. There was wide admiration for the aerial attacks that the LTTE made. The statement made in Colombo that the Indian radars failed to detect the LTTE planes, shocked a considerable section of the people of Tamil Nadu. They were stunned that there was secret help to Sri Lanka with equipments and intelligence. In fact the assistance to Sri Lanka made many in Tamil Nadu feel that they were being letdown. There was an air of anger and hurt in Tamil Nadu.

The strafing in Chencholai, killing more than sixty children provoked the Tamil Nadu assembly to condemn it by a resolution.

The Mutur massacre of young boys, (4th August 2006), the shelling and killing of people in Philip Nery church at Allapidi, (August 15 2006), the attack at Pesalai Church (June 17, 2006) killing and injuring many, killings at Padagu Thurai, bombing in Illupakavadi (Jan 2 2007) and the lack of protest by powers on all these, along with apprehension of clandestine intelligence and logistic support provoked many Tamil Nadu politicians and public, to openly criticize the Central and State Governments for their silence. The sympathy for the Tigers was so much that people started cropping up pictures and flags of Tigers openly defying police and the ban on the organisation. Many public meetings and processions were conducted in different parts of Tamil Nadu in support of Tamils of Sri Lanka and against the onslaught on them. Groups of intellectuals formed organizations and expressed their sympathy in the form of processions, meetings and discussions in the halls. The Central Government offices were blockaded, and even an army convoy of an organization of Central Government was attacked in Coimbatore.

The killing of Prabhakaran and others in the field provoked sympathy even with the non- committed. The press especially, Tamil language news papers wafted up the sympathy for the Tamil Tigers. However the DMK (Dravida Munnetra Kazhagam) leader blamed the tiger leader for not being diplomatic but intolerant and was criticized by his rivals for not putting in his best to prevent the final onslaught and the ultimate denouement. The AIADMK (All India Anna Dravida Munnetra Kazhagam) leader who had been against the Tigers also expressed its concern for the trapped Tamils in Sri Lanka. Students, who were not aware of the earlier criminal proclivities of the militants including the assassination of Rajiv Gandhi, lawyers and cine artists were agitated. This was capitalized by local champions of Tigers.

The processions, public meetings, demonstrations, exerted enormous pressure on the law and order machinery. Of late, such effusion of sympathy for the fallen tiger leader is on the decline. Nevertheless, people are disturbed over the living conditions of people in the IDP camps in Sri Lanka. The conditions in which the Tamils live in the camps are poignantly portrayed in the press. The Tamil Nadu Chief Minister and the leader of the opposition are repeatedly expressing concern over the conditions in the camps and desire quick settlement of IDPs.

Present Situation

The alleged sighting of Chinese in the patrol boats in Palk straits is viewed with concern by the Tamil fishermen. The media is highlighting this as a serious security threat to the country. The photos of Chinese marked tents pitched in Katchativu in the North were also given a lot of coverage in the press. The information of a Chinese company being awarded fishing rights in the North of Sri Lanka make the fishermen feel insecure and think that they might have to face new enemies soon. The Tamil fishermen are confused. They wonder why he should not fish in the sea where he and his forefathers were fishing prior to the conflict.

They are unable to comprehend why they are shot at even after the war has ended. This confusion results in his abstention from fishing for days together or his threats to sail enmass to Katchativu and court arrest. A section of fishermen are banking upon and confabulations that are going on among the fishermen of both the countries.

There is widespread concern for the IDPs in the camps. Almost all sections of people, political parties and the Government desire quick settlement and normalcy. Further most of the refugees settled in Tamil Nadu are not in a mood to go back to Sri Lanka as they are not absolutely sure of the security situation in Sri Lanka. However a few refugees are getting back to the island mostly to see their properties, friends and relatives and return. As the refugees have developed vested interests, deep roots and relationship with local population, they are hesitant to move back. Added to this are the welfare measures in Tamil Nadu that are an advantage for them. The refugees are not sure whether the Indian educational certificates their children have would be recognized in Sri Lanka. They are also not sure whether they will be able to get back the lands they left in Sri Lanka in the absence of documents which at the time of their flight they had abandoned. They are also not sure whether they would get jobs. Many of the refugees are not sure whether they should have Indian citizenship or Sri Lankan citizenship for their children born in India. The refugees may well demand for citizenship for themselves and their children born in the refugee camps. The Chief Minister of Tamil Nadu once floated the idea of citizenship for them but it was opposed by the leader of the opposition and scholars as it would have implications on refugees in India from other countries. Later "Permanent Residentship", a concept alien to the Indian constitution was advocated but there was no progress on that.

A new trend that is noticed among the refugees these days is the attempt to go to Australia by boats. Touts have been visiting various camps and enrolling refugees to put them on boats and send them to Christmas Island. Attempts at such trafficking have been unearthed by police and the agents have been brought to book. Such attempts were scorched in Kollam, Puducherry, Ooty, and Kuttralam.

More importantly a tribunal is conducting an inquiry on the ban on LTTE and MDMK (Marumalarchi Dravida Munnetra Kazhagam) and a few interested groups are appearing before the tribunal to lift the ban.

LONG DISTANCE REACTIONS TO THE CONFLICT AND THEIR RAMIFICATIONS

Laksiri Fernando

The final stages of the war between the Sri Lankan government (GOSL) and the Liberation Tigers of Tamil Eelam (LTTE) generated a complex web of 'action-reaction matrix' between the country and the outside world that could be considered rather unprecedented in recent histories of internal wars with external ramifications. These reactions and their consequences still reverberate and provide the opportunity to understand (1) the internal-external mix in conflicts (2) international relations between the countries of the West and the East (3) the role of international non-governmental organizations (NGO) in internal conflicts and (4) more importantly the effects of Diaspora nationalism on conflicts in general.

While the above research benefits are in more general terms, the study of external reactions to the Sri Lankan conflict, and particularly of their nature, are of paramount importance considering their implications on (1) the country's present and future security and peace (2) ethnic relations and social harmony in the short and the long term (3) foreign or external relations particularly with the Western countries and (4) the future development of the economy and also the society.

External reactions to internal conflicts or upheavals are not unusual in history, but the magnitudes are different from the past to the present. The French revolution in the late eighteenth century created both support and opposition in England and the American Revolution, a decade before also had a similar response. Major powers usually have involved themselves in internal affairs of other countries under various pretexts and even smaller powers have sent troops to neighboring countries in support of friendly rulers or in aid of rebellions, depending on the circumstances or interest. All these can be characterized as sorts of international or outside reactions to internal affairs of other countries.

The present circumstances after the WWII are however different in terms of internal conflicts or external interventions. There are two sets of norms developed by the United Nations to govern these two interrelated trajectories but unfortunately only one set is emphasized or rather over emphasized. The first are the rules and principles that the member countries should follow on its own volition in respect of its citizens and in governance. These are by and large the human rights norms in the spheres of civil, political, economic, social and cultural. In addition is the International Humanitarian Law (IHL). While the IHL is meant to govern the wars between the sovereign states in respect of border, regional or international confrontations, they are also increasingly supposed to apply to internal conflicts without much reflection or modification.[1]

The other set of norms are equally or much more important for the survival of the international system. Member States and even the UN should follow these norms that are related to the rights of the states and their sovereignty and territorial integrity. They also cover the 'right to development' within a favorable international environment without coercion or oppression. These norms embodied in the UN Charter prevents intervention and interference except in particular circumstances, sanctioned through strict and due procedures. While both sets of norms and rules are important and interrelated, it might be argued that the

---

[1] President Mahinda Rajapaksa said before the 65th UN General Assembly on 23 September 2010, "In this context, it is worth examining the capacity of the current international humanitarian law to meet contemporary needs. It must be remembered that such law evolved essentially in response to conflicts waged by the forces of legally constituted States, and not terrorist groups. The asymmetrical nature of conflicts initiated by non-state actors gives rise to serious problems which need to be considered in earnest by the international community." Ariyarathna Athugala (ed.), *President at the UN*, (Colombo: Department of Information, Government of Sri Lanka, 2010), p. 20.

norms in respect of human rights or humanitarian law may render meaningless and unworkable unless the second set of norms are adhered to. There are several loopholes in both sets of international norms, and on both accounts, non-state actors (i.e. terrorist organizations or even NGOs) appear not to respect either human rights or non-interference.

There are two main ways that the conflict in Sri Lanka has been characterized, one as an ethnic conflict and the other as a terrorist problem. There is no denial among many analysts or external parties that the situation contained both elements but the dispute has been about the key characteristics, what was predominant and to what proportion or extent.[2] The reactions of external parties or the 'long distance reactions' referred to in this chapter depended largely on these two different perceptions directly or indirectly. In addition, there were parties or actors mainly some non-governmental organizations that at least pretended to be 'neutral' on the subject and tried to focus on human rights norms and their alleged violations almost completely ignoring either the character of the conflict or the sovereignty of the country.

Given the permissible length of the chapter and considering its required cohesion, this chapter takes only three layers of reactions to the conflict in Sri Lanka particularly during the final stages of the battle between the GOSL and the LTTE. They are (1) the Diaspora reactions (2) reactions by the international non-governmental organizations, particularly the International Crisis Group (ICG) as an example and (3) the reactions of some selected Western Governments and the UN. The discussion on these reactions is preceded by a short recounting of events to which external forces were reacting.

Recount of Events

Any recount of events may be subjective depending on how you approach the events and from what perspective. It was a fact, however,

---

[2] Arshi Saleem Hashmi, "Conflict Transformation from Ethnic Movement to Terrorist Movement: Case Studies of Tamils in Sri Lanka and Mohajirs in Pakistan," *Policy Studies 45*, (Colombo: Regional Centre for Strategic Studies, 2008.)

that the declared policy of the President elected in November 2005, Mahinda Rajapaksa, was for negotiations with the LTTE nevertheless strongly deviating from the past policies and positioning strongly against separatism, homeland claim and self-determination. "I will not permit any separatism," he said.[3] He criticized the past saying that he was deeply convinced that Sri Lanka needed to think from a fresh perspective and devise a new approach if it has to find a sustainable solution to the conflict in the North and the East. External interferences into the issue have made the situation more complex. In addition, he criticized the ceasefire agreement (CFA) signed in February 2002 by the then government and the LTTE, claming it was signed in 'haste and in a short sighted manner.' On the issue of negotiations, he however declared, "I shall initiate direct talks with the Liberation Tigers of Tamil Elam. I also intend to meet their leader and other representatives for such discussions."

A peculiar aspect of the events was the indirect support of the LTTE for the Rajapaksa Government to come into power in 2005 by forcing a boycott by the Tamil voters who would otherwise have by and large voted for the opposition candidate, Ranil Wickremasinghe. Wickremasinghe who was reputed to have close connections with the Western governments was instrumental in initiating a peace process under the patronage of the West, mediated or facilitated by Norway in 2002. It was that peace process that Rajapaksa was criticizing. It appears that the LTTE somewhat opened the way for Rajapaksa government not with a peace strategy but with a war strategy. The idea was to isolate the government as much as possible in the West without a 'safety net.'

There were two rounds of talk in 2006 but the last round in Geneva failed in October even without the two parties sitting together. The international community could not do much to rescue the situation. On November 27 that year, Velupillai Prabhakaran declared his final struggle for Eelam. He said, "It is now crystal clear that the Sinhala leaders will never put forward a just resolution to the Tamil national question." On

---

[3] *Mahinda Chinthana*, Presidential Election 2005, p. 26. All quotations in this respect are from the above document.

the question of peace he further said, "Therefore, we are not prepared to place our trust in the impossible and walk along the same futile path."[4] He called upon the international community and the Tamil Diaspora to support the Eelam cause of self-determination.

By this time, the dispute over Mavilaru had already erupted. The dispute arose when the LTTE forcibly closed the sluice gates of Mavilaru in July 2006 which supplied water for cultivation for over 30,000 families in the area. By early August, the Sri Lankan armed forces managed to capture the area and open the gates. This was the beginning of a long battle to gain control of the LTTE held areas, and step by step, the government forces succeeded. Some of the main incidents and events are discussed in the following paragraphs.

In January 2007, the government captured Vakarai, an eastern stronghold of the LTTE. In March, the LTTE launched its first air attack on the country's only international airport. In July, the government declared that it has captured Thoppigala, the last jungle stronghold in the East, but it took another few months to take complete control of the area. During the eastern operations, there had been serious allegations of human rights violations and the government initially allowed internationally monitored investigations but the efforts became stalled by March 2008 due to disputes.

In October 2007, the LTTE mounted its biggest suicide assault on the north-central air base at Anuradhapura and the strategy seemed to be to cripple the government's air power. However, in November, the LTTE political wing leader, S. P Thamilselvam, was killed by a military drone air attack.

In January 2008, the government terminated the ceasefire agreement formally indicating its full scale intended assault on the LTTE areas in the North. In March the government held elections to nine local

---

[4] 'Heroes' Day' speech by LTTE chief V elupillai Pr abhakaran a vailable onl ine at ht tp:// www.satp.org/satporgtp/countries/shrilanka/document/papers/29nov2006.htm accessed on 27 January 2011

government councils and the devolved Provincial Council in the East indicating its dual strategy of military and political. It was almost at the same period that the government launched its strategy in the North. Without directly moving on the A9 road, the highway to Killinochchi and Jaffna, like in the past, the government troops encircled the area by first moving to the north-west and then to the north and thereafter coming from north to the south towards Killinochchi, the stronghold of the LTTE.

The troops captured the Madhu area in April 2008 and moving further north overtook Pooneryn in mid-November. As it was reported, "The army now controlled the entire western coast of the country, effectively cutting off the LTTE's most direct supply lines across the narrow Palk Strait."[5] It was at this juncture the President Rajapaksa made an appeal saying, "In this situation my clear message to Prabhakaran and the LTTE is to lay down their arms and come forward for discussions with us forthwith."[6] In the author's opinion, this was a clear juncture where the international community could have supported the government's call and persuaded the LTTE to lay down arms. If this was done there was a clear possibility of saving many lives. There can be many reasons why this did not happen. Perhaps the 'international community' did not believe that the LTTE could be defeated. As some government sources suspected, 'perhaps there was a hidden expectation that the LTTE should win.' Whatever the reason, Prabhakaran declared that 'capturing Killinochchi is a day dream.'"[7]

It was after the capture of Killinochchi that the international community got completely alarmed. A major reason for the concern was the large number of trapped civilians within the LTTE held territory

---

[5] Sarath Kumara, "Sri Lankan Troops Capture LTTE Stronghold of Pooneryn." *World Socialist Website.* 20 November 2010.

[6] "Pooneryn falls: Lay down arms now- President tells LTTE" *Asian Tribune*, 15 November 2010 available online on http://www.asiantribune.com/node/14208. accessed on 7 May 2011.

[7] *Tamil Sydney* quoted Prabhakaran telling Nakkeeran, a magazine in India in early January 2009.

now confined only to around 200 square kilometers. The number estimated was between 150,000 and 200,000 thousand. Already around 100,000 had escaped from the fighting area to government camps. India also expressed valid concerns direct to the Sri Lankan government. While there were protests and reports by the Amnesty International and Human Rights Watch on the deteriorating situation, the EU was the first to put pressure on Sri Lanka with its economic muscle over the country.

The government called for surrender to terminate offensive and even declared several amnesties to the LTTE. For the benefit of the civilians, 'safe zones' were declared although maintaining them 'safe' was a difficult task. The EU pressure was for the government to declare an unconditional ceasefire. In early February there were several large scale protest marches in France, Germany, UK and Switzerland mainly by the Tamil Diaspora. In March, the Office of the UN Human Rights Commissioner directly accused the government. The government in turn accused the LTTE for using civilians a human shield.

During the Sinhala and Tamil New Year in mid April 2009, the government suspended military action to allow the civilians to escape from war torn areas. It was only a partial success as the LTTE forces were holding them as hostages. The highlights of the pressure tactic by Western governments during the period were the visit of the British Foreign Secretary, David Miliband and the French Foreign Minister, Bernard Kouchner, to Colombo in late April. The pressure however was not that successful. The request was for a complete ceasefire and even there were rumors in Colombo that some Western forces were planning to rescue the LTTE leaders. It is possible that the Western pressure – unconstructive as it was - in fact compelled the government to expedite the military operations leading to the complete liquidation of the LTTE leadership by 18 May 2009 whether some of them were ready to surrender or not.

Reaction of the Diaspora

It is a well known and a well accepted fact that political solidarities exist beyond borders. These solidarities are obviously strong when they are linked to common ethnicity or religion. Often these solidarities are called 'trans-border nationalism' and intermittently they show even irredentist tendencies.[8]

The Tamil population in Sri Lanka is around 3.1 million and in South India around 62 million. While this has been a concern for Sinhala nationalists after independence or even before, there is a degree of acceptance of this solidarity in the country today considering its obvious nature and circumstances. The solidarity has also fluctuated over time and two noteworthy peaks of camaraderie have been around 1983 and 1987. It is not clear however whether there was solidarity in the same intensity during 2009 when the final battle between the two parties took place. It may be possible that on the recent instance in 2009 there were other forces moderating the influence or solidarity to a greater extent unlike in the past.

While there are still around 60,000 Sri Lankan Tamils in exile living in South India, the main Diaspora that we refer to here are in Europe and North America. Elsewhere, except South Africa, the numbers appear insignificant. From Colombo, the distance to Chennai is merely 682 km and from Killinochchi it is even less at 328 km. Nevertheless, the reactions and protests came from the 'long distance places' such as London, Paris, Geneva, Toronto, Sydney and San Francisco. Distance from Colombo to London is 8,714 km, Paris 8,518 km, Toronto 14,027 km and San Francisco 14,547 km. It is interesting to probe this phenomenon and its distinction from Chennai.

Apart from what was mentioned earlier as 'moderating Indian factors,' there were other reasons why trans-border nationalism has subsided or subsiding between India and Sri Lanka. In trans-border nationalism, which may be common to Diaspora as well, it is often one's own political grievances that lead to external solidarity. With federalism and devolution, and other measures in India, it appears that Tamil nationalist grievances in South India have subsided. Second and perhaps

---

[8] Rogers Brubaker, *Nationalism Reframed: Nationhood and the National Question in the New Europe*, (Cambridge: Cambridge University Press, 1996), p. 5

more important is what Kishore Mahbubani has argued.[9] It is the growing economy, liberalization and more expanded life opportunities that have changed the mindset of the ordinary people in Tamil Nadu. Added to this is the nature of the LTTE that many well meaning Diaspora elements failed to grasp or conveniently ignored.

There are many reasons why strong Diaspora reactions came about when the LTTE was about to be defeated, or before and even after. The Tamil Diaspora in the West was the main lifeline of the LTTE for some time. The bottom line perhaps was the numbers. It is estimated that there are around 700,000 Tamils who left Sri Lanka with some bitterness after the events in 1983 who now live in major capitals in the West and North America.[10] The number estimated for Canada is 250,000, United Kingdom- 150,000, France- 65,000 and Germany- 60,000 and Australia-53,000. Although the number in the United States is only 35,000 and scattered, nevertheless, the groups were well organized by the LTTE.[11] Many of the Diaspora groups are concentrated in capital cities, Toronto being one of the main centers in North America. In addition, there are over two million Tamils from India who are in these countries and there are organizations which bring them together on a common platform.

There are many other or more profound reasons linked to the present age. As Benedict Anderson has argued, "electronic communications, combined with the huge migrations created by the present world-economic system, are creating a virulent new form of nationalism, which I call long-distance nationalism."[12] While commenting on the "Canadian 'Tamils' in supporting the murderous Tigers of Jaffna," he also noted,

---

[9] Kishore Mahbubani, *The New Asian Hemisphere: The Irresistible Shift of Global Power to the East*, Public Affairs Program, New York, 2008, p. 11-14 .

[10] Dhananjayan Sriskandarajah, "Tamil Diaspora Politics," *Encyclopedia of Diasporas*, Springer, 2005. p. 492.

[11] It is believed that around 45 LTTE offices still function in the US. Rohan Guneratna before the Lesson Learnt and Reconciliation Commission. *Sunday Observer*, 14 November 2010.

[12] Benedict Anderson, "Western Nationalism and Eastern Nationalism: Is there a difference that matters?" *New Left Review* 9, May-June 2001 available online at http://www.newleftreview.org/?page=artivle&view=2320

"But there are millions of other long-distance ethno-nationalists who are by no means necessarily committed to fanaticism and violence."[13] Then what made some of the Tamil Diaspora committed to LTTE fanaticism and violence?

There cannot be much dispute that political activism of the Tamil Diaspora was controlled by the LTTE until recently and even today. No other Tamil party was allowed to function by them in many countries. The Tamil Diaspora undoubtedly was not a total creation of the LTTE. The July 1983 riots against the Tamils and the ensuing war between the government forces and the LTTE were the main reasons. However, the process of seeking asylum abroad, except perhaps initially in India, has had a particular pattern and most of the efforts were coordinated by the LTTE. Or in other words, the LTTE networks in Diaspora emerged out of this process. The LTTE created easy avenues for the Tamils to migrate and professional human traffickers were employed for the task.

It was mainly from these sources that the protests came when the government of Sri Lanka intensified its military actions against the LTTE in early 2009. There were major demonstrations in South Africa, Australia, New Zealand, Washington DC, New York, San Francisco, London, Paris and Geneva. In London, the protesters occupied the Westminster square for several hours in April 2009. In Canada, a 'human chain' surrounded a large part of downtown Toronto.[14]

There was a strong reaction on the part of the Tamil Diaspora when the LTTE was defeated in May 2009. The following is a glimpse of what was reported on the BBC website. "We are very angry and every single Tamil is crying over this victory? The Sri Lankan government has merely made a territorial gain at the moment. There are LTTE supporters all over the place and all over the world. Unless we have a solution for the Tamil people, this problem will continue." [15]

---

[13] ibid.

[14] Karen Parker before the US Senate Committee on Foreign Relations, 24 February 2009 available online at http://www.tamilnet.com/art.html?catid=13&artid=28525

[15] Vasuki Muruhathas, Lawyer, London in "Voices: Tamil Diaspora in shock", BBC News, 19 May 2009 available online at http://news.bbc.co.uk/2/hi/south_asia/8056176.stm.

The above perhaps was a 'general feeling' of the Tamil Diaspora irrespective of whether they directly supported the LTTE or not. Today everyone knows that the government's victory is not merely a 'territorial gain.' The point is that, whatever the myths, illusions and ideals that govern any nationalism, in the long run, the people have to come to grips with realities if they want to make an impact in politics and improve the fate of their destinies. However this might take time.

An important question is, what factors led to this Diaspora activism which sustained LTTE terrorism for such a long period of time? Apart from what can be called the 'long distance nationalism,' it appears that certain dislocations related to the host country also were responsible for Diaspora activism. The difficulties in accessing desirable employment, feeling of alienation in a different cultural setting and perhaps the felt discrimination in the new society were some of the reasons for continued activism. Nevertheless, 'long distance nationalism' is still strong. This became evident when the LTTE activists managed to force the Oxford Union to cancel President Rajapaksa's scheduled address on the 2 December 2010. Apart from the World Tamil Forum (WTF) and its counterpart, the British Tamil Forum (BTF), it is reported that several of British politicians were involved in the protests organized at the Heathrow airport and in front of the Dorchester Hotel where President was staying.[16]

Reactions of the NGOs

There has been an obvious sympathy for Tamil militancy from non-governmental organizations within the country and abroad at the beginning of these movements. Apart from human rights concerns, a certain ideological affinity was the reason. The state was an antagonistic institution for both movements and most often the NGO functionaries came from radical or left wing orientations. After the demise of socialism, many of the radical intellectuals who were at the helms of non-governmental organizations both nationally and internationally were easily

---

[16] Hemantha Abeywardena, "The Scale of Protest against President Rajapaksa: Strom in Ceylon Tea Cup," *Asian Tribune*, 5 December 2010.

attracted towards radical nationalism, ethnic rights and more particularly the theory of self determination. There were undoubtedly other elements in the NGO sectors who were either with a missionary seal or strong legal positivist orientation who perceived issues in a rather 'black and white' manner without due consideration for a country's socio-economic context or historical evolution.

In the 1980s, the human rights concerns that they advocated were largely valid. Since 1977, there had been a pattern of attacks against the Tamil residents in Colombo and suburbs and in the Hill country, almost every two years, culminating in a major onslaught in 1983, killing around 2,000 and displacing over 80,000 people which strengthened the militant claims for a separate state. It was in this context that the nexus between the Tamil militancy and the NGO sector was first created and at time there were other organizations apart from the LTTE who were active in the international scene. However thereafter, the situation significantly changed particularly in respect of the Tamil community and the good offices of the Indian government was largely responsible for the changed situation. The change also came, to an extent, at the expense of the Sinhala youth militancy. There were different types of human rights violations in the late 1980s in the South but the NGOs or the international community in general was not so concerned about the overall situation.

The above prognosis, if correct, gives rise to serious concerns about the credibility and objectivity of the international non-governmental organizations. While the number killed in 1983 were around 2,000, during 1987-89 at least over 30,000 were confirmed to have disappeared. There were organizations who were concerned about the latter situation but they were mainly investigative organizations without much muscle for influencing the policy of the UN and thereby the government of Sri Lanka.[17]

By the end of 1980s, the LTTE had completely hegemonised the militant movement virtually eliminating all the rival factions from

[17] Eduardo Marino, Political Killings in Southern Sri Lanka. (London: International Alert, 1989), Pages. 8-11.

effective involvement in politics in the country or abroad. However this was not a concern for the NGOs or the international community who were supposed to bring a reasonable solution to the conflict in Sri Lanka. Equally important is their rather non committal position on the Indo-Sri Lanka solution to the ethnic conflict and Tamil grievances in the form of extensive devolution of power through a constitutional amendment. If the international community was firm and supported the Indo-Lanka solution at that time, persuading or forcing the LTTE to accept it, perhaps the unfortunate incidents later or prolongation of the war could possibly have been avoided.

A major mistake by the international non-governmental organizations at that time was to focus their critical and corrective eye only on the state or state actors virtually ignoring what the non state actors or even the terrorist organizations had been indulging in. This came about by following purely a positivist legal approach to human rights with slightly a prejudicial view on the Third World state. Norway compiled an annual report on *Human Rights in Developing Countries* covering selected countries including Sri Lanka. It was only at later stages that this mistake was recognized, thanks to the Human Rights Centre at the University of Oslo. Some of the international NGOs like the Amnesty International followed suit but even then their 'shaming or blaming' was quite unbalanced until today leaving the impression that the states are solely or largely be responsible for human rights violations in Third World countries. In practice the approach encouraged and gave way to the propaganda by anti-state forces to gather political momentum against these countries.

There was no international effort to prevent the break out of the Eelam War II in mid-1990s despite the fact that almost all the main elements for a reasonable political settlement were incorporated in the Indo-Lanka solution. When over 2,000 Indian peace keeping soldiers were killed, no international organization considered it as a war crime. The LTTE began the Eelam War II with a massacre of 600 unarmed policemen in the East. Few months into the events, nearly 30,000

Muslims were forced to flee Jaffna with only 24 hours notice, reminding how Pol Pot evacuated Phnom Penh in 1975. The effort here is not to relate all the 'war crimes' that the LTTE apparently had committed during their war effort, but to highlight that the international community was by and large silent on these instances. The situation was the same when both the Eelam War III and the Eelam War IV broke out. No substantive international effort was made to prevent these outbreaks other than calling for ceasefire and negotiations.

It has to be admitted that it was the legitimate right and the duty of the Sri Lankan state on behalf of its citizens to free or liberate the country from terrorism, following of course the domestic as well as international legal norms governing the conduct of such kind of operations. This was exactly the situation when Eelam War IV was precipitated by the LTTE, closing the sluice gates of Mavilaru in July 2006 and depriving water for over 30,000 families in the East. By that time it had been estimated that nearly 90,000 people had already died because of the three cycles of separatist war since July 1983.

There cannot be any doubt that deviations from international norms or domestic law must have occurred but there is no evidence or indication so far to say that major violations have taken place or violations were committed intentionally. Some unauthentic reports from UN sources claimed the demise of around 7,000 civilians during the last stages of the war, but the experts on the events estimate the civilian deaths to be not more than 2,000.[18] As the armed forces were quite strong in numbers and the morale was high with victory at hand the excesses in any frenzy would have been minimal. Although no key leader was found to be alive, it is exceedingly possible, that given their ideology, that all fought to the end. LTTE is the movement which invented suicide bombers and the cyanide capsule to prevent capture or surrender. Apart from the leaders, over 12,000 fighting cadres were captured or surrendered including middle rung leaders during the last stages of the war.

---

[18] Rohan Gunaratne before the LLRC, *Sunday Observer*, 14 November 2010.

While the government has appointed a Lessons Learnt and Reconciliation Commission (LLRC) to probe into these and other matters, what has prevented a genuine dialogue between Sri Lanka and the rest of the world on this matter is the unfounded accusations, threats of war crimes and similar charges which might give rise to the resurrection of the LTTE.[19] The most vociferous has been the International Crisis Group (ICG). It issued a report on "War Crimes in Sri Lanka" exactly after a year of the end of the war in May 2009 and called for a war crime investigation by the UN. The tone of the report was quite punitive as if it has found the truth and it has the necessary authority over the Sri Lankan government. For any reasonable Sri Lankan, the tone might be quite distasteful. In the executive summary of the Report it says, that "evidence gathered by the International Crisis Group suggests that these months saw tens of thousands of Tamil civilian men, women, children and elderly killed, countless more wounded, and hundreds of thousands deprived of adequate food and medical care, resulting in more deaths".[20]

However, nowhere in the report does it say or indicate how these figures have been arrived at. 'Tens of thousands' or 'hundreds of thousands' do not mean any exact figure or even an approximation. They are inflated figures even from what has been said about 7,000 civilian deaths earlier on. After accusing "top government and military leaders potentially responsible" for war crimes, the report says in passing that "there is evidence of war crimes committed by the LTTE and leaders as well" followed by the rather gleeful mention that "most of them were killed and never faced justice."

The language of the report appears quite rhetoric and whenever it refers to an alleged violation, it adds almost as a ritual "men, women, children and elderly" into the picture. There are over fifty instances in a

---

[19] There are other quarters who have expressed concern. The group of Elders has been among them including Kofi Annan, Mary Robinson and Martti Ahtisaari. Careful study of their statement in August 2010 might highlight the enormous gap of perception between the 'insiders' and the 'outsiders.' Some of the violations that they attribute completely are unknown to the present author .

[20] International Crisis Group, *War Crimes in Sri Lanka*, Asia Report No. 191, 17 May 2010.

48 page document where this phrase has been used. Intentional shelling of civilians, hospitals and humanitarian operations are the main charges against the government and the LTTE is accused of killing or wounding 'many' civilians and inflicting suffering on them without giving numbers. It is abundantly clear that if there is any empirical basis for this report, it came from the LTTE sources with little evidence here and there from some civilians.

The most outrageous are the recommendations. It rather commands the Sri Lankan government to "Cooperate fully with international efforts to investigate alleged war crimes." It recommends the government to "Try LTTE cadres suspected of war crimes in open court with international oversight or release them if there is insufficient evidence." It asks several governments including India not to "extradite LTTE suspects to Sri Lanka unless there are guarantees of humane treatment," but requests "target sanctions, including travel restrictions on Sri Lankan officials and members of their families, unless and until the government cooperates with international efforts to investigate alleged war crimes." There are no recommendations whatsoever to sanction the LTTE activities in these or other countries.

It is a known fact that several of international non governmental organizations have come to the aid of the remaining LTTE outfits to carry on their work in different guises directly and indirectly. It is also known that several organizations in fact have distanced themselves from the LTTE and even the Sri Lankan issue. When the Provisional Transnational Government for Tamil Eelam was first mooted in July 2009, the Swiss NGO, the SOS Racism was the first to declare its support to the outfit.[21]

Perhaps most worrying is what Robert Templer, International Crisis Group's Asia Program Director said in February 2010. After releasing the

---

[21] It's General Secretary, Karl Grunberg declared "Despite exile, repression, disappearances, ethnic cleansing or, more accurately, because of these evils, the rights of the Tamil people have to be protected. The right of the Tamil people neither to be oppressed nor discriminated, their right for self determination, all their basic human rights and the humanitarian law have to be ensured them in Sri Lanka and abroad."

latest report from the ICG on *The Sri Lankan Diaspora after the LTTE*, he stated quite admirably that "new Diaspora initiatives attempt to carry forward the struggle for an independent state in more transparent and democratic ways." He has noted his only disagreement as "but they must repudiate the LTTE's violent methods."[22] What is missing here and in many NGO perceptions is that the connection between the LTTE's violent methods or terrorism and the separatist objectives.

Government and UN Responses

The reactions of foreign governments or the UN to the last stages of the conflict in Sri Lanka have been significantly different to the Diaspora or the NGO sector. They also differ with each other in the sense that some were more understanding of the position of the Sri Lankan government than others. The most empathetic of the situation undoubtedly was India. The government of Sri Lanka made it abundantly sure that all necessary information and details were communicated to the Indian government. This was also the case with Pakistan but to a lesser extent. Although China did not have a direct stake or close interest on the issue, as a matter of friendship or strategic concern the country gave its fullest support and cooperation in defeating the LTTE. Russia also supported the Government having had a similar experience with Chechen guerillas.

The West was significantly different and Japan by and large followed the same line as a co-chair of the peace process along with Norway, the US and EU. Their positions and reactions were to a large extent understandable. It is possible that many of the Western countries did not anticipate a complete defeat of the LTTE and perhaps thought that a stalemate might occur in the last stages when a ceasefire might be in order and the stalled peace process could be restarted. This was in fact a miscalculation.

There were repeated calls for ceasefire from Western governments

---

[22] Thomson Reuters Foundation, Alert Net, 23 February 2010.

[23] On 23 January, Germany called for ceasefire and EU followed suit on 23 February.

and the UN officials since January 2009, more intensified than before.[23] The abrogation of the Ceasefire Agreement (CFA) signed between the GOSL and the LTTE in February 2002 was a major concern. There were around 300,000 civilians trapped in the conflict zone and they were largely used by the LTTE as a human shield. The situation was considered a humanitarian crisis but it was clear that the process of conflict perhaps had reached the 'point of no return.' A request by Mexico to address the issue in the Security Council was not allowed by Russia. Therefore, there was no debate on the situation of Sri Lanka in the highest body of the UN.

It is perhaps with this realistic assessment of the situation, that many governments and UN officials, more particularly the Secretary General, tried their best to minimize the damage to the civilians. The government of Sri Lanka, on the other hand, appeared to fulfill major humanitarian concerns of the international community. Although both matters are controversial and disputed, it is in addressing these concerns that the government placed a moratorium on the use of heavy weapons and created no-fire zones with major efforts at rescuing the trapped civilians. A better understanding was created when the Foreign Ministers of Britain and France met President Rajapaksa in April 2009 just several weeks before the final battle ended, although the Swedish Minister could not be accommodated.

If one needs to take a look at the general world opinion on the defeat of terrorism or the LTTE, however one may want to characterize it, the best way is to study the resolution at the UN Human Rights Council on 27 May 2009 which was adopted with a record of 29 to 12, with 6 abstentions. Some of the salient elements of the resolution might be quoted. It categorically reaffirmed "the respect for the sovereignty, territorial integrity and independence of Sri Lanka and its sovereign rights to protect its citizens and to combat terrorism." Then it condemned "all attacks that the Liberation Tigers of Tamil Eelam launched on the civilian population and its practice of using civilians as human shields." It welcomed "the conclusion of hostilities and the liberation by the Government of Sri Lanka of tens of thousands of its citizens that were kept by the Liberation Tigers of Tamil Eelam against their will as hostages, as well as the efforts by the Government to ensure the safety and security of all Sri Lankans and to bring permanent peace to the country."

There were 12 recommendations in the resolution for the Sri Lankan government and the international community to follow. In conclusion it urged "the international community to cooperate with the Government of Sri Lanka in the reconstruction efforts, including by increasing the provision of financial assistance, official development assistance, to help the country fight poverty and underdevelopment and to continue to ensure the promotion and protection of all human rights, including economic, social and cultural rights."

Since the end of the war in May 2009, there has been certain pressure exerted on Sri Lanka by some Western governments for several and different reasons. One immediate concern was the internally displaced people and their situation. The most concerned country of course was India and its approach, like on many other issues appeared to be different to the Western approaches. The IDP issue or the humanitarian issues in general are professional issues for the UN and their concerns were rather valid which the government did its best to accommodate. More importantly, as the war ended and apparently the LTTE was out of the scene, the Western governments opted to exert pressure on Sri Lanka to resolve what was understood as the Tamil national question. An immediate political solution was their demand. However, the government has taken the position that for a comprehensive political solution, the country might need some time to weigh all the issues and concerns. The President has quipped that forging a political solution 'is not like producing instant noodles.' More elaborately, he stated to the UN General Assembly that "the entire focus of our nation is now on building a lasting peace; healing wounds, ensuring economic prosperity and guaranteeing the rights of the whole nation to live in harmony. We are mindful that in order to fulfill these aspirations, economic development and political reconciliation

---

[24] President Mahinda Rajapaksa, United Nations 65th General Assembly, 23 September 2010.

must go hand in hand.[24]

There are other issues of contention and most of all are the so-called war crime charges. Apart from the ICG Report in May 2010, that we have already commented on was the Report of the US Department of State to the Congress on "Incidents during the Recent Conflict in Sri Lanka." Unlike the ICG Report, it categorically stated that "The United States recognizes a state's inherent right to defend itself from armed attacks, including those by non-state actors such as terrorist groups." It also stated that "The United States also expects states and non-state actors to comply with their international legal obligations." The report related the matters of 'children in armed conflict,' 'harm to civilians and civil objects,' 'killing of captives or combatants seeking to surrender,' 'disappearances' and 'humanitarian conditions.'

The 69 page document however stated "This report compiles alleged incidents that transpired in the final stages of the war, which may constitute violations of IHL or crimes against humanity and related harm." It further said, "the report does not reach legal conclusions as to whether the incidents described herein actually constitute violations of IHL, crimes against humanity or other violations of international law." It also stated that "Nor does it reach conclusions concerning whether the alleged incidents detailed herein actually occurred."

It is also important to note the observations and recommendations by the Foreign Relations Committee of the US Senate on the broader subject of US-Sri Lanka relations, dated 9 December 2009, and titled "Sri Lanka: Re-charting US Strategy after the War." It stated that "As Western countries became increasingly critical of the Sri Lankan Government's handling of the war and human rights record, the Rajapaksa leadership cultivated ties with such countries as Burma, China, Iran and Libya…" "This strategic drift will have consequences for U.S. interests in the region. Along with our legitimate humanitarian and political concerns, U.S. policymakers have tended to underestimate Sri Lanka's geo-strategic importance for American interests. Sri Lanka is located at the nexus of crucial maritime trading routes in the Indian Ocean connecting Europe and the Middle East to China and the rest of Asia…." The final conclusion in essence was to say that "The United States cannot afford to 'lose' Sri Lanka…"

It is in the above context that the appointment of the UN Panel of Experts to advice the Secretary General on 'accountability' issues should be viewed. It is understandable that the UN cannot simply ignore the 'final stages' of the war given their magnitude and the intensity and also the ferocity of the non-state actor involved. This is irrespective of the emotional charges leveled against the government by the Diaspora or the self-serving accusations of some non-governmental organizations. It is customary of the UN to examine the comparative compliance of international law, of course with exceptions or discretion applied in the case of 'big powers,' on cases such as Sri Lanka. While the government appointed LLRC might appease many of the concerns of the international community, it might be in order to submit 'at least one comprehensive official explanation' before the UN Panel by the government of Sri Lanka. As the Chairman of the LLRC has already stated, "If there were atrocities, the government too must apologize."[25]

Conclusions

This chapter is limited to an overview on external reactions to the internal conflict in Sri Lanka, particularly during the last stages of the war. It examined and reviewed three main layers of reactions from (1) the Sri Lankan Tamil Diaspora (2) the international non-governmental organizations and (3) the governments of the West and the UN.

While it may be the case that 'trans-border nationalism' between Sri Lanka and South India is changing in a positive direction, the Diaspora nationalism or the 'long distance nationalism' of the Tamil community abroad is still strong and may pose a challenge to the dual purpose of 'reconciliation and development' in the country. While there are so many

---

[25] *Sunday Island*, 24 October 2010 available online at http://www.island.lk/ index.php? page_cat=article-details&page=article-details&code_title=9674 accessed on 7 May 2011

reasons why the Diaspora sentiments by and large are still bitter, the best breakthrough to change the situation might be through efforts at reconstruction and political engagement with all concerned sections within the country particularly in the North and the East. The effort of political engagement also should be extended to where the Diaspora live, taking measures to make them engage in development efforts in the country at large, not confining to the North or the East.

It might be the case that the attitudes or the approaches of many non-governmental organizations would not be possible to change in the foreseeable future particularly on human rights. There is an apparent failure on their part at least to listen to the views of others on human rights. This might not mean that all accusations that they make are factually incorrect. There is a failure to appreciate the human rights conditions in countries in a holistic manner and to devise measures to improve them in a constructive way. Apart from some elements of double standards, the punitive approach alone will not work. What Sri Lanka could do is to have patience, ignore the offenses, and try to put forward its views and analysis objectively before the 'international community,' whatever the 'community' means.

Some of the reactions of the Western governments during as well as after the last stages of the war are largely understandable. They in fact were modest and helpful. As shown in this chapter, these views however are not necessarily the 'world opinion.' While the Sri Lankan government may ignore or resist what appear to be 'interferences,' there is a need to constructively engage with these governments for the betterment of our own society and betterment of the world community. The most important is to engage with the UN on matters that have been raised and pursued.

SRI LANKA: TRANS-BORDER CONSEQUENCES OF AN INTERNAL CONFLICT

N. Sathiya Moorthy

Despite the general perception to the contrary, the political and electoral impact of the ethnic issue, violence and war in Sri Lanka on neighbouring India, particularly southern Tamil Nadu, was and is much less than on the security front – and for more reasons than one.

Possibly, nowhere else in the world has an internal conflict of the kind has had its wide-ranging and continuing impact on other nations, their peoples, polity and governments as the ethnic issue, war and violence in Sri Lanka. The trans-border impact and consequences of the conflict was, and continues to have had its direct political impact across the world wherever the Sri Lankan Tamil Diaspora has taken roots since the 'ethnic issue' hit the roof in the mid-Fifties. The vibrancy and enterprise of the Diaspora community combined with years of State assault on their legal and constitutional rights ensured that the insults, injuries and images that they carried with them overseas did catalyse a new public awareness and political thinking in host-nations. It was thus that much of Europe, including the UK across the English Channel, the US, Canada and Australia, not to leave out the nations of South-East Asia, with their varied forms of governments and political administration, became a part of the 'ethnic problem' for the Sri Lankan State, though not always a part of the solution, which anyway was eluding the stake-holders. The UN was not left out, either, particularly in the concluding stages of 'Eelam War IV' (2006-09), when the Sri Lankan State forces trounced the LTTE, and eliminated their iconic leader, Velupillai Prabhakaran. Better or worse still, at a crucial stage in the war, the Sri Lankan Government began acting on indications that the propagandists of the LTTE may have neutralised the Government of Eritrea, for the latter to confer legitimacy on a separate 'Tamil Eelam' State if and when the militant outfit were to declare one. Reports indicated that the Colombo Government may have neutralised such efforts through diplomatic channels – though it could not succeed as much in dousing the flames of human rights violations and political solution to the ethnic issue that the Diaspora Tamils could whip up on the streets of western nations – and through that their political class, who had become as much dependent on their votes as that of any other immigrant/local community for winning elections at different levels.

It did not end there, however. Even in countries where the Sri Lankan Tamil Diaspora did not have any substantial presence or influence, as in South Africa, the Tamil-speaking citizenry from the common Indian roots provided a platform for their financial and other illegal trades that were aimed at funding an ethnic war back home. When the war peaked in the 2006-09 period, even such nations became central to the political campaign of the Sri Lankan Tamils in regions of the world where they did not have any substantial presence earlier. So much so, when the Tamils of Indian Origin in Malaysia became part of a larger agitation of a larger Indian migrant population in the country, the local Government agencies would identify some leaders of their Hindu Rights Action Force (HINDRAF) movement as allies of the Liberation Tigers of Tamil Eelam (LTTE), the militant group that was using both conventional war and terrorist attacks in their fight for a separate 'homeland' in Sri Lanka. No proof of such linkages were either sought – or, exactly given. It was taken for granted, so to say. So in the post-war situation in Sri Lanka after the death of LTTE supremo Velupillai Prabhakaran in May 2009, the Sri Lankan State mainly turned its security focus to South-East Asia. Not very long after, they had in their custody, Kumaran Pathmanathan *alias* 'KP', whom Prabhakaran resurrected from the sidelines, to name him the head of the international division of the LTTE, when certain defeat on the war front was already staring him on the face in Sri Lanka.

Impact on India

However, the larger, greater and immediate impact continues to be felt mainly in and by northern Indian neighbour, particularly in and through the south Indian State of Tamil Nadu, its polity and society. It is but natural for any nation in the neighbourhood of another nation in distress having to absorb certain fallout, whether they are of natural disasters like earthquakes, floods or even a tsunami, or of man-made conflicts like insurgencies and terrorism. As the centre-piece of South Asian geo-political architecture and socio-economic changes influenced by, and influencing the global evolutionary processes in these areas, India could not have hoped to be otherwise. It already had its own share of inherent problems visiting and revisiting the nation and the peoples from the days of Independence and Partition, when the post-war colonial British rulers decided to reassess their positions and possessions, and return home before the consequences of their continued occupation became too strong to repel, and too weak to ignore. The creation of Pakistan (1947) first, and the birth of Bangladesh later (1971) meant that India was involved in the birth of two nations in less than three decades. Even where it was not a party or direct stake-holder in the birth of Bangladesh, India got involved – in more ways than one.

The fallout of such perceptions and actions continue to be felt by India in the form of cross-border terrorism. A defeated/defeatist Pakistan leadership, already suffering from the perceived baggage of Partition, chose cross-border terrorism as a tool of containment of perceived Indian expansionism or whatever. Even without the creation of Bangladesh, India had faced insurgency, in the North and the North-East, aided and assisted by nations like China and Pakistan since birth. Yet, the insurgents in these cases were mostly Indian nationals, given to wrong advice and methods. That cannot be said about Jammu and Kashmir in particular, where from the word go, the involvement of Pakistani nationals, taking the name of *razakars*, or 'revolutionaries', had actively participated in the half-successful insurgency/war of the late Forties. Thus was born 'Pakistan-occupied Kashmir'. Over the years, particularly since Pakistan re-drew its strategy and tactics for 'dealing' with India, the border State of Jammu and Kashmir – and a few other parts of India – have been the victim of the involvement of both Pakistani and 'non-Pakistani, non-Indian' terrorists in action within India's territorial borders. The early wave of Pakistan-induced terrorism in the northern border State of Punjab first, and Jammu and Kashmir later, also saw the forced migration of a section of the local population from their homes into refugee camps run by the State.

It is however in the case of Sri Lanka that India's politico-administrative engagement and socio-emotional involvement have remained long and continuous in more direct terms than in the case of Bangladesh, which India had helped in the creation and legitimisation. It is true that the 'Bangladesh issue' at birth involved the forced exodus of a million people from then East Pakistan into adjoining States in India. Their socio-political impact continues to be felt in States like West Bengal and Assam, where the induction of 'foreigners' into the job-market and voters' list have had their far-reaching consequences. The exodus strained the finances of the Indian States in a critical time of its economic history, to begin with, unprepared as the Governments at the Centre and the State of West Bengal were, for housing and feeding those million people, tending and caring to them as only fellow human beings should and could do. Yet, it was also the cause and justification for India having to intervene directly – the anticipation having prepared the nation and the people for what is now known as the 'Bangladesh War' of 1971. India having recognised Bangladesh at birth only months earlier in the same year, it could also be described as the only war in which India got directly involved on behalf of a friendly, beleaguered neighbour. The Indian military engagement in Sri Lanka was to follow years later, in 1987.

History and Historicity

As is known, the linkages between India and Sri Lanka date back to centuries, if not more! The great Indian epic *'Ramayana'* speaks about a god-in-human form from India annihilating a King of Lanka after the latter had coveted his wife and taken her prisoner. According to Buddhist chronicles in Sri Lanka, Mahinda and Sangamitta (or, Mahendra and

Sangamitra, the children of Emperor Ashoka of Kalinga, now forming part of the East Indian State of Orissa) had taken the religion to the island-nation. Sinhala-Buddhists across Sri Lanka revere the 'Bo' tree in Kandy, as the representation of one that Princess Sangamitta had brought with her, after the Buddha was believed to have attained *'nirvana'*, or spiritual salvation, under the mother-tree. Centuries later in the post-Christendom, the Chola Kings from southern Tamil Nadu had sent out naval expeditions to Sri Lanka while the Sinhala rulers were known to have taken brides from the Pandya and Pallava royalty. The shared history of the Tamil-speaking people in the two countries is as much a reality as their shared origins, religion, culture and language are still unclear. In more recent centuries, the increasing exchanges involving the Tamils of recent Indian Origin, taken to what was then Ceylon under the common British ruler, as interred labour to man the tea plantations in the central highlands of the island-nation are well documented. So is the continuing familial and trade linkages between the Tamil-speaking Muslim communities across the Palk Strait.

Independence for India on 15 August 1947 and for Sri Lanka a few months later on 4 February 1948 redrew national boundaries on the shared seas, and thus introduced legal restrictions that were unknown to the people of these parts all along. The 'ethnic war' since the mid-Eighties in the island-nation complicated issues and concerns for the security forces in the two countries, particularly after the LTTE acquired maritime and naval capabilities. Suffice is to point out that even at the commencement of the ethnic strife that followed the anti-Tamil pogrom in Sri Lanka in July 1983, the affected population could and did rush to the Indian shores in whatever passed for a boat, with the hope and confidence that their Tamil and non-Tamil brethren across the Palk Strait would be for them – as they did. So much so, at the height of the refugee influx, Tamil Nadu housed close to 250,000 Tamils from Sri Lanka, in special camps put up by the State Government with aid and assistance from the Union Government. The rest, as they say, is history, until the assassination of Rajiv Gandhi, the former Indian Prime Minister tipped to return to power at the end of the elections that were already under way, by an

LTTE suicide-bomber, reversed the mood in Tamil Nadu and rest of India in 1991. However, in more recent years and months, the conclusive 'Eelam War IV' in Sri Lanka did trigger fresh anxiety in the Tamil population in India and the polity elsewhere in the country, too, on the ultimate fate that awaited their linguistic brethren in Sri Lanka. If however such anxieties did not turn out into sure-support for the LTTE-centric propaganda that was as high-pitched as it was unconnected with the immediate priorities of the local population, it was not without reason. Results of the federal parliamentary polls from Tamil Nadu in May 2009 showed that sympathy for the suffering populace in Sri Lanka should not be confused with support for the methodology of the LTTE, then claiming to be the 'sole representative' of the latter.

India and the two 'JVP Insurgencies'

The LTTE-centric war, violence and terrorism were not the only ones to imperil Sri Lanka since Independence. Before it, and alongside, too, there were the two 'JVP-led insurgencies', in 1971 and 1987-89. On both occasions, the militant-left, Janatha Vimukthi Peramuna, or the People's Liberation Front, launched insurgency operations aimed at upsetting the State and targeting government property and leaders, as also civilians, alike. Neither had any direct impact, nor did they evoke any Indian interest other than at the official-level, as became the case with the ethnic issue, war and violence. There was no public response to the JVP-led insurgencies in India, one way or the other, despite the fact that the first such insurgency of 1971 also coincided with the emergence of the left-militant Naxalite movement across the country, including the south Indian States of Tamil Nadu (then Madras), Kerala and Andhra Pradesh. Tamil Nadu also witnessed massive anti-Naxalite police action during the Eighties but that again had nothing to do with the second JVP insurgency in Sri Lanka that was to follow only years later.

On both occasions, the official reaction/contribution from India ended up helping the Sri Lankan State put down left militancy in the country. During the first insurgency of 1971, a Colombo Government caught unaware, appealed to India for military help, and New Delhi obliged by sending Indian Air Force (IAF) helicopters, for the Sri Lankan troops to fight the insurgents. During 1987-89, the induction of the Indian Peace-Keeping Force (IPKF) into the Tamil-speaking North and East in Sri Lanka was accompanied by a mandated de-induction of the Sri Lankan troops from those parts. These troops were then deployed in the Sinhala-speaking areas where the second JVP insurgency was brewing, particularly in opposition to the India-Sri Lanka Accord, which had made the IPKF induction possible in the first place.

While the JVP's political stance against India is well known, and it continues to remain a key element in the party's five-point charter even after it had shed militancy as a creed, post-'89, there was, and is, nothing to suggest that the left-leaning JVP had any deep association or linkages with any anti-India militant force in India. Whatever ties were there, they were confined to the political Left in India, particularly the CPI. However, in the light of the JVP's position on the 'ethnic issue' in Sri Lanka, the CPI chose not to extend the customary invitation to the JVP, for the party's State convention in Tamil Nadu and the national conference in 2008-09. Yet, neither the political, nor the militant impact of the internal conflict in Sri Lanka pertaining to the 'JVP insurgency' was felt in India, particularly the southern States, where access was theoretically possible for the JVP cadres on the run during 1987-89. Nothing of the sort seemed to have happened - not certainly on a scale that demanded public attention and governmental notice in India. Even if there were stray cases of JVP cadres and leaders wanted by the Sri Lankan security agencies escaping to/through India, there numbers were a handful, if at all – and were no way comparable to the massive exodus witnessed at the height of Sri Lanka's anti-Tamil Pogrom of 1983. This was so despite the claims that as many pro-JVP Sinhala youth, particularly boys and girls in their college-going age, had fallen victim to the two years of the anti-insurgency operations in 1987-89, as have died in the 'ethnic war' that lasted three decades. Their numbers are put at around 75,000 each.

Of course, the collateral damage suffered by the civilian Tamil population may be more in the case of the 'ethnic war' than was with the 'JVP insurgencies', but at focus here is the cross-border impact of an internal conflict. In comparison, the trans-border consequences of internal conflicts across India's land borders in the North, West and the East have been continual and consequential. The best example is that of the 'Bangladesh movement'. Right from the creation of a separate nation to more recent times, along the Chittagong Hills, internal conflicts in the erstwhile East Pakistan, first, and Bangladesh, since, has been felt by and in India. Even in the case of Nepal, the leftist Maoist insurgency has left an indelible mark along the shared borders between the two countries, and on the Government of India's Nepal policy. That cannot be said about the JVP – whether militant or otherwise, though the reverse is the truth when it comes to the 'internal conflict' in Sri Lanka pertaining to the local Tamil population. Suffice is to point out that the impact of the 'ethnic issue' on the people, politics and policies of the Government of Tamil Nadu and on the Indian Government have been next only to that triggered by the Pakistani army action on the Bengali-speaking population in what was then East Pakistan. Unlike in the case of Bangladesh, the 'ethnic issue' in Sri Lanka has had a longer innings, running up to decades. So did its consequences for Tamil Nadu and the rest of India, in political terms and policy options.

India & Tamil Nadu – Why, When and How?

No discourse on the Sri Lankan ethnic issue, war and violence would be complete without reference to the 'Tamil Nadu factor'. Such a discourse could take place anywhere in the world, and not confined to India or Sri Lanka. It would be so even if one were to discuss the creation of Bangladesh. Yet, if one were to assess the trans-border consequences of the internal conflict in Sri Lanka, on the Indian neighbour, the long innings of such impact would be more in the case of the Sri Lankan ethnic issue than the Bangladesh War. Before beginning to delve into the subject, one should acknowledge that Tamil Nadu did not create the problem, *per se,* nor was it party to whatever early processes that had created the 'ethnic issue' – or even the internal support that the Sri Lankan Tamil groups began enjoying in India. Even the worst critics of India's role in the ethnic issue would not say that Tamil Nadu was a part of the problem from the beginning. Nor could Tamil Nadu claim to be a part of the solution, as yet. Again, it owes mostly to the attitude and approaches of the stakeholders in Sri Lanka, starting with the State and the Government. Tamil Nadu was an inadvertent partner by geographical accident, as the mass exodus from across the seas in the aftermath of Pogorm-'83 showed. It was humanitarian in nature, to begin with. It could have been so even if the Sri Lankan victims were not Tamils. It is true that ethnicity-related socio-political factors took over later, but that was the effect of, and not cause for whatever happened in Sri Lanka.

Going beyond the 'Tamil Nadu factor' was the charges levelled against India on its arming and training of Tamil youth, for them to be able to defend themselves and their men, women and children. The charge at the time was not that the Sri Lankan State and governmental machinery took an active part in the mayhem that was unleashed against the Tamil civilian population all across the country, in the aftermath of the Liberation Tigers of Tamil Eelam (LTTE) ambushing a Sri Lanka Army (SLA) convoy, killing 13 soldiers in the Tamil-majority Northern Province. It was more about the security forces and the police personnel remaining a mute spectator as political goons identified with the ruling party of the time, as also anti-socials that were encouraged to do so, indulged in wanton raping and killing of Tamil civilians in large numbers, looting and burning their homes and businesses. A commercial interest too was at times cited as among the causes for the riots. On earlier and later occasions however, the Sri Lankan State, particularly a partisan police and an ill-prepared armed forces did overplay their role, in what was then seen as a beginning of lawlessness by a majority of the Sri Lankan officialdom and as chauvinistic by a smaller group. That this smaller group comprised 'Sinhala-Buddhist chauvinistic elements is what did not go unnoticed – but unchecked, still.

It did not mean that no personnel from the security forces, including the police, were involved in the atrocities that were perpetrated on the Tamil community. There were individual cases of wanton and heinous misbehaviour on the part of some just as many others were lauded for the way they had protected the hapless Tamil victims of Pogrom-83 from the Sinhala marauders. Either way, the Sri Lankan State and the security forces might not have been the intended targets in the minds of those who thought about India having to train and arm the Tamil youth. It was possibly the national guilt and global shame of having let down an identifiable and select section of the citizenry in their hour of grave crisis that had blurred the vision so much that the Indian efforts at peace-building in Sri Lanka were not seen in perspective. At subsequent stages, if the Indian training for the Sri Lankan Tamil youth included preparations for standing up to the armed forces, it owed to the inability of the Government in Colombo to appreciate the harm that had been done to the Tamil-speaking community, already. The point was and is simple: India and Tamil Nadu entered the scene neither on their own, nor at the invitation of the Tamils. They were left with little option.

While talking about India's engagement in the Sri Lankan ethnic crisis since the Eighties, reference is often made by anti-India critics to New Delhi wanting to protect its strategic interests in the shared Indian Ocean neighbourhood during the 'Cold War' era. Likewise, reference is also made about India getting involved in the anti-Bengali mayhem unleashed by the undivided Pakistani State on the nation's eastern wing, earlier, in 1970-71 – and fighting a war with Islamabad, that led to the liberation of Bangladesh. In Sri Lanka, as in Bangladesh earlier, no one has charged New Delhi with fomenting ethnic trouble or abetting with the State to harass, humiliate and harm the ethnic minorities in ways that would demand reprisal by the victims. If the reference is still to India wanting to neutralise the Sri Lankan plans to provide port and oil-tanker facility to the US at the height of the 'Cold War' in which New Delhi identified with Moscow, greater clarity needs to be thrown at the existing circumstances of the time. If anything, it was Colombo that had persistently called for making the Indian Ocean a 'Zone of Peace', and protested loudly when the UK allowed the US, leader of the NATO, to set up a large military base in Diego Garcia, off the southern coast of Sri Lanka. Throughout, India had backed Sri Lanka in its efforts in this direction, and also stood to benefit from giving shape to the shared concerns for a weapons-free Indian Ocean neighbourhood. If anything, it was Colombo that broke the cordiality and cooperation when in the name of ushering in 'market economy' in 1977, Colombo granted strategic concessions to nations that were then perceived as being unfriendly, if not outright adversarial to India. Earlier in 1971, only months after New Delhi had helped Colombo militarily in neutralising the 'first JVP insurgency', Sri Lanka did not think twice before granting re-fuelling – and landing – facilities for the Pakistan Air Force (PAF) aircraft to shuttle between the western and the eastern wing of the divided nation. It did not seem to have occurred to the Sri Lankan authorities that such an action would have not only upset India but would have also provided PAF with an opportunity to snoop down on India, if not target it directly along the southern flank. Even one successful hit would have been enough to change the mood in India, if not the method of India's armed forces.

Here again, Tamil Nadu did not have any role to play until after the mass exodus of Tamil civilian victims from Sri Lanka beached along the State's shores in their tens of thousands, with no food to eat, no clothes to wear and no money to spend. Their shattered lives and sickened bodies were all that they had. If all this had not moved the people of Tamil Nadu – whether the victims from Sri Lanka were Tamils or not – it would have then become a greater cause for worse concerns about their mental makeup and general disposition. At one stage, as many as 250,000 Tamils were housed in the refugee camps, erected all across Tamil Nadu, with each one of these victims having a worse tale than the others' for the neighbourhood population to shed tears for their plight. It was possibly the first time that many in the interior villages in the Tamil Nadu districts away from the southern coast had heard of Sri Lanka, or the ethnic issue – which had been raging as a political issue almost since the island-nation became independent in 1948. In turn, the humanitarian concerns that the people of Tamil Nadu had for the victims from Sri Lanka forced the political parties in the State not to ignore the 'ethnic issue' that had taken a definite shape across the Palk Strait. This, despite the fact that the dominant 'Dravidian polity' in the State at the time had had a long history of projecting pan-Tamil issues and promoting political causes that painted the federal government in poor light, in terms of addressing

the political concerns of the Tamil-speaking people in the country and
the developmental demands of Tamil Nadu, as the State came to be
known later.

Given the mood and methods of the people at large and those of
peripheral political parties wanting to ignite a political crisis out of a
humanitarian situation that was more real than any other that the State
had witnessed, neither the mainline polity in Tamil Nadu, nor the
Government in Chennai could have stayed quiet, or indifferent to the
emerging situation, for long. In this context, comparison needs to be
drawn with the reaction of the parties and Government in the State to
the 'ethnic situation' in Tamil Nadu as it unfolded. The Dravida Munnetra
Kazhagam (DMK), the pan-Tamil political party still in its infancy, passed
a resolution in its annual conference at Pudukottai in 1956. The Madras
State Assembly, as Tamil Nadu used to be called at the time, too passed
a resolution. Even earlier, when independent Sri Lanka decided to
disenfranchise Tamils of Indian Origin and render them Stateless soon
after the country became independent, the Government of India and the
Government of Tamil Nadu were circumspect in their reaction. As Prime
Minister, Jawaharlal Nehru had held that Indians living overseas, having
decided to stay back in those countries, should abide by the laws and
needs of those nations. Nor should New Delhi interfere in what essentially
was an internal affair of those countries, by seeking to present the case of
peoples of Indian origin in those countries, or seek to represent them,
Nehru had held.

Politics of 'Ethnic Issue'

There is a general perception that the competitive nature of the
'Dravidian polity' in Tamil Nadu may have influenced the Government
of India's approach towards the 'ethnic issue' and its fallout in Sri Lanka.
As already explained, Tamil Nadu was a later and accidental entrant in
the matter. Hence, neither the State Government, nor the political parties,
had any vested approach or dynamics when it all began. At no time was
their approach pro-active, with the initiative for either political action, or
otherwise, emanating in the State. Theirs was essentially a re-active action

and approach, where their perceptions may have influenced their decisions. If their perceptions were at variance with those of either Colombo, or even New Delhi, it owed to the general mood of their cadres and at times the public at large, nearer home in Tamil Nadu. It may have been 'biased' when interpreted in a certain way but was purposeful in the larger context and considering the ground realities – both in Sri Lanka and also nearer home. As far as the latter was concerned, the public mood was influenced by pro-LTTE elements in Sri Lanka and elsewhere as by the pro-Tamil sympathy that the ethnic war entailed, otherwise. In the 'IT era' when 'information' travelled fast, and access to such information was also greater in an ever-developing Tamil Nadu than in many other parts of India, the inevitability of propaganda influencing public opinion could not have been avoided. Nor could the mistaken notion that propaganda was reflective of public sympathy be erased as fast as it spread. While the Sri Lankan State did not have the equipment and energy, the Government of India, and that in Tamil Nadu, did not have the intention. In a way, the greater politicisation of the Sri Lankan issue in Tamil Nadu had more to do with the public mood – where it was not induced by the initiatives elsewhere, including New Delhi.

The pan-Tamil parties may have exploited it also to explore the electoral advantage that the issue may have provided, but that was neither the essential basis for their decision, nor could they have exploited it beyond a point. The results of the federal parliamentary polls in Tamil Nadu in May 2009 should be an eye-opener in the matter. Strongly criticising the ruling Congress-DMK combine at the Centre and the in State for their handling of the 'Sri Lankan affairs' as the ethnic war there reached its climax, the Opposition AIADMK-led alliance had hoped to make it big in the parliamentary elections in India. The results showed that it was not to be. The Congress-DMK combine, of which the pan-Tamil, Dalit-centric Viduthalai Chiruthaigal Katchi (VCK) was a minor partner, won 28 of the total 40 seats from Tamil Nadu and adjoining Union Territory of Puducherry. In a way, the only time that the 'Sri Lankan issue' influenced elections in Tamil Nadu, or elsewhere in India, was in 1991, when the 'Rajiv Gandhi assassination' caused the complete rout of the DMK in the State and the consequential 'limited victory' for the Congress-led combine, of which the AIADMK rival was a partner. In comparison, the 'Indira Gandhi assassination' in 1984 had contributed to her Congress Party sweeping the parliamentary polls so very completely.

The reasons are not far to seek. One, in an era of globalisation, the emerging generation of youth in Tamil Nadu had ironically become inward-looking, caring only about the individual self and his or her personal demands and expectations. They did not have time for larger issues of common concern. This could remain so for a long time to come. On the streets of Tamil Nadu, one could see evidence to the growing indifference of the voter to the political class and issues unless it touched their lives more directly – than just emotionally. Gone are the days when a political rally by one of the major parties in the State could gather a million people for well-prepared conferences, and at least a 100,000 for campaign meetings in district headquarters. Today, making even 5,000 committed cadres to gather at any political rally has become near-impossible. The local media is full of stories, particularly during election time, as to how political parties organise 'paid crowds' who are formed into groups and are shuttled from one rally to another in hired trucks and buses, at times in their thousands. Two, with the passage of time and the advancement of pan-Tamil issues and concerns overall during four decades of 'Dravidian political administration' in the State since 1967, the ageing constituency of ideology-driven generation has become increasingly marginalised. Their limited survival – sans growth, hence – owed to their acquiring new political identities in the interim. It was the inevitable birth of parties like the MDMK and PMK that vocalised those ideologies, but in such strong terms and shrill voices that their real appeal and reach were misconstrued. The election results showed the real reach of their appeal.

This is not to say that the Centre and the Tamil Nadu Governments were uninfluenced by the developments in Sri Lanka, and the consequential events in Tamil Nadu. At one stage in the early career of the 'ethnic issue' in Tamil Nadu, DMK leader M Karunanidhi, then in the Opposition, even mooted a 'Cyprus-like' solution for solving the ethnic issue in Sri Lanka. This was considered controversial at the time. Throughout the early years of the ethnic violence and consequent arms training for the Tamil youth from Sri Lanka, the Government of then Tamil Nadu Chief Minister, the late M G Ramachandran actively cooperated with the Centre. The AIADMK, first under MGR and later under his political-heir and Chief Minister, Jayalalithaa, had sought to influence the Centre's policy on Sri Lanka, from time to time, moved as they were by reports from across the Palk Strait – often travelling through the more circuitous routes through western nations, where all the LTTE had relatively better access after the 'Rajiv Gandhi assassination'. The charismatic leader that he was, M G Ramachandran or MGR undertook a day-long token fast as Chief Minister, to call the Centre's attention forcefully on the plight of the Sri Lankan Tamils in their native land.

If this wall got broken down in more recent years, particularly through the conclusive 'Eelam War IV' in Sri Lanka, it also had to do with the 'communication revolution' of the email-internet-sms era, where greater access to information became possible, sitting in one's study, either at home or office. In comparison, access to information from Sri Lanka in India, through 'Old Media' tools like news chapters or even television continued to remain limited and mostly State-controlled. The host State' in a democracy like India played little or no role in dissemination of such information. Where however a distinction needed making but was not made while assessing the real impact of the ethnic issue, war and violence in Sri Lanka on impressionable minds in India related to information regarding any 'neo-converts' that the events and consequential efforts may have produced. It only helped the 'already-converted' to reinforce their beliefs that now bordered on faith without actually helping to expand the base of such believers in numerical or electoral terms, particularly in Tamil Nadu. Yet, there is no denying that younger elements in Tamil Nadu have got their first real exposure to pan-Tamil issues of the kind that have been forgotten for and by a full generation.

There is a history to what constant references to 'pan-Tamil' polity meant in the Tamil Nadu context. For a region where the British ruler first set his political foot in undivided India, what is now Chennai is where the East India Company installed its first politico-administrative set-up in the country. Madras as the city came to be known for 335 of its 350-year long history was also where the Britons established the first modern courts in India. Though they spread their wings fast enough, and also developed Calcutta, or Kolkata, where they shifted their headquarters, and later Bombay, now Mumbai, their love for Madras was not altogether dead. It was not without reason. By a stroke of good luck, and of a pen, the Muslim Nawab of Arcot, had bequeathed the revenue-collection powers for all that the kingdom had surveyed to the East India Company, for the military help that a rag-tag army a young clerk, Robert Clive, in vanquishing a blood relation. The rest, as they, is history. But woven into that history is also the history of the revival of court-patronage of the kind that the forgotten upper castes – who had also formed the upper class – in an era gone-by, had got used to, but missed after the famed Tamil kingdoms of the Cheras, Cholas, Pandiyas and the Pallavas fell to disuse. Competition for British patronage took familiar and familial lines, with the result, the upper caste Brahmin community ended up cornering all the plum jobs that were available to the 'natives', first in the East India Company and later in the district administration that they fashioned. Left out of the favours' list, particularly in proportion to the numbers that they represented, the non-Brahmin upper castes founded the Southern India Liberal Federation, commonly known by the name of its mouth-piece, as the 'Justice' Party.

Around the time, Gandhiji, the 'Father of the Indian Nation', took the Indian National Congress (INC) to the masses, over the head of the upper class structure that the British rulers had helped fashion in 1885, if only to play bridge between the rulers and the ruled in the aftermath of the 'First War of Indian Independence' in 1857, the Justice Party had already formed an 'elected' government in what was then the Madras Presidency – comprising much of the present-day Tamil Nadu, over which the East India Company had acquired revenue-collection rights from the Nawab of Arcot, centuries earlier. As the name went, the Justice Party made 'social justice' its political agenda, and distanced itself from the freedom movement that the Congress under Gandhiji enunciated and fought for. The chief beneficiaries were however the non-Brahmin upper castes, not necessarily the forgotten downtrodden sections of the population. Having achieved its early goals in terms of reservations for jobs and higher education for the non-Brahmin communities, the Justice Party and Government had to give way to the Congress, whose mass-appeal became infectious through the Thirties of the 20th century. Out of this frustration and given the socio-political vacuum that Gandhiji's Congress had produced was born the 'Self-Respect Movement' of the late *'Periyar'* E V Ramaswami Naicker, whose non-political Dravidar Kazhagam (DK) soon gave birth to the politically-oriented Dravida Munnetra Kazhagam (DMK), in the early years of independent India, 1949, to be precise.

Taking a leaf out of Gandhiji's political experience and experimentation *viz* the ruling class and their language, the Dravidar Kazhagam (DK) had added opposition to Hindi and northern India as a part of the anti-Brahmin creed that it had inherited from the Justice Party. Out of this admixture was born the pan-Tamil identity, which when stoked in the form of the anti-Hindi agitation in the mid-Sixties, contributed to the DMK capturing political power in Madras State in 1967. Out of the DMK was born the breakaway AIADMK – with continuing affinity for the larger 'pan-Tamil cause' even through the years of its inevitable transformation as a more moderate and all-inclusive political party, first under MGR and later under an equally charismatic Jayalalithaa. The AIADMK, for reasons of politics and public appeal, may have wiped off some of its pan-Tamil masking, aided as it was by the social welfare programmes initiated by the State Government, through the 'MGR years' and even earlier under the DMK Governments of party founder, the late C N Annadurai and Karunanidhi. But that did not mean that issues of common concern did not arise for the larger population in Tamil Nadu – particularly pertaining to river-water disputes with neighbouring States. Given the complexities of the issues and the constitutional questions that they often raised, the Union of India and the Supreme Court of India were often called upon to deliver justice to Tamil Nadu and its people. In the perception of the Tamil people in the country, and hence their leadership, the constitutional institutions called upon to render justice to the State and its population, were often found wanting. What was thus essentially a common concern of the Tamil population in the emerging circumstances then came to acquire the 'pan-Tamil' tag that was almost forgotten, otherwise. The 'Sri Lankan ethnic issue', from time to time, got added on to the list – both because the victims in that country shared the language and culture of their brethren this side of the Palk Strait – and with whom they would later claim, they had the 'umbilical cord relationship'.

What did it add up to?

The Sri Lankan ethnic issue did not exactly influence elections in Tamil Nadu to the same extent it impacted on the campaign, as in 1991 and 2009, to a greater extent, and in 1989, to a lesser degree. In 1984, when Tamil Nadu faced both parliamentary polls and Assembly elections at the same time after the assassination of Indira Gandhi and hospitalisation of alliance-partner and Chief Minister M G Ramachandran in the US, the 'sympathy wave' caused by the twin-developments swept through the electorate in the State. The impact of 'Pogrom-83' in Sri Lanka, while having its effect on the polity and society in the State after the mass exodus of refugees, did not influence the electoral results, one way or the other. The competitive nature of the 'Dravidian polity' at this stage also witnessed the two Dravidian majors, namely, the ruling AIADMK and the Opposition DMK parent, seeking to outdo each other in arguing the case of the Tamils in Sri Lanka with the Government of India, during this period, and even later. Even during the run-up to the 1991 elections, ahead of the 'Rajiv Gandhi assassination', the LTTE-centric approach of the dismissed DMK Government had caused a huge embarrassment to the party, particularly after the LTTE killing of rival EPRLF militant leader Padmanabha and his men in a Chennai apartment when Karunanidhi was Chief Minister. In the rest of the elections that followed, other than 2009, Sri Lanka was never really an issue for the Tamil Nadu voter – and hence the policy-maker, either at Delhi or in Chennai, for him to look at Colombo or Jaffna, exclusively through Tamil Nadu.

Where the competitive pan-Tamil politics of Tamil Nadu influenced the political leadership, and hence the policy-maker in Delhi, there was a strong justification for their arguing their case on the points that they had made and in ways they made their arguments. Be it public protests by every political party in the State over the past decades, or the public fast by Chief Ministers M G Ramachandran in the Eighties and M Karunanidhi in 2009, they had sought to distinguish their concern for the larger Tamil community and their forfeited rights inside Sri Lanka from any support for militancy or terrorism, as the case may be. If the Tamil Nadu polity empathised with the militant Tamil youth in the mid-Eighties, it flowed from, and was within the parameters of the policies enunciated and implemented by the Centre. Where M G Ramachandran, Jayalalithaa or Karunanidhi were engaged with either the Centre or the Tamil political/militant groups from Sri Lanka at the official-level, it either had the Centre's blessings or acquiescence. It was thus that the MGR Government and M G Ramachandran as Chief Minister served the twin-purpose of providing a bridge between the Centre and the LTTE even while communicating to New Delhi, the strong and evolving sentiments of the Tamil Nadu population on the Sri Lankan issue. Barring a few and less significant aberrations in comparison, the DMK under Karunanidhi, whether in power or not, was careful in not crossing the 'Lakshman *rekha*' in matters of foreign policy and security issues – both relating to Sri Lanka, in this case. Karunanidhi, particularly when he was in power, was more than aware than the rest that the Constitution of India conferred on the Centre, exclusively rights and responsibilities over foreign and security policies of the Indian State – and their implementation. Where he had erred, as he did by boycotting the reception given to the IPKF when they returned from Sri Lanka when he was Chief Minister, it had more to do with a domestic policy, where the State had the constitutional right in the matter.

If it was in bad taste, and more so when compared to the fast that his *bete noire*, MGR, had undertaken, that alone was the compromise the likes of Karunanidhi and MGR were willing to make — either from the ethnic or electoral point of view. Neither had staked their Government in aid of the ethnic issue, or any other concern of pan-Tamil identity. Nor did Jayalalithaa do so when she became Chief Minister in 1991. Her protest fast on the 'Cauvery water dispute', while stressing the concerns and demands of the State and its people, was not unconstitutional. Whatever surprise element was there in a Chief Minister of an Indian State undertaking a public fast, targeting the Centre, had gone after MGR did so on the Sri Lankan issue years ago. Otherwise, the likes of MGR and Jayalalithaa, as the moderate faces of the Dravidian polity in Tamil Nadu, lent greater credence to pan-Tamil causes in their time than Annadurai could have attempted in his short-lived tenure as Chief Minister (1967-69), or Karunanidhi, through his five terms as Chief Minister in four decades (including the term, since 2006). Given the public perception of individual leaders and their known positions on issues such as these, public protests by MGR and Jayalalithaa on pan-Tamil concerns of the kind only diluted the seriousness of the affair than should have been otherwise. It was thus that Jayalalithaa's maiden Independence Day speech from the ramparts of Fort St George, the seat of power in Chennai (15 August 1991), calling upon the Centre to rescind the 'Kachchativu Accord' with the Sri Lankan Government, got noticed more in Colombo and Delhi than in Tamil Nadu.

The DMK, which had taken certain liberties at one time, was doubly cautious after the 'Rajiv Gandhi assassination'. The party did not want a repeat of the stunning electoral blow that it suffered in 1991, when public perception linked the erstwhile Karunanidhi Government to the freedom of movement that the LTTE had enjoyed in the preceding years. In the aftermath of the Rajiv Gandhi assassination, not only the DMK but other mainstream political parties in the country also became convinced that an outfit like the LTTE, purportedly behaving as the 'sole representative' of the Tamil-speaking people in Sri Lanka, could not be trusted to keep its word, or not to do the unthinkable. Even otherwise, the two Dravidian majors have drawn a clear distinction on the constitutional front. The DMK which has not tired of demanding more powers for the States in India and has identified sectors and areas where the Constitution needed amendment in this regard, has not mentioned foreign policy, defence and security, in this regard.

This approach of the party was also reflected in the DMK-led Government's initiatives and reactions on the Sri Lankan front, independent as they were from the political statements and initiatives emanating from the party, from time to time. It was no different in the case of the AIADMK, where Jayalalithaa as Chief Minister in 1991, did call for India taking back Kachchativu islet that it had ceded to Sri Lanka, but did not refer to the 'Sri Lankan ethnic issue' in the same vein. Even her very reference to the 'Kachchativu issue' should be construed as Jayalalithaa's way of seeking to project a larger cause when she was engaged in a love-hate relationship with her Congress ally, ruling the Centre – and the Machiavellian Prime Minister, the late, P V Narasimha Rao. The aberration in her case flowed from her demand for India sending the Army to rescue the holed-up Tamil refugees in the crumbling northern stronghold of the LTTE in May 2009. Read with her other statements made on this occasion and also around the time, this one too sounded anti-Sri Lanka and against the Government and leadership of President Mahinda Rajapakaksa. Yet, the fact remains that the Tamil civilians in their tens of thousands were held by the LTTE under duress, as 'human shields' and as 'hostages'.

Twin Tracks from Tamil Nadu

Looked at in perspective, there were two components to the 'Tamil Nadu reaction' and consequent impact on the national politics and policy/ policies on the Sri Lanka front, influenced as the former was by the events in the island-nation. One was the larger issue of 'Tamil rights and issues' in Sri Lanka and the consequent relation to LTTE terrorism, violence and the larger war. Tamil Nadu's moods and methods in this regard were influenced by the ground situation and developments in Sri Lanka. Where the Tamil felt aggrieved and targeted, either in a single incident or as a political collective over a period, at the hands of the Sri Lankan security forces or otherwise, Tamil Nadu sympathised and empathised with them. This was not restricted to either the peripheral polity or the entire polity. The larger population the State – at times including migrants from other parts of the country for long – identified with the human cause. That they happened to be victimised time and again did touch a cord in the Tamil population in the State. It argued for a greater Indian engagement and involvement in Sri Lankan affairs, for New Delhi to be able to influence Colombo's course in the matter. On the LTTE front, the DMK and the AIADMK were cautious, not to cross the 'Lakshman rekha'. The caution continued even through the decisive 'Eelam War IV', whose end-game coincided with Elections-09 in India.

The Tamil political support for the cause of their brethren across the Palk Strait did not have anything to do with the politics of the State. While pan-Tamil and peripheral political parties and groups did seek to identify with the LTTE, and even sought to market the outfit's purported justification for the 'Rajiv Gandhi assassination' to the local population, the DMK and the AIADMK as the mainline Dravidian parties resisted the temptation through and through. While they were demonstrative in their support for the 'Tamil cause' in Sri Lanka, and their larger cadre-following and support-base meant that any public display of their support made bigger and better news, speakers at the rallies organised by these parties at all levels were restrained in the verbal exhibition of their sympathy and empathy. Every remotest display of any identification with the LTTE however was carefully shunned with great care and precaution. If they still were loud and clear about their support for the suffering Tamils in Sri Lanka, the reasons, as already explained, were not far to seek.

To be precise, it was not just the regional parties, even national parties in Tamil Nadu toed the line and ended up reflecting the public mood in the State, just as they were taking up the cause of the State in internal Indian matters such as the 'Cauvery water dispute' or the 'Mullaiperiyar issue' with neighbouring Indian States such as Karnataka and Kerala – or, the 'Sethusamduram Canal Project'. In the case of Sethusamduram, A B Vajpayee as BJP Prime Minister had announced the clearance for the project by the Centre. His Congress successor, Prime Minister Manmohan Singh and party president and ruling alliance chairperson, Sonia Gandhi, launched project, in their turn. In between, the higher judiciary in the country had thrown out all objections to the project. This could also be said of the Cauvery and Mullaiperiyar disputes, where technical teams and quasi-judicial commissions had been involved, either at the instance of the Centre or the higher judiciary, or both. Yet, when the chips are down, Tamil Nadu finds itself stymied by new committees, set up at the instance of the higher judiciary, or new hurdles in the implementation of the projects, which the Centre is either incapable or unwilling to clear. It was thus that the political forces with which Prime Minister Vajpayee was identified were the ones who revived religious sentiments as among the reasons for reviewing the Sethu Canal Project. Given the inevitable political confusion that seizes a national party, particularly the one in power at the Centre, based as it is on the divided loyalty of its States units on issues such as the Cauvery dispute or the Mullaiperiyar row, the political parties and their perceived pan-Tamil identity end up taking the blame, often. Because they are unwilling to shed that identity for historic and contemporary socio-political reasons, and also the fact that the cause that they end up espousing are for real, the pan-Tamil identity would continue to stick – as long as those issues remain alive.

If anything, in the final phase of the armed conflict in Sri Lanka, which brought in further untold miseries to the local Tamil population ('Eelam War IV, 2006-09), the so-called national parties in India were the ones that became more vociferous than the two 'Dravidian majors'. The Communist Party of India (CPI), Communist Party of India-Marxists (CPM) and the Bharatiya Janata Party (BJP) became more vociferous than the Congress rival at the national-level in voicing their concerns over the plight of the Tamil population. In this, the CPI and to a lesser extent, the CPM allowed the thin-line dividing the Indian concern for the suffering Tamil population in Sri Lanka and support for the LTTE to be blurred. In the company of their new-found Tamil Nadu allies in the long run-up to parliamentary polls in 2009, the CPI and CPM in particular got themselves heard louder than ever before on the Sri Lankan issue, both in Tamil Nadu and in New Delhi.

On a more recent development such as the arrest of Gen Sarath

Fonseka (retd), former Sri Lanka Army chief and common Opposition candidate for the presidency, the BJP, for the first time commented publicly on what was deemed an exclusive internal affair of Sri Lanka – with no overt implications for India. The Congress, having been in power at the Centre through the crucial years, had a 'vested position' on the Sri Lankan issue, owing to the 'Rajiv Gandhi assassination' in particular. Even then, the party had drawn the distinction like any other, between the 'ethnic issue' and 'LTTE terrorism'. Where its voice was raised on the former, it was as clear as the rest. On the latter, it was louder than others. Overall however, as parties heading the Government at the Centre during different times over the past decade and more, the Congress and the BJP were circumspect in their public pronouncements, just as their regional counterparts in the DMK and the AIADMK in Tamil Nadu. This was particularly so whenever the respective party was heading the Government at the Centre. At other times, they had generally maintained a relative low-profile on matters concerning the southern neighbour when compared to their decision and more vocal positions on Pakistan, Bangladesh or even Nepal.

The second element in this regard pertained to domestic politics, where political parties in Tamil Nadu first, and their counterparts at the national-level began playing a calculated game of one-upmanship. The 'ethnic issue' in Sri Lanka came in handy for these parties and their leaders. Their needs and demands fell into two or three different categories, all independent but dovetailed at the same time. One was to be able to retain that section of their party cadres and voters, who were at askance about the less-than-expected action/reaction from their respective leaderships to a given situation or development in Sri Lanka. The other owed to the need for individual political parties in Tamil Nadu to appeal to a larger section of the population (*read:* voters), to be able to strengthen their weakening political/electoral base. Years of Independence and 'Dravidian political administration' had rendered all kinds of 'isms superfluous, irrelevant or both, particularly with the new-generation voters who were born into the benefits earned for them though sacrifices made by and in an earlier generation. Yet another aspect was the need and opportunity for political parties, be they at the regional-level or at the national-level, to use the 'Sri Lankan issue' as an occasional trigger to send out what essentially was/ is an 'electoral message' to their partners and counterparts at the other end.

To this should be included, Chief Minister Karunanidhi's statement of 13 February 2010, wherein he said that his DMK party would not remain silent if the re-elected Rajapaksa presidency did not give the Tamils of Sri Lanka, their political dues (in terms of power-devolution). He said that they would take up the issue with the Centre. Read between the lines, it was his own way of responding to the earlier indication flowing from political *bete noire* Jayalalithaa that the AIADMK was anxious to have the DMK's Congress ally cross over to her side in time for the State Assembly elections in 2011. Obviously, Karunanidhi was not satisfied with the public pronouncements of alliance-loyalty by Congress spokespersons at the national and State-levels. His statement, in the form of a question-answer session, that he penned as always, was aimed at addressing the non-Congress parties in the State, all of whom had a common thread of understanding on the 'Sri Lankan issue' – and wanted the DMK to give them the much-needed leadership.

Otherwise, his chief ministerial initiatives, in the form of the State Assembly passing two resolutions in as many years since the breakout of 'Eelam War IV' were in the nature of putting an early lid on a legislative debate on a sensitive subject, which had the potential of causing 'diplomatic embarrassment' to the Government of India. Even his accompanying statement on the arrest of Gen Sarath Fonseka on 13 February 2010 was as carefully worded as his earlier pronouncements on the ethnic issue. Without naming anyone and in his typical style, Karunanidhi reminded his constituency and readers about all the past killings in Sri Lanka. Clearly, he was referring to the LTTE killings as well, but more to all the charges by the pan-Tamil movements nearer home and afar about the leadership that Gen Fonseka had played at the ground-level in 'Eelam War IV', in which tens of thousands of Tamil civilians had reportedly been killed, a substantial number of them, purportedly in cold blood. His loaded statement also made a reference to Alexander the Great and recalled for the benefit of President Rajapaksa, how the Greek invader had treated King Porus of India with dignity befitting a war-hero even after the latter had lost the battle. The comparison between the traditional war that Porus lost and the election battle in which Fonseka was defeated was not lost on the discerning reader.

If someone wanted to make a comparison between the victorious Alexander and President Rajapaksa, possibly, Karunanidhi would not have come in the way. Read together and interpreted – which often has to be the job of Karunanidhi-watchers in Tamil Nadu – the twin-statements of his were asking/appealing to President Rajapaksa to find an amicable solution to the 'ethnic issue' to the satisfaction of the Tamil people and polity in Sri Lanka. And if need be, he would be forced, Karunanidhi was telling his Congress ally at the Centre, he would have to take up the 'ethnic issue' in Sri Lanka, for joining hands with prospective non-Congress, non-AIADMK political spectrum in the State and the Centre. This would be so, considering that the DMK, as the ruling party in the State and as a partner in the Congress-led coalition Government since 2004, cannot take a strong position against the Centre on issues such as price rise, inflation and unemployment, other common cause over which anti-Congress parties in the State and at the national-level have very definite positions.

Yet, it was only like any other issue that the DMK – or, the AIADMK in its place – could have and would have taken towards facilitating the formation of a new electoral alliance, or breaking up of an existing alliance, purely with the poll chances in Tamil Nadu in mind. Thus, it used to be the 'democracy card' for contesting against the Congress at the end of the 'Emergency era' in 1977, during which period the Centre had sacked the first Karunanidhi Government. Later, it was 'stability card' that the DMK used to back the Congress in the parliamentary polls of 1980 and the BJP in 1999. The DMK also used the traditional 'anti-Hindutva card' to put down the BJP through most parts of their intervening political career in the State and national-levels, respectively. Likewise, the DMK would use constant references to the party's 'Social Justice' plank and its contributions towards the uplift of the downtrodden sections of the masses while in power as a bait to woo the two Left parties, as and when the party needed them as a prospective electoral ally.

Through much of MGR's lifetime at the helm of the AIADMK that he founded, the party used the 'stability card' to back the Congress at the Centre. Jayalalithaa as his political heir and successor too used it, both for and against the Congress and the BJP, from time to time. Her criticism of a non-ally was harsher than that of the DMK rival or the AIADMK founder. Yet, M G Ramachandran too had used issues of democracy to back the Janata Party and subsequently the Janata Dal Governments at the Centre, headed respectively by the late Morarji Desai and the late Charan Singh. It was the Charan Singh-led Government that found the AIADMK nominating two Ministers– the first time a 'Dravidian party' from Tamil Nadu had found a berth in the Union Council of Ministers. MGR also used the 'democracy card' to campaign against the Indira Gandhi Government dismissing the State Government headed by him after the 1980 parliamentary polls. Needless to say that MGR won on the 'sympathy wave' caused by the dismissal, though there were other equally important political and electoral factors that had contributed to the defeat of the Congress-DMK alliance.

To both the DMK and the AIADMK, the use of the 'Sri Lanka card' to form an electoral alliance or break the existing one, or even to play one up over the other, was borne out by other existing circumstances as well. Their use of the 'Sri Lanka card', as already explained, was akin to their using any other electoral plank or issue to make and break alliances – and to try and bag as many more votes as possible, or to ensure that they did not lose votes that might otherwise come their way. This should be read into their competitive behaviour in relation to the various Tamil groups from Sri Lanka, particularly the militant youth, in the early days of the break out of the 'ethnic issue' in the Eighties – with near-immediate impact in Tamil Nadu. Whether it was appealing to the sentiments of the moderate Sri Lankan Tamil leadership of the time, or in accommodating the militant Tamil youth groups, particularly the LTTE, AIADMK Chief Minister M G Ramachandran had the first choice, compared to the parent DMK rival. In allowing this to happen, the Sri

Lankan groups were the one that set the agenda rather than their Tamil Nadu counterparts. Whether it was the moderate Tamil United Liberation Front (TULF) or the militant LTTE, their preference for the AIADMK as the party in power and for MGR as the most charismatic political leader in Tamil Nadu was natural. The DMK was thus left with having to do business with those Tamil groups, political and militant, that were not on the same side of the LTTE, for instance, back home. The competitive politics of the Sri Lankan Tamil groups in their country rather dictated the competitive politics of the Dravidian parties when it came to the 'ethnic issue' – rather than the other way round.

It is not as if the 'national parties' were/are bereft of playing competitive politics of the kind. There is no denying that in the early years of the ethnic conflict in Sri Lanka, the two communist parties, stung as they were still by a global ideology, had problems identifying with the Tamil groups from Sri Lanka and their cause. Their preference for left-leaning Tamil groups from the island-nation was known, however. It also needs recalling that during that phase of the 'ethnic issue' in Sri Lanka, barring the moderate TULF, which was the political mainstay of the community, most groups, including the LTTE, had liked to be identified as left-leaning. Until the mid-Nineties, the BJP did not have any great hopes for Tamil Nadu, and would not want to be drawn into issues that were seen as 'divisive' by its hardcore support-base elsewhere in the country. However, the need for the BJP to expand its electoral base beyond the traditional 'Hindi belt' in central India, and reach out to the non-traditional South and East of the country, meant that not only did the party have to identify with the Tamil voters but also associate with whichever party that was willing to do business with this political voice of 'Hindutva'. For a time, it was the MDMK and the PMK that came first, followed by the AIADMK and the DMK, later.

However, with their organisational and electoral weaknesses showing up ahead of the parliamentary polls of 2009, and consequent desperation exposed even more than in the past, the CPI, CPM and the BJP used the 'Sri Lanka card' in Tamil Nadu in ways the two 'Dravidian majors' had hesitated to do, particularly since the 'Rajiv Gandhi assassination'. It was the CPI thus that launched the first credible political protest on an issue identified with the Sri Lankan situation at the height of the 'Eelam War-IV'. The party started off with focussing on the problems faced by the Tamil Nadu fishermen at the hands of the Sri Lanka Navy (SLN), and staged a protest in Chennai, with participation from peripheral pan-Tamil groups, including the PMK, MDMK and the VCK, however representative they otherwise might have been. At the end of the day, it turned out to be a 'pro-LTTE' protest.

The role of the CPM was no less contradictory and controversial in the matter, but it was the BJP that should take the cake. At the height of the campaign for the 2009 polls, a veteran BJP leader in Tamil Nadu provided space for M K Shivajilingam, a Member of Sri Lankan Parliament belonging to the LTTE-centric Tamil Nationalist Alliance (TNA). Earlier, the CPI was known to have allowed such presence and speech by Tamil MPs from Sri Lanka. Until then, the presence of pro-LTTE elements from Sri Lanka in protests organised in Tamil Nadu had been confined to pan-Tamil parties like the PMK, MDMK or VCK, or other pan-Tamil groups and organisations. Against this, the DMK and the AIADMK were known to have studiously and consciously avoided encouraging the presence of 'overseas speakers' on their political/electoral platform, lest they should be construed as encouraging foreigners to interfere in the domestic political processes in India. Post-war, as already mentioned, the BJP also took a strong position against the arrest of Gen Fonseka in Sri Lanka. Karunanidhi's aforementioned observations on the matter came only days after BJP's Leader of the Opposition in Parliament, Mrs Sushma Swaraj, had demanded Fonseka's release, forthwith.

All this does not mean that the Tamil Nadu parties were either using the 'Sri Lanka card' to line their own political and electoral pockets, and did nothing more. Their concern for the Tamils in Sri Lanka was/is real. It flowed from the twin combination of the inescapable humanitarian angle and the inexplicable 'umbilical cord' bond, as they perceived it. Considering that most international voices in favour of the Tamils in Sri Lanka – and against the Government in Colombo – have come from people who are physically, politically and ethnically separated by long distances, the concerns that emanated in Tamil Nadu have to be seen in perspective. Apart from proximity that could be related to constant exposure, caused in turn by early political positions, even the continuing stance of the pan-Tamil peripheral parties and groups in Tamil Nadu on the 'Sri Lankan situation' owed to a combination of factors and sentiments, all of which have not been understood in New Delhi, leave alone Colombo or elsewhere. After a point, it was the greater and constant interaction with the LTTE and other pro-LTTE leaders in Sri Lanka, and the competition among the pan-Tamil groups in Tamil Nadu to be identified and become acceptable and acknowledged by the LTTE leadership that contributed to their voice becoming louder and shriller, from time to time. This again did not mean that their concerns were any less genuine.

Social and Societal Influence

The 'Bangladesh War' witnessed a massive exodus of the affected population from the then East Pakistan into adjoining States in India. At one stage, the Government of India was providing shelter and food to one million refugees from across the border. Post-war and after the consolidation of Bangladesh as a nation, many of these refugees stayed back in India. Many more of their brethren have continued to pour into India, owing to lack jobs in their country and the relative availability of relatively cheaper labour for the Indian masters. Today, down South, up to the last Indian town that is in Tamil Nadu, you have boys from Bangladesh villages doing odd jobs in restaurants and shops, construction sites and elsewhere. They are illegal migrants, whose presence is known but neither recorded until they get into the police-net for a specific crime, nor acknowledged as contributing to cheap and competitive labour in India. It's akin to the 'Mexican influx' into the US, despite laws and systems to stop illegal migration on such a scale.

It suits everyone to have them around – and not acknowledge their presence. In the case of the Bangladeshi refugees, as is the case with their Mexican counterparts in the US, it makes good politics, mainly for those opposed to illegal migration, for one reason or the other. In the Eighties, the 'anti-foreigner' youth movement in Assam owed to the large-scale presence of Bangladeshi refugees in the State, with their names having been added to the local voters' list and thus being used to 'manipulate' election results. In more recent times, it has suited sections of the 'Hindutva forces' in the country, to identify the Bangladeshi migrants with their religion, and extend the argument to paint them all as prospective, if not possible terrorists. While the BJP may have become more circumspect in its public pronouncements on the subject after the party came to head a Government at the Centre and not wanting to hurt the sentiments of a 'friendly neighbour', that cannot be said of the party's Shiv Sena ally in western Maharashtra State. The Shiv Sena launched a massive protest to have all Bangladeshis evicted from Maharashtra, but citing possible links to anti-India terrorists as among the causes, even though the party has always protested against people from other parts of India coming to Mumbai, the nation's business capital, in search of livelihood.

The social and societal influence of the Sri Lankan Tamils in Tamil Nadu, and through it, the rest of India, needs to be seen in a similar setting. The mass exodus of Sri Lankan Tamils in the aftermath of 'Pogrom-83' was not as large as that of Bangladeshi nationals in 1971. It owed both to the relative demographic strengths and also the absence of a shared land border between India and Sri Lanka. A 20-km sea-lane divided/connected the two countries at the closest points, both happening to be Tamil-dominated areas – the Northern Province in Sri Lanka and Tamil Nadu coast in India. Yet, escaping to India from the harsh realities of their native country meant that the victimised Tamils of Sri Lanka had to risk traversing the harsh seas, which became riskier for a variety of reasons. One, they depended on the local fisher-folk to deploy their fishing vessels to organise the transport. There are not many recorded occasions when the fishermen were known to have ferried the affected people free of cost or at nominal rates that would have met their operational costs and family expenditure. After a time, the fishermen saw a windfall-in-waiting. This was more so in the case of the fishermen from the Tamil

Nadu coast, who charged exorbitant amounts of money for risking their own lives in the process. Not all the Tamil people affected first by the riots of 1983 and later by the war and violence could afford the high cost of travel, which did not guarantee safe-landing. This was because even at the worst of times for the Sri Lanka Navy (SLN), their patrols could and would intercept the 'refugee vessels'. When the LTTE's 'Sea Tigers' began dominating the Sri Lankan side of the shared seas with India, they were known to have hunted 'refugee vessels', to take away able-bodied youth and children, to serve their militant/military cause. This made the cross-over as riskier as any other for the peace-loving among the prospective refugees.

There were also 'cultural reasons' of a kind that contributed to fewer Tamil-speaking people from Sri Lanka landing in Tamil Nadu as refugees than might have been the case otherwise. First, the Sri Lankan Tamils were/are a proud people than can be understood – steeped as they were in their understanding of their relative standing even *viz* their Tamil Nadu counterparts. Early interactions of many of them as refugees with their Tamil-speaking hosts showed up a 'cultural gap' of a kind that had made them dominant in the domestic Sri Lankan society and polity – despite they being the numerical minority when compared to the Sinhala majority in the country. This meant that not all the affected Tamils in Sri Lanka after 1983 or even in the early years of the war wanted to land in Tamil Nadu or the rest of India as refugees. This would be borne out also by the fact that when opportunities beckoned, most intended refugees would manipulate their way to the western world, where they would keep their education, job and pride as much intact as was possible under the circumstances. This took the form of many of them using India in particular as a spring-board to seeking political asylum in western countries and settling down their for good. Over time, they also regained some of their personal glory, jobs and education in the host-nations. Citizenship for many of them in those countries and their consequent projection as a vociferous section of the local electorate with the 'Eelam cause' to call their own made them a relatively strong political force by their own right.

This was not the case in Tamil Nadu or elsewhere in India. There was sympathy for the Sri Lankan Tamils and their larger cause in India through and through. It got demonstrated better in Tamil Nadu mainly because the exposure that the local population got early on to the human problems faced by the people across the Palk Strait. At that stage their shared language helped better communication and understanding than what could be seen and visualised. Yet, it was also the time that the average Tamils in the State were coming into any contact with their 'blood brethren' (?) from Sri Lanka than any time in the past. Prior to the refugee-influx, there was no great interaction or exchanges of the kind between the Tamil-speaking people between the two countries other than in select areas. Through the post-Independence era and even later to a lesser degree the 'Boat Mail' train-cum-shipping service would disgorge students, traders and pilgrims from one country to the other, most of them Tamils. The students were mostly from Sri Lanka wanting to pursue their higher studies in India, particularly at Tiruchi, Madurai or Madras, now Chennai. On the return trip, the 'Boat Mail' would take teachers from southern India, particularly Tamil Nadu and Kerala, to various schools in Tamil and Sinhala-speaking areas in Sri Lanka.

Traders from the two countries, mostly Muslims, have maintained business and familial contacts almost to date, but the linkages between the fishermen communities in the two countries got mostly broken after the advent of the ethnic war in the country – with only risk-bearing groups and individuals venturing to transport men, material or medicines, the latter two linked to the LTTE's 'war efforts'. The Upcountry Tamils of recent Indian Origin were not to make use of the contact-points or communication facilities between the two countries as much as the Sri Lankan Tamils or the Muslim community, as poverty and the practice of the estate owners retaining the family members of an intended traveller to the Indian mother-land as a bargaining chip to ensure that the latter did not make good his escape. Yet, there was no constant contact and exchanges between the Tamil-speaking population of the two countries as latter-day terminologies like 'umbilical cord connection' would indicate. Yet, there was no denying the deep and strong identification that 'Sri

Lankan Tamils' as a community had for India, which they still continue to consider as their 'mother-land', the leaders of the freedom movement from Tamil Nadu and the rest of India, and also the pilgrim-centres in the State, such as Tiruchendur, Madurai, Palani, Chidambaram and even Tirupati. To the list has been added in recent times, Buddhist pilgrim centres in north India, and Christian and Muslim centres of religious reverence in Tamil Nadu and elsewhere in the country.

Yet, the contacts between Tamil-speaking individuals and communities across the Palk Strait were not as vast and varied as is being perceived to be in terms of identifying the political and humanitarian causes of the Sri Lankan Tamil community as those of individual Tamil-speaking people in Tamil Nadu. That's a fallacy on which most perceptions about the 'Tamil Nadu factor' in India-Sri Lanka relations on the 'ethnic issue' have been built over the past decades. The contact with the refugees in their camps and easy communication through the language that they shared brought the plight of the Tamil people in Sri Lanka right before the eyes of their counterparts in Tamil Nadu. There is a vast difference between the Tamil as spoken in the two countries, particularly in terms of diction, choice of words and even in the construction of sentences. The song intonation of the spoken by the Sri Lankan Tamil community could at best be identified as coming close to the closely-knit fishing community in the southern Tamil Nadu district of Kanyakumari, particularly in and around the coastal town of Colachel. It was this societal pressure from the Tamil people in the State, to the plight of the people in Sri Lanka that first forced the political class at all levels, to take up their issue. Until then, as mentioned elsewhere, the Tamil Nadu polity's engagement with the ethnic issue in Sri Lanka, raging almost since Independence in 1948, was minimal, non-committal and non-controversial.

With the result, even when there was mass exodus of the kind that India witnessed from Sri Lanka, there was not much of social interaction of the kind that was expected of the peoples speaking the same language, claim common ancestry to a shared culture, and also the religious linkages established by Hinduism /Saivism for most parts (which however has not barred Sri Lankan Tamil Hindus to go on a pilgrimage to the Balaji Temple at Tirupati, also in southern India, where the presiding deity is identified with the Vaishanvite denomination. If these interactions however produced mixed-marriages those were few and far between. It owed to a variety of reasons. First, the refugee status of the Sri Lankan Tamils arriving on Indian soil did not provide for sentiments of the kind. There was then the reservation of the Sri Lankan Tamil to mix freely with their Indian counterparts, despite the common language link and shared traditions. They saw themselves as culturally and even linguistically superior to the Tamils in India – which tendency continues to date. Their references to the lifestyle and practices of the local Tamils were derisive at best. When the two peoples began mixing freely and comfortably came the 'Rajiv Gandhi assassination', which confined the refugees to their camps – as they needed to be secured from possible attacks from the locals. Barring few exceptions, the trend continued for long, what with the Sri Lankan Tamils in the camps eyeing western destinations as their ultimate goal. Their alternative aim was to return home on an early date.

When near-normalcy was restored post-assassination, the camp inmates were wary of everyone around, as families apprehended possible abduction of their able-bodied youth and children of either gender, by LTTE recruiters, for being forcibly transported back to Sri Lanka, for fighting the armed forces of that country. This meant that older people would prefer going out of the camps to undertake odd jobs, to bring in the extra money beyond the monthly dole that the Governments in Delhi and Chennai were giving families over the past 25 years and more. The police men on duty at the camps would turn a blind eye, if only out of sympathy for the families, whose children had to be cared for and daughters, married off – all of which required money. In between, there emerged a time before the Rajiv Gandhi assassination when the freedom that the camp inmates enjoyed in going about freely in the neighbourhood meant the availability of cheap labour and domestic helps than was available otherwise. This, coupled with reported and unreported incidents of drug-trafficking and peddling by some of the Tamil militant groups and youth inmates of the camps, such other cases of moral turpitude involving a legal angle, and their constant quarrels with the locals over a variety of issues, real and imaginary, were all beginning to be seen as a social situation waiting to explode.

The incident in the crowded Pondy Bazar area of Chennai, in which LTTE supremo Prabhakaran and fellow-militant leader Uma Maheswaran of the People's Liberation Organisation of Tamil Eelam (PLOTE) used guns at each other in broad-day light, highlighted the extent of freedom that the Sri Lankan Tamils had come to assume on the non-militant, non-political front in Tamil Nadu. This was followed later by the Tamil Nadu police cracking down on the LTTE and other militant outfits, not owing to the 'Pondy Bazar incident' but by Prabhakaran's adamant position on political negotiations with the Sri Lankan Government, facilitated by India. All these however also had a sobering effect on the refugee camp inmates, so did the strong feelings of the local community against the Sri Lankan Tamils in the aftermath of the 'Rajiv Gandhi assassination'. The refugees, where they were already not living with/as families outside the camps since arrival in the Eighties, were confined mostly to the camps. It was also when they began turning to West more than in the past. But for a series of events such as these, there was a distinct possibility that the groundswell of disaffection that began showing up in Tamil Nadu against the Sri Lankan Tamil refugees and the militant groups (who were known to be brandishing their weapons in street-corner shops and the like in interior villages) may have taken a turn for the worse. It is possibly in the absence of greater interaction, forced by circumstances that a situation like the 'Assam foreigners issue' did not develop in Tamil Nadu.

Strategic and Security Concerns

Incidents like the 'Pondy Bazar shootout' involving Prabhakaran were few and far between, yes, but then the arrival of Tamil militant youth in Tamil Nadu also exposed the locals to weapons and violence as a way of life, some still argue. It is not as if there did not exist before them other violent groups like the Naxalites or even local pan-Tamil militants. In due course, a local breed of 'Islamic terrorism' also entered the scene, with none-too-infrequent blasts on select targets across the State. The 'Coimbatore serial blasts' of 14 February 1998, in which at least 59 people lost their lives was a culmination of such terrorist strikes involving 'anti-Hindutva' groups as different from contemporary attacks involving 'Kashmiri groups' outside the north Indian State of Jammu and Kashmir or later-day *jehadi* terrorists. The 'Khalistan terrorism' of the early Eighties did not impact on Tamil Nadu, or any other south Indian State directly. But that cannot be said of 'Sri Lankan Tamil militancy'.

More than individual incidents, including the 'Rajiv Gandhi assassination', their presence in large numbers and the freedom that they might have enjoyed, or they had extracted, in terms of movement and militarization, contributed to the slow but poisonous spread of 'gun culture' across the State. This has since become a major law and order problem in Tamil Nadu, though the LTTE or other Tamil militant groups from Sri Lanka cannot be directly blamed for any or all of them, directly. In comparison, other militant groups, be it of the local pan-Tamil variety, or the Naxal or anti-Hindutva kind, were not known to have made a rash display of the weapons at their disposal. It is unclear as yet if any of these groups from across the seas, particularly the LTTE, had aimed at impressing upon the local youth, the might of their muscle power, and thus get new recruits from their midst for fighting their war back home. If anything, some of the non-LTTE groups were believed to have toyed with such ideas or tried out some of them, but the LTTE, at least after a point, became convinced that they should not involve local Tamil youth in their militant exercises, anxious to avoid cadre-indiscipline on the one hand and losing public support and sympathy, on the other.

Yet, the image of Prabhakaran wielding the gun did send out wrong signals to the local youth – not necessary about the cause, but about the methods. This included some youth who joined some pan-Tamil militant groups from within the State with or without linkages to the LTTE or other militant groups from Sri Lanka. For some of the Muslim youth of the generation, the LTTE provided the basis for conviction to the cause and the consequent methods. Thankfully, there are not many cases of the

Tamil militants in Sri Lanka inspiring many bank heists and like in Tamil Nadu. Whatever happened in Tamil Nadu in the Seventies and early Eighties may or may not have drawn inspiration from Sri Lanka, but they also dropped the methods as it died a natural death in the island-nation. Thankfully, the local militant groups did not adopt the later-day methods of the Sri Lankan Tamil militants, be it in funds-raising or creating business ventures or money-laundering. Against this, the LTTE, particularly over the past decade or so, was believed to have been running a network of businesses, including truck and transportation networks, just as their global shipping businesses. The aim was to make legit money and at the same time also provide a legit link for transporting their illegal goods – medicines, weapon parts and other war-material, including petrol, diesel and batter, etc.

Independent of the inspiration that the LTTE and Prabhakaran may have provided local Tamil militant youth in anti-government politics and acts of violence targeting the Indian State, many of the pan-Tamil groups from Sri Lanka were known to have taken to drug-trafficking in a big way to make money for fighting their wars back home. Thus, evolved linkages between international drug-traffickers in the Af-Pak region and Sri Lanka, where Tamil Nadu became the transit point. There were also recorded instances of these facilities being used by the LTTE in particular for transporting war material from along the Pakistani border, or open-store procurements from places as distant as Mumbai, for being illegally shipped to the war zone in Sri Lanka. This became relevant as an 'act of terror' in India after the LTTE was banned in the aftermath of the 'Rajiv Gandhi assassination'. There is no knowing if the State apparatus had gone soft from time to time, depending on the lack of militant activity in Sri Lanka, or whether the LTTE itself was going slow at times, but there is enough evidence to suggest that war material was being smuggled out of India, or through India, to Sri Lanka for and by the LTTE. In some of the cases, the couriers, particularly involved in money-laundering for the LTTE in the 2006-09 period had claimed that they did not know the linkages involving a terrorist organisation of the kind. They knew they were doing something illegal and unacceptable by the

Indian Government, but claimed that they did not have a clue to the LTTE links.

There are at least major incidents of violence involving Sri Lankan militant groups that got staged in India, rather Tamil Nadu. Of them, the Rajiv Gandhi assassination and the 'Padmanabha killing' (19 June 1990) of fellow Tamil militant group leader from the EPRLF involved the LTTE. They were deliberate acts of violence aimed at silencing whom the LTTE wanted silencing. Close to a score each perished with the two killings. However, there has been no incident of the kind in India, particularly targeting Indian victims, involving either the LTTE or other pan-Tamil militant groups from Sri Lanka, after the Rajiv Gandhi assassination (21 May 1991). The 'Padmanabha killing' in a middle-class apartment building in a crowded residential locality in the heart of Chennai was another act of daredevilry involving the LTTE. All assassins made good their escape, until their leader, 'One-eyed Jack' Sivarasan paid with his life when the Indian security agencies surrounded his hideout in Bengaluru (then Bangalore) when the manhunt for the Rajiv Gandhi assassination reached its climax. In the first incident of the kind involving a Sri Lankan Tamil militant group in India, 33 persons were killed and 27 others injured in a bomb-blast at the Chennai Airport (August 1984). Kathiresu, the leader of the infant 'Tamil Eelam Army' (TEA) from Sri Lanka had intended for the bomb to go off at the Colombo Airport but owing to a mix-up, it went off in Chennai. To that extent, it was an 'unintended blast' on Indian soil but then India would have been embarrassed and answerable if the blast had occurred on Sri Lankan soil, instead.

If the 'Meenambakkam airport blast' did open the eyes of the Indian security agencies as to what awaited them over time, it was the Padmanabha killing six full years later that surprised them. The 'Rajiv Gandhi assassination' less than a year later shocked them – and also embarrassed them. In the case of the 'Padmanabha killing', there were doubts and possible indication of indifference on the part of the Tamil Nadu authorities to apprehending the LTTE assassins, who freely motored a few hundred kilometres against a police-alert and returned to their Sri

Lankan base by speed-boats within hours. Two commissions of inquiries, headed by Justice J S Verma and Justice Jain Commission that probed different aspects of the 'Rajiv Gandhi assassination' referred specifically to the complacency exhibited by the Tamil Nadu police and civil authorities in the immediate aftermath of the 'Padmanabha killing' and concluded that it may have contributed in no small way to the climate and environment that made Rajiv Gandhi assassination possible. The influence that the LTTE wielded at the time, whether in political and/or emotional terms, or otherwise, was a major impact of domestic insurgency in Sri Lanka impacting on the scheme and system of governance, with particular reference to maintenance of law and order, and crime-detection, in India, particularly Tamil Nadu.

While piloting the parliamentary resolution on the dismissal of the DMK State Government headed by Chief Minister Karunanidhi only months after the 'Padmanabha killing', Prime Minister Chandra Shekhar said that Central intervention was necessitated by an 'anti-national act'. He did not elaborate at the time. However, down the line after the Rajiv Gandhi assassination, that too in the midst of fresh parliamentary polls, Tamil Nadu administered the worst-ever debacle on the DMK since the party's founding in 1949 and entering the electoral arena in 1957. There was no evidence or even time for the voters to conjure up any conclusion against the DMK based exclusively on the Rajiv Gandhi assassination. But their suspicions and surmises flowing from the earlier 'Padmanabha killing', particularly the shocking way in which the crude and cruel act was played out in the heart of the State capital, and subsequent media indications that the police had instructions not to stop the escape vehicles of the assassins, was enough to do the DMK in. The chastened party never ever looked at militant groups of the LTTE kind – which was also the sole surviving agency – with the same kind of sympathy, empathy or possible support as may have been available to the outfit prior to the Rajiv Gandhi assassination. It also meant that the DMK, like many other individuals and agencies, may have felt fooled and cheated by the LTTE, which had no qualms in embarrassing the party and Government that had empathised with it after the death of AIADMK Chief Minister M G

Ramachandran on 24 December 1987.

In way, it was the LTTE's hand in the 'Rajiv Gandhi assassination' that impacted on Tamil Nadu, and consequently Indian politics and policy-making on matters of ethnic issue than anything domestic such as the perceived nature of 'competitive Dravidian politics' of the DMK-AIADMK variety. But it was the security concern that it highlighted that caused even greater concern. That a ruthless militant group with access to weapons and commitment to the cause to be able to have its suicide-bomber(s) assassinate public figures in this country was both a shock and shame for India's sovereignty, territorial integrity and even the security agencies. It was said that the Indian intelligence agencies had not exactly ruled out the possibility of the LTTE targeting Rajiv Gandhi, particularly in Tamil Nadu. However, when the gruesome killing took place, its impact was felt severally. Combined with the planning and execution of the 'Padmanabha killing' only months earlier, which included the escape of every member of the assassination team back to base in Sri Lanka's North, the 'Rajiv Gandhi assassination' convinced the Indian security agencies that the LTTE had a free run of the shared seas between the two countries. It was a fact known to the Indian intelligence agencies for some time, but the truth, as it unfolded the way it, was hurting. Considering that the LTTE was acting against Indian interests and concerns, it became clear that anyone in its place could do worse damage.

From the mid-Eighties on, the LTTE's 'Sea Tigers' wing had acquired a lot of lethal power at sea – which however it used only against the Sri Lanka Navy. The LTTE speed-boats, often acquired from the West, manned by committed cadres who knew the seas in those parts better, cornered and destroyed SLN craft in convincing ways, time and again. This in turn dampened the naval cadets and demoralised them. The turn-about came in 'Eelam War IV', when SLN also deployed small, specialised teams that would pay back the 'Sea Tigers' in its own coin, through precision, surprise strikes. Through this period, the SLN, coordinating its intelligence-sharing with countries such as India and the US, also drowned as many as 12 LTTE commercial vessels on the high seas when they were engaged in smuggling weapons and ammunition for the fighting cadres. As the continuing post-war recovery of weapons and ammunition from the LTTE dumps in Sri Lanka showed, the destruction of the commercial fleet by the SLN demoralised the cadres than disarming the outfit. But in terms of factors of internal and external (sea-lane) security, the message and lessons for India was clear. That the southern coastline was as vulnerable as the land borders in the north. It is anybody's guess how the message did not get the attention it deserved. For, ahead of the 'Mumbai serial blasts' of 1993, followed by the more shocking '26/11 Mumbai attacks' of 2008, the 'Padmanabha killing' and the 'Rajiv Gandhi assassination' showed how the Indian shoreline was vulnerable, and required high-intensity security on a constant basis. However, they seemed to have been dismissed as connected yet isolated incidents. The focus then seemed to have been more on the capabilities and commitment of the LTTE, and not on the porous nature of the coastline in these parts – extended to other regions in the country. Yet, when the message dawned, India would shore up its coastal security along the Tamil Nadu border in particular, but along the south Indian coast, otherwise.

The Indian mood and methods changed when it became clear in the early years of the new millennium that the LTTE may have acquired air-power as well. In the days and weeks following the 'Rajiv Gandhi assassination' a decade ago, the intelligence agencies were working on the possibility of LTTE using gliders and remote-controlled toy-planes to hit at targets, particularly in Chennai. The name of post-poll AIADMK Chief Minister Jayalalithaa often got a mention in this regard as a possible target in the tension-ridden months of 1991. Given the LTTE's track-record *viz* India in the Nineties, Indian security agencies became concerned about two distinct possibilities. One was the theoretical possibility of the LTTE air wing targeting Indian assets on Indian soil, in retaliation for New Delhi's perceived political support and non-lethal military aid to Sri Lanka in fighting the ethnic war. This included prestigious and nuclear and space-technology installations along Tamil Nadu's southern coast, but extending up to the fringes of the Chennai coastline up north. This included the upcoming Koodamkulam nuclear power station and the Kalpakkam installations. The first was still under construction, but Kalpakkam, near Chennai, had been in operation for decades. Closer to the Sri Lankan coast in the south were the Liquid Propulsion Testing Centre at Mahendragiri in Tamil Nadu, and the pioneering Vikram Sarabhai Equatorial Test Launching Centre, both of the Indian Space Research Organisation (ISRO). The Indian Navy and Coast Guard had contingency plans to secure these installations all along, and the possibility of LTTE strikes – just as other anti-India terrorist groups from across the country's northern borders – too had not escaped their calculations, either. But the possibility of surprise air-strikes added a new dimension.

Though New Delhi insisted that its military supplies to Sri Lanka did not include any lethal weapons – which alone forced Colombo to approach countries such as China and Pakistan not favourably disposed to India – the LTTE and much of the rest of the Sri Lankan Tamil community would not believe it. Nor would their local political supporters in India accept it. They were convinced that India was supplying lethal weapons to the Sri Lankan State to target the LTTE, and by extension the Tamil population in crowded communities where the outfit took its battles with the Government troops. Thus, in the eyes of the Indian agencies, there existed a possibility of the LTTE wanting to 'teach India yet another lesson', though in the aftermath of the loss of popularity and support in Tamil Nadu in particular, had made the organisation a little wiser. The security agencies also did not rule out the possibility of the LTTE reviving its old calculations, as had happened with the 'Rajiv Gandhi assassination' ahead of the 1991 polls – and drawing its own conclusions. In sheer desperation of continuing to lose the war in Sri Lanka, the possibility of the LTTE indulging in a daredevil act that it thought would stall the Sri Lanka Army on its track nearer home could not have been overlooked, either.

The second reason for India getting concerned about the LTTE air-wing was the possible violation of the Indian air-space in the course of the Sri Lankan air war, or in the process of LTTE deploying its air assets for clandestine movement of men and material from across the Indian shores, where it had stock-piled war-effects. It's hard to expect any such violation of the Indian air-space to go undetected or challenged, but any LTTE violation of the Indian air-space in pursuit of its immediate goals in relation to the Sri Lankan State would have meant that the Sri Lanka Air Force (SLAF) would be tempted to come after them in a hot pursuit. Given the short distance, formal exchanges of intelligence and deployment of Indian Air Force (IAF) or naval-air assets by New Delhi, to stop the LTTE aircraft from violating the Indian air space would not have come in time. In turn, this could have led to diplomatic incidents involving the two neighbours, who were still at repairing the political damage from the past – when the IAF undertook 'Operation *Poomaalai*' in Tamil, or 'Operation Garland' in July 1987, to air-drop food and medicine to the beleaguered Tamil civilians in Sri Lanka's Tamil-majority North after the SLA had cornered the LTTE. In the post-Cold War world, both nations, particularly India as the bigger and powerful neighbour, needed to avoid that.

There was a more important reason and cause however. The acknowledged birth of the LTTE air-wing meant that Sri Lanka needed not only flying machines capable of taking them on – which anyway it had, but engaged in bombing land-based targets or ferrying men and material. The SLAF in particular required radars capable of identifying the LTTE flying-objects. India, having looked the other way when Sri Lanka went to Pakistan and China for weapons and ammunition to fight the LTTE, could not do so when it came to their radars operating from Sri Lankan soil – installed and possibly manned by their agencies. Given the long-standing adversity, New Delhi felt uncomfortable about the possibility of unfriendly nations having a foothold in Sri Lanka and with capability to peep into its skies at will. This meant that not only did India have to offer Sri Lanka a pair of 2-D radars, install them and operate them it also needed to strengthen its own air defence mechanisms along the shores from across Sri Lanka. Earlier, when the 'Sea Tigers' acquired vast powers, the Indian Navy and Coast Guard had increased and improved their watch along the southern Tamil Nadu coast. The Navy thus installed an air-wing station in southern Thanjavur district. In preparation for the LTTE air-wing, the IAF installed radars along the southern Tamil Nadu coast. Air sorties from the Indian sides also increased during the period.

Suddenly, the southern Tamil Nadu coast looked vulnerable, and needed to be guarded and protected. It was a direct consequence of the LTTE's increasing strength and capabilities – like the creation of sea and air wings – within Sri Lanka. However, the air-wing, still in its infancy, when the LTTE was forced to come out displaying its assets, if only to make a propaganda pitch when cadre-morale nearer home and Diaspora belief overseas were low, did not acquit itself as well as the 'Sea Tigers', which took years to mature. By the time the LTTE deployed the air assets, without any coordinated battle-plans other than to try and demoralise the Sri Lankan State and the Sinhala population, through selective air-strikes, the battle had turned fully against it. From there, it had become difficult for the LTTE air-wing to turn the tables. This led to a situation in which the LTTE was forced to deploy its limited air assets in pursuit of what were basically political, and not military targets, and lose them all in the bargain. It is anybody's guess if a more careful and calculated deployment of LTTE air assets, or the possibility of the outfit being able to induct more aircraft to its fleet, would have made any difference to the threat-perceptions for India. But definitely India would have been concerned, given that the political pitch in Tamil Nadu, particularly from the peripheral pan-Tamil groups publicly identifying with the LTTE in the end years of 'Eelam War IV', was becoming shriller by the day.

What Remains for the Future?

Insurgency of the LTTE kind as used to be known and identified may have gone from the Sri Lankan soil. It is most definitely so for the present. The iconic dominance that Prabahkaran had over not only the Tamil polity but also the larger community in the island, and over the Sri Lankan nation of his times, is too difficult to rebuild or revive by another person in his place. A lot would depend on what the Sri Lankan State has to offer the defeated Tamil community and polity in terms of a political solution. It would also depend on what the Tamils, nearer home and afar, think that they are capable of, and would want to do in the future in terms of politics and public life in their home-country. Even if the emerging situation and circumstances were cause the revival of Tamil militancy of some kind, comparisons would be drawn. Individuals would evaluate the stakes before wanting to enrol, whether in a political movement of the Tamils or a militant outfit of whatever shape and shade – if the idea were to press for the causes that the LTTE held close. It could be 'power devolution' as the LTTE understood or a 'separate State' as it had aspired for. These are issues that are fraught with possibilities for Tamil Nadu – hence, for India.

If a situation as the one outlined were to emerge in Sri Lanka, now or later, the dependence of a future generation of Tamil politicos or militants wedded to their cause, as it may stand at the time, would be tempted to use Tamil Nadu and the rest of India as their base. Throughout the post-Independence period, there were no great exchange-visits involving ordinary politicians between the two countries. Barring Ministers at New Delhi and Colombo, politicians were not used to visiting each others' countries, to know its people, their politics and problems as one would have expected – at least during the early decades of Independence. It is equally true of the politicians from Tamil Nadu visiting Sri Lanka. Barring the controversial, illegal visits to Sri Lanka undertaken by the likes of MDMK leader Vaiko in the early Nineties, and VCK's Thol Thirumavalavan and a few others during the relatively peaceful first half of the Norwegian-brokered cease-fire period (2002-07), visits of the kind were confined to a section of the Tamil polity from the island-nation coming to India with their woes and demands. Among them, Tamil United Liberation Front (TULF) leader A Amirthalingam, slain later by the LTTE, remained a State guest in Tamil Nadu for long. Over the decades of war, many other Tamil political leaders had shifted their families to the safety of Tamil Nadu, which in turn necessitated their frequent visits to Chennai or to other towns in Tamil Nadu.

The ice was broken when 10 members of Indian Parliament, all of them from Tamil Nadu, visited Sri Lanka after the conclusion of the war, and were taken to the camps for the internally-displaced persons

(IDPs). There has not been a visit of the kind since, nor is anyone talking about one. It is hard to expect the post-war Tamil generation in Sri Lanka that feels strongly about alleged victimisation by India alongside the Sri Lankan State, wanting to involve the Tamil Nadu polity in any of their future political/militant endeavours. Yet, there is a silent, strong section that still feels that their ends cannot be met without Indian engagement and blessings. Yet, in terms of Tamil militancy, if it were to rear its head again on Sri Lankan soil, Tamil Nadu would provide the natural sanctuary for them. It may not be the training ground as it was in the mid-Eighties as the rest of India was, thanks to the indulgence and initiative of the Indian Government, but it could still be the only base outside of Sri Lanka for a future militant group to stockpile its weapons and other supplies needed for a long drawn-out engagement with the Sri Lankan State. Unlike the Seventies and the Eighties, when left-militancy in Sri Lanka passed by India, any future revival of the JVP kind of insurgency in that country too would consider the wisdom of engaging with the Naxalite militants in India, for sharing experiences, weapons and even training. Tamil Nadu could still provide the landing-base for them all, but they could also choose other parts of the country – particularly Kerala, for the purpose. It could not be the same again.

Linked to the LTTE militancy and smuggling of war material from and through India over the past decades is another socio-economic issue that has been crying for a political solution between the two Governments and their peoples. The "fishermen's issue" involving the folk along the southern Tamil Nadu coast and their constant harassment by the Sri Lanka Navy (SLN) has been a huge cause for political embarrassment in New Delhi, with frequent pressure building up from Chennai. Close to 500 fishermen from southern Tamil Nadu have lost their lives over the past years in mid-sea incidents, reportedly involving the SLN, and so is the community's loss in terms of seized or destroyed boats, fishing-net and catch. Governments at the Centre and in the State could not ignore the frequent protests by the affected fishermen, and their staying away from the sea for a few days to a few weeks in a row. From time to time during the three-decade war, the "fishermen's issue" has reached a diplomatic flash-point of some kind, but in the last few years in particular, dexterous and delicate handling by the Governments at Chennai, Delhi and Colombo, with adequate understanding from the Sri Lankan Deputy High Commission for southern India, has helped ease tensions.

It is true that Tamil militancy was not the cause for the genesis of the "fishermen's problem" involving the two countries and their governments. It owed to the traditional culture of shared fishing in the shared seas. With only a 20-km stretch of sea separating the two coasts at the shortest-point, time used to be when fishermen from one coast in the Tamil-speaking areas would have members of their families in the other coast. This also helped in sharing of the catch and profits, and also leading to further social contracts in terms of marriage between the younger generations across the seas. Proximity and constant exchange of visits also meant that the fishermen carried much-needed goods from one shore to another, and make profits from the sale of those goods to the local population. Over time, this got institutionalised as 'informal trading' between the two countries, in which certain fishermen families and those from other communities along the coastline were wholly engaged, at times to the detriment of their fishing interests. The money was big, the risk of having to sit out at the sea for long hours, and at times days, was less – and the need to bargain for the price of their catch with middle-men on landing along the coast was non-existent. They were the masters, they quoted the prices, and people paid.

It is here that the Independence for India and Sri Lanka in quick succession caused a certain unease to begin with, and concerns after the Tamil militants, particularly the 'Sea Tigers', entered the scene. Independence from the common British colonial rulers led to relatively strict enforcement of the maritime borders between the two countries, and also the respective laws pertaining to passport, visa and customs. The post-Independence era also saw a boom in the arrival of white-goods into India, from the West, through Singapore and then Sri Lanka. On their return voyage, these traders would carry handloom textiles, for men and women, rice, grams and whatever that sold in Sri Lanka. While there had been problems from time to time during the pre-militancy period, the advent of the 'Sea Tigers' as a force to reckon with in the shared seas, interfered with the traditional ways of living in these parts. The Sri Lanka Navy suspected, not without proof, that some of the fishermen traditionally engaged in non-formal trading, were now smuggling war-goods for the LTTE. There were more serious issues of LTTE battle-ready boats camouflaging as fishing vessels, launching suicide-attacks on Sri Lankan naval craft from time to time. On occasions, 'Sea Tigers' boats had also taken cover in the midst of the hundreds of fishing boats that dotted the seas, to speed away at the last-minute and hit their SLN targets. Such attacks comprised surprise conventional-strikes and 'suicide-boat hits'.

Linked to the LTTE-centric security concern on the Sri Lankan side and the political protests against the Sri Lankan State in Tamil Nadu is the 'Katchathivu issue'. It flowed/flows from India transferring the ownership and possession of the tiny, 285-acre islet, off the Tamil Nadu coast, to Sri Lanka in 1974 as part of the redrawing of the international maritime boundary (IMB). The legal and technical issue flows from the SLN barring Indian fishermen from Tamil Nadu visiting the islet, for drying their nets, resting and for the annual St. Antony's Church feast, though through most of the war years even their Sri Lankan counterparts were barred from all such activities. Though the enforcement of the Agreement by the Sri Lankan authorities was not strict in the early years, the advent of 'Sea Tigers' and other sea-borne activities of the LTTE, at times involving Indian men and boats, meant that they began enforcing the sovereignty and territorial integrity clauses, to deny 'poaching' by the Indian fishermen near the Katchathivu issue' area. Quoting from the text of the India-Sri Lanka Agreement on the subject, it is often argued that the very fact that the Indian fishermen were given freedom to dry their fishing nets on the islet implied that they could fish in the neighbourhood seas. The burden of such a position was that the transfer of ownership and possession of the islet was a techno-legal decision and should not come in the way of the traditional livelihood of the Indian fishermen in the neighbourhood. From time to time, there have been political and non-political demands for India seeking re-possession of Katchathivu issue', or at least obtaining a lease-in-perpetuity so as to facilitate fishing and visitation rights for the Tamil Nadu fishermen. New Delhi has publicly declined to do the first and has maintained a stoic silence on the latter.

Between them, the two inter-linked concerns of "fishermen's problem" and the "Katchathivu issue' issue" have been exploited by interested sections within the peripheral pan-Tamil polity in Tamil Nadu and others over the past years. This does not mean that the problems of the fishermen are unreal or imagined. The fact is that the fishermen from Tamil Nadu have not come to terms with the political reality of two nations and their borders. These issues *per se* would have come up on the anvil in time, and may have been addressed at the political-cum-community levels by the Governments and people concerned. But the advent of Tamil militancy in Sri Lanka and the arrival of 'Sea Tigers' added a totally new element to what essentially should have remained a political discourse, aimed at arriving at a mutually-satisfying solution to what essentially would have remained a "fishermen's problem". It needs to be recalled that in the decades that followed Independence for the two nations and the years before the ethnic issue, violence and war became a security concern for the two nations, there had been instances of the fishing community from the Tamil-speaking areas in India and Sri Lanka clashing in the mid-seas over the catch or poaching. The traditional war between neighbourhood fishing communities along the long Indian coast over "poaching in each other's seas" (?) continues to date, with individual communities 'arresting' the alleged intruders and their boats, and releasing them only after obtaining a huge cash-ransom for the loss of catch that they believed was theirs. There was no recorded incident of such ransom-paying involving the Tamil-speaking fishermen from the two countries in the past.

Post-LTTE, the direction that the "fishermen's problem" took during the war years continues to haunt bilateral relations in ways that could become a diplomatic deadlock between the two nations. On the one hand, it is linked to the demand-supply situation in the seas, particularly for select fishes for which there is a specific palate and thus a market in either country – or, overseas. Through most of the war years, the Tamil fishermen in Sri Lanka had to sit out, after the Government banned fishing along the coast, apprehending 'LTTE involvement' of some kind or the other. Their adventurous cousins from across the Palk Strait would take the risks of not only violating the international maritime boundary but also facing the SLN. The number of fishing boats from Tamil Nadu thus violating Sri Lankan territory and the existing order than banned fishing for all in what was ear-marked as 'High Security Zone' (HSZ) in the seas as much as in land were in their hundreds, if not thousands. They kept away from the seas only during the 45-day fishing ban period imposed by Governments in India in more recent years, to facilitate breeding, but would not budge even after being challenged by the Sri Lanka navy, mid-seas, time and again. The Indian Navy and Coast Guard have not been able to do much about it, either.

The end of the war means that the Tamil fishermen from Sri Lanka too are returning to their neighbourhood seas. This in turn could lead to situations in which they may want to establish their traditional rights over the Sri Lankan seas, leading to mid-sea quarrels with their counterparts from India. During the Norwegian-brokered CFA period, there had been instances when the 'Sea Tigers' or Tamil fishermen from Sri Lanka, then allowed to undertake limited fishing activity, would 'arrest' poachers from India and hand them over to the LTTE leaders along the coast. The Government of India, which has been negotiating freedom for Tamil Nadu fishermen taken prisoner by SLN throughout the war period, then used to count on the good offices of the Sri Lankan counterpart, to obtain freedom for those in LTTE custody. Better or worse still, as a professional organisation charged with securing the maritime boundary and interests of the country, the Sri Lanka Navy (SLN) will not feel comfortable about violations of any kind by Indian fishermen for a long time to come. Their loss of naval assets and personnel to the 'Sea Tigers' through the war years may have tempered their thought process and strategic/tactical thinking. Any addition of a fishermen's row between communities in the two countries could only complicate bilateral relations on this score than it would have done otherwise. There is realisation in the capitals concerned that it could be a constant irritant in bilateral ties between the two nations, only that there is no clear way out of a possible mess, which was introduced by the LTTE's militant posturing on the seas and their consequent need for 'cover' and support from the fishermen communities along the two coasts and their boats, mid-sea.

Through the era of ethnic war in Sri Lanka, pan-Tamil sections of the polity and society in Tamil Nadu have been made to believe – and, in turn, they too have tried to make others believe – that the problems facing fishermen from the State in the shared waters with Sri Lanka and the Katchathivu issue' issue were only a part of an overall conspiracy/ strategy to deny the Tamil community their due place and share even in the Indian scheme and system. Their arguments have been purportedly bolstered by other issues and concerns affecting the larger Tamil Nadu population, one way or the other, owing to domestic Indian developments. Included in the list are constant irritants like the 'Cauvery water dispute' relating to Karnataka, the 'Mullaiperiyar row' with Kerala and the more recent 'Pallar issue' involving the third neighbouring State of Andhra Pradesh. As mentioned, you also have the 'Sethusamudram Canal Project', where Sri Lanka too had raised objections, citing environmental reasons – which a section of the Indian elite too support. It is another matter, parties such as the AIADMK and leaders like Jayalalithaa have often argued against the Sethu project, for instance, after having promised the Tamil masses, their dream project of a century in the party's election agenda. It is also where 'competitive Dravidian politics' often has reared its head – and not as otherwise believed to be. On all these issues, however, the Tamil Nadu Government and the average Tamil on the street feels aggrieved. They are unlike any other that the pan-Tamil Dravidian polity had flagged and highlighted during the early decades of Independence. Unlike the conceptual concerns that made the DMK take up the anti-Hindi agitation as a focal issue in the Sixties and make a huge success of their public protests in the State, the river-water disputes involving all three neighbours, for instance, is a livelihood problem every individual in Tamil Nadu, almost every day. Despite being identified as among the foremost industrialised States in the country, Tamil Nadu easily remains agrarian in character. The younger generation that throng engineering colleges that dot the landscape as nowhere else too depends on the family's agriculture income for seeing them through professional courses. The political and judicial handing of Tamil Nadu's concerns at the highest levels over the decades has not inspired confidence or found a satisfactory solution that would solve the problems on hand.

Be it as it may, what might have remained a social problem, and at best a political issue, now threatens to take a militant shape – if not in the immediate future, thanks to the exposure that the peripheral groups and individuals have had from the LTTE on the one hand, and their LTTE-centric conviction that the Tamils of the world have been denied justice in whichever land they lived. This perception is also finding oral and physical expression in some way among the Indian origin Tamils in countries such as Malaysia, where they had been taken as interred labour, some 150-200 years ago, by the common British colonial ruler. The Malaysian Government had officially charged the local 'Hindraf Movement' of the local population of Indian origin, as playing second-fiddle to the LTTE. Tamils formed a vociferous section of the Hindraf leadership when they protested against the imposition of Malaysian laws in 2008, and were put behind bars. Unlike in the past, Tamil-origin leaders from among the Hindraf hierarchy visited Tamil Nadu and toured India, among other nations, extensively, to project and promote their cause, and establish contacts. It coincided with the ethnic war reaching a peak in Sri Lanka, when the Tamil-dominated Penang State Assembly in Malaysia, passed resolutions that were seen as pro-LTTE in content and character. A Tamil Minister in Penang State, S Ramaswamy, has been visiting Tamil Nadu often and addressing conferences organised by pan-Tamil groups with distinct identification with the LTTE, both during and after the ethnic war in Sri Lanka.

Post-war in Sri Lanka, pro-LTTE groups in Tamil Nadu have also been inviting Tamil political leaders and those sympathetic to the 'Tamil/ LTTE cause' to Tamil Nadu, for addressing rallies that however remain poorly attended – compared to the war-time sympathy that the mainline Dravidian polity was able to whip up in a controlled and calibrated measure. Though there are no known contacts between pan-Tamil groups from other countries and their counterparts in Tamil Nadu, the long years of ethnic strife in Sri Lanka, particularly during the months of 'Eelam War IV', have made an indelible impression on the 'IT-driven' generation that has access to information on their tables and their drawing rooms, 24 X 7. Suffice to recall that the pro-LTTE protests staged by sections of the Tamil-speaking community in South Africa, most of them of Indian origin, were on the internet within minutes for those who wanted to follow the global propaganda in this regard. Likewise, the weeks-long Hindraf protests in Malaysia were covered by the international television networks as they had not done with the 'Sri Lankan ethnic issue' through decades. Picked up by their poor cousins from Tamil Nadu, they were watched in all homes in the State that watched the telly for its daily diet of local news.

Combined with the fact that the younger generation in the impressionable age-group in the State have been exposed to pan-Tamil issues, concerns and methods, both nearer home and afar, where their jobs have taken them outside the country – and also thus provide opportunities for interaction with their Tamil brethren from Sri Lanka and elsewhere – it remains to be seen if and how it all shapes up in the coming years. It may not be that easy for anyone to whip up a great political cause, based on any or all of these 'pan-Tamil concerns' but it only takes a few impressionable minds to give 'action-orientation' of a kind to their expectations and frustrations. Politics and public support could start off from there – though it should be said to the credit of the security agencies in Tamil Nadu and at the Centre that they have been able to manage and control the emerging situation at the height of the 'ethnic war' in Sri Lanka to satisfaction and relief. How long and how far would it hold is a concern that would keep them occupied from time-to-time on the physical front, and forever conceptually, owes to the 'LTTE hand' in the affairs of what essentially was localised pan-Tamil concerns, much of which the pro-active policies of successive Dravidian polity Governments in Tamil Nadu had addressed effectively through the past four decades.

Likewise, it may not be a direct fallout of the internal conflict in Sri Lanka, but the end of the 'Cold War' during the decades of 'ethnic strife' in the country has stirred the shared Indian Ocean waters between India and Sri Lanka as none else may have done in recent times. The arrival of the US armada, in the face of Afghanistan-based terror-strikes on American land in the form of 9/11 attacks, the emergence of China as a prospective super-power, the revived hopes of Moscow for a share in the global strategic sphere as politics and economy on the home front stabilises, and the interest of the European Union to carve out a niche for itself in the global affairs are all the main reasons behind the greater and constant global interest in the Indian Ocean Region (IOR), with particular reference to the 'energy sea-lanes' from the Gulf-Arab region to the rest of the world. A superior regional power with global role and ambitions, India finds itself at the cross-roads. Every move and method of its immediate neighbours is cause for further cooperation and concern at the same time. Sri Lanka is no exception. The years of ethnic violence and war has caused Colombo to move closer to Pakistan and China, two of India's traditional adversaries, thanks mainly to the 'Tamils factor' and past Indian involvement, if only to obtain weapons and ammunition that New Delhi would not sell Colombo for prosecuting the war on the LTTE.

Post-war developmental demands of Sri Lanka too has its approaching Beijing for aid and assistance, China being the only country with massive stocks of surplus funds in an era of global depression – and also has the willingness to spend or invest. It was indirect fallout of the ethnic war, but for which the decades of destruction and consequent neglect of the Sri Lankan developmental agenda would not have suffered as much. India, while having the willingness and commitment to rush to the aid of Sri Lanka, including the war-ravaged Tamil areas of the country, does not have the kind of reserves that China can mop up. Yet, the constant and continuing involvement of nations such as China in the affairs of a next-door neighbour like Sri Lanka, with the world ahead of the Indian Ocean wide open through its door, is a concern that New Delhi can hardly overlook, whatever the commitments that may come its way from the Colombo side. Combined to this is also the 'energy-related threats' to international actors that may emerge from the Sri Lankan side, in the form of rump groups of 'Sea Tigers' that may take the example of the Somali pirates elsewhere. What is good for the south of Sri Lanka seas could be more so for the northern seas that it shares with India – particularly if these rump groups of LTTE or future militant outfits of the kind were to use Tamil Nadu as a base and the shared waters as an initial source for their funding, as well. Though neither of these aspects seem to have drawn the attention of security agencies in either country, or the rest of the world already, this is something that they can overlook only at peril to their national security and territorial concerns in particular cases.

Lasting Impact?

Weeks after the LTTE had lost the self-initiated 'Maavilarau battle' after it had unilaterally broken the cease-fire accord and sought physical control of the sluice-gates of the river in the Eastern Province of Sri Lanka through militant/military means, Sri Lankan Tamil Diaspora interlocutors landing in Tamil Nadu had a few points to make:

- The Tamils' struggle, including insurgent means sans LTTE's terrorist methods, would continue even if the outfit were to lose the 'ethnic war' ultimately.

- The 'Sri Lankan Tamil community' would like to whip up whatever sympathy that they could obtain from their brethren in Tamil Nadu, with the hope of pressuring the Government of India to help and aid the Tamil struggle – or, at least to try and ensure that New Delhi did not aid and support the Colombo Government.

- Despite what may be said in public, the 'Eelam struggle' did not exactly count on the Tamil Nadu polity and society to back them, given the perceptible memories flowing still from the 'Rajiv Gandhi assassination' in particular. The 'Eelam cause' and movement required Tamil Nadu more for keeping the Tamil language and culture alive – for the Diaspora in particular to keep its younger generation that had been brought up on a diet of western thinking and values in western setting. Thus, the Diaspora's younger generation needed to be exposed to popular Tamil media like films, television serials and magazines. If a section of it could be used (manipulated?) to serve the immediate cause, the better. If not, no harm done.

- The LTTE or any future pan-Tamil militant group from Sri Lanka would not hesitate to seek the blessings of its enemy's friend's enemy, if that alone would help. (The reference was to China, based on the allusion that India could "continue to support the Sri Lankan State" against the Tamils fighting for a separate homeland in that country.

It's anybody's guess how the Diaspora interlocutors of the type could start thinking and talking about a future without the LTTE, as they had done after the outfit had lost only the 'Maavilaaru battle' in 2006. Yet, there could be no two opinions about sections of the Sri Lankan Tamil Diaspora funding and financing Tamil films being made in India in a big and in a near-open way around the time the 'Eelam War IV' was on. With the war peaking back home in Sri Lanka, what with the LTTE too requiring all the moral and political support that it could muster across the world, including Tamil Nadu – and through Tamil Nadu, the rest of India, starting with the Government in New Delhi. That was also when the Tamil filmdom in India joined sections of the Tamil Nadu polity favourably disposed to the LTTE's cause, in staging public protests against the Sri Lankan Government – where sentiments and speeches against the Indian Government too got varied expression. Earlier, sections of the Tamil filmdom had also taken the lead in taking up the 'Cauvery water dispute' in earlier years. There were clear indications during the anti-Sri Lanka protests of the Tamil filmdom that film personalities were being threatened to fall in line. There were also instances of overseas rights-holders of certain Tamil films and/or overseas financiers of others forcibly indicating their mood against stars who would not cooperate with the organisers of such agitations. Months after the conclusion of 'Eelam War IV' and the robust defeat of pro-LTTE elements in the federal parliamentary polls in Tamil Nadu, individual film actors in the State began speaking their minds – as to how they were being forced to participate in public protests and rallies against their own wishes. The allusion was obviously to the anti-Sri Lanka protests in the earlier months and years.

The Diaspora funding of Tamil filmdom thus needs to be read in the context of the averments already made. So should be the competition among popular pulp magazines in Tamil being published from Tamil Nadu to spread the cause of the LTTE even months after the conclusion of the 'ethnic war'. With the Sri Lankan Tamil Diaspora forming a substantial readership-based, particularly for the web editions of such magazines, it is anybody's guess if the editors could have overlooked commercial considerations while deciding to reflect the common Tamil sentiments that they shared on the 'Sri Lankan Tamil cause'. This trend has continued even months after the end of 'Eelam War IV' in Sri Lanka. What more, Tamil media references to domestically sensitive issues like the Cauvery water dispute, the Mullaiperiyar dam row and the Pallar imbroglio, not to leave out the 'Sethusamudram canal controversy' all now have a discernible tinge of pan-Tamil perception attaching to them. Some magazines write in a way that could be seen as whipping up the sentiments that were ignited in a new-generation of Tamil Nadu youth by the mood and methods that they had adopted at the height of the 'Eelam War IV'. Others are more subdued. In turn, from time to time, issues such as these have the propensity to keep the political flame on related issues alive.

As pointed out already, the fallout of the revival of pan-Tamil sentiments on the political plane in Tamil Nadu has more to do with domestic politics than on influencing the Government of India's policies on the Sri Lankan ethnic issue, *per se*. Yet, at two desperate moments in their electoral career, the DMK in the Seventies and the AIADMK in 2006, still tended to side with parties and groups that were seen as pan-Tamil from the pro-LTTE angle. Otherwise, even the pan-Tamil sentiments expressed by those groups and parties, including the two Dravidian majors, or national parties like the communists and the BJP, were not confined to the Sri Lankan issue alone. They had covered larger domestic issues of grave concern to the common man in Tamil Nadu, both from the sentimental front as also the more serious livelihood front. The end result is that while the direct sentiments and political influence borne by Tamil Nadu, and through it the Government of India, may have overshot the 'Sri Lanka ethnic issue' in electoral terms, the residual impact on elements that could be convinced of the LTTE's ways and methods to achieve their own confused ends in the Sri Lankan context may be the 'lasting contribution' (?) of the internal conflict in Sri Lanka to the polity, society and security of Tamil Nadu and rest of India. More than anything else, it is this that the Government of India should be concerned about – and to this end, New Delhi should address Tamil Nadu's concerns on domestic issues as the Tamils' concerns over the 'ethnic issue' in neighbouring Sri Lanka.

CONTRIBUTORS

Brig K Srinivasan (Retd) a defence and security analyst, while in service has been involved in addressing internal conflicts in Jammu and Kashmir. At Centre for Security Analysis, he guides and supervises the work of research fellows. His areas of interests include conflict resolution & peace building, disaster management and role of civil society in conflict situations. He is an active member of the working group on non-traditional security of Regional Network of Strategic Studies Centres set-up by NESA Centre, National Defence University, Washington.

Ms Ancy Joseph is research assistant at the Centre for Security Analysis, Chennai. She has written articles on the conflict and the current affairs of Myanmar as well as on internal conflicts in South Asia. As a Research Assistant at CSA, she assists the Executive Director in carrying out the Center's programmes and projects. She holds a Master of Philosophy Degree in Public Administration and Masters Degrees in International Studies and Public Administration from the University of Madras. She also holds a Post Graduate Diploma in Business Administration from the Technical Education Department, Government of Kerala.

Hon (Prof.) G.L. Peiris is presently the Foreign Minister, Government of Sri Lanka. He has held a number of high positions in the Government of Sri Lanka including Minister of Constitutional Affairs, Ethnic Affairs and National Integration, Justice and Constitutional Affairs, External Trade and Deputy Minister of Finance. Prof. Peiris was Professor of Law, Dean of the Faculty of Law and later Vice Chancellor of the University of Colombo before he took to politics. He held Fellowships from the Universities of Oxford, Cambridge and London. He was a Rhodes Scholar of the University of Oxford (1968-1971) and has been a Visiting Scholar to several prestigious Universities in UK. He has published numerous books and articles in research journals and has delivered numerous lectures in Sri Lanka and abroad.

Prof. S.I. Keethaponcalan is currently the Head of the Department of Political Science and Public Policy, University of Colombo, Sri Lanka. He has served as Visiting Professor at University of Bradford, England, Kotelawala Defence Academy, Ratmalana, Sri Lanka and Department of International Relations, University of Colombo. He also served as national consultant to the international team that evaluated the European Commission Assistance to UNDP's Mine Action Support Project in Sri Lanka in 2008. He obtained his Ph.D in Conflict Analysis and Resolution from Nova Southeastern University, Florida, USA. He writes a regular column on ethnic conflict and peace process in Sri Lanka in the Thinakkural (Daily Voice) a leading Tamil weekly and has published a number of articles in the local newspapers in Sri Lanka on the domestic and international issues. He has written extensively on the ethnic conflict, conflict resolution and peace process in Sri Lanka. Some of his recent publications include *Conflict and Peace in Sri Lanka: Major Document*; *Sri Lanka, Perspectives on the Ceasefire Agreement of 2002*; *Interim Administration: A tool for Conflict Resolution*; Currently, he is engaged in studying *Failure of a Non Violent Struggle: Revisiting the Non- Violent Struggle Carried Out by the Sri Lanka Tamils headed by SJV Chelvanayakam for Regional Autonomy.*

Prof. Gamini B Keerawella is currently the Head of Department of History, University of Peradeniya, Sri Lanka. He obtained his Ph.D in History from the University of British Colombia, Vancouver, Canada. He is also founder member of Social Scientist Association and Director, Institute of International Studies (IIS). He was also Advisor to the President on Peace matters from 2002-2003 and 2004-2005; he was a member of the Security Advisory Council, Presidential Secretariat from March – October 2003. He has published extensively on Modern Sri Lankan History, Strategic History of India Ocean, Human Security and Post Colonial State building and National Integration in South Asia.

Some of his recent publications are *From National Security to Human Security: Evolving Security Discourse in Sri Lanka* and *Japan in South Asia in the Context of New Discourse on Peace and Security*. He has also presented papers at various international conferences and seminars.

Mr. Deshal de Mel holds a Masters Degree in International Political Economy from the London School of Economics. His areas of interest are international trade, regionalism, SAFTA, Indo –Sri Lanka Free Trade Agreement, trade in services and the international aid architecture. Along with academic research Mr de Mel has been involved in the formal trade negotiations of the India–Sri Lanka Comprehensive Economic Partnership Agreement between 2005 and 2008. His most recent research has been in macroeconomic policy, post conflict economic priorities in Sri Lanka and governance issues related to political and economic devolution of power to ensure sustainable peace. He has been involved in consultative and collaborate work with USAID, UNIDO, UNECAP, ADB, World Bank,

Dr. V. Vivekanandan is Convenor, Alliance for Release of Innocent Fishermen (ARIF) which was set up in 1997 by a number of trade unions, fishermen associations and NGOs in India concerned about the plight of fishermen who are arrested and detained for long periods for crossing the Indo-Sri Lanka maritime border. He has also been Chief Executive of the Trivandrum based South Indian Federation of Fishermen Societies (SIFFS), a federation of village level fish marketing cooperatives of small scale fishermen. He founded the Fisheries Management Resource Centre (FishMARC), a NGO to promote fishermen coops in other parts of India. He also works closely with the National Fish workers Forum of India (NFF), a federation of fish worker trade unions fighting for the rights of the fishing communities and preservation of fish resources. He is also a member of the International Collective in Support of Fish workers. He holds a Post Graduate Degree in Rural Management from the Institute of Rural Management in Anand, Gujarat.

Mr. A X Alexander, IPS (Retd) is former Director General of Police, Tamil Nadu and has been in the Intelligence Department of Tamil Nadu Police for the best part of his 37 years career.

Prof. Laksiri Fernando is Director of the National Centre for Advanced Studies in Humanities and Social Sciences (NCAS). He has held positions of Secretary for Asia/Pacific of the World University Service, Geneva (1984-91), and Executive Director, Diplomacy Training Program, University of New South Wales (1995-97). He has been a Visiting Professor recently at Ryukoku University, Japan, and University of Sydney, Australia. His publications range from labour to political economy, human rights to constitutional issues. He is author of books *Human Rights, Politics and States: Burma, Cambodia and Sri Lanka; A Political Science Approach to Human Rights* and *Police Civil Relations for Good Governance* among others. His educational background includes BA (Ceylon), MA (New Brunswick) and PhD (Sydney).

Mr. N. Sathiya Moorthy is a journalist and political analyst with a degree in law from the University of Madras. He has worked for / associated with most major newspaper groups in India, both in English and local languages for over 30 years. At present he is the Director of the Chennai Chapter of the Observer Research Foundation (ORF), the multi-domain Indian policy think-tank headquartered in New Delhi. He is a keen observer of the Sri Lankan political scene and India-Sri Lanka relations. He writes a weekly column on related issues and topics in the 'Daily Mirror', Colombo.

CSA PUBLICATIONS

CONFLICT RESOLUTION AND PEACE BUILDING

1. Conflict Resolution and Peace Building in Sri Lanka

2. Federalism and Conflict Resolution in Sri Lanka

3. Peace Process in Sri Lanka: Challenges & Opportunities

4. Conflict Over Fisheries in the Palk Bay Region

5. Conflict in Sri Lanka: The Road Ahead

6. Peace and Conflict Resolution: Emerging Ideas

7. From Winning the War to Winning Peace: Post War Rebuilding of the Society in Sri Lanka

8. Internal Conflicts in Myanmar: Transnational Consequences

9. Internal Conflict in Nepal: Transnational Consequences

10. The Naxal Threat: Causes, State Responses and Consequences

SECURITY STUDIES

11. US and the Rising Powers: India and China

12. Maritime Security in the Indian Ocean Region: Critical Issues in Debate

13. Public Perceptions of Security in India: Results of a National Survey

14. Essential Components of National Security

CIVIL SOCIETY AND GOVERNANCE